Collaboration in International Rural Development

Collaboration in International Rural Development

A Practitioner's Handbook

GEORGE H. AXINN
NANCY W. AXINN

SAGE PUBLICATIONS
New Delhi/Thousand Oaks/London

First published in 1997 by

Sage Publications India Pvt Ltd
M–32 Market, Greater Kailash–I
New Delhi 110 048

Sage Publications Inc
2455 Teller Road
Thousand Oaks, California 91320

Sage Publications Ltd
6 Bonhill Street
London EC2A 4PU

Published by Tejeshwar Singh for Sage Publications India Pvt Ltd, phototypeset by Line Arts Phototypesetters, Pondicherry and printed at Chaman Enterprises, Delhi.

Library of Congress Cataloging-in-Publication Data
Axinn, George Harold, 1926–
    Collaboration in international rural development: a practioner's handbook/George H. Axinn, Nancy W. Axinn.
      p. cm.   (c: alk. paper)   (p: alk. paper)
    Includes bibliographical references and index.
    1. Rural development—International cooperation. I. Axinn, Nancy W. II. Title.
HN49.C6A95 307.1′412—dc21   1997   97–27342

ISBN: 0–7619–9200–6 (US-hb)   81–7036–652–6 (India-hb)
        0–7619–9201–4 (US-pb)   81–7036–653–4 (India-pb)

Sage Production Team: Malathi Ramamoorthy, O.P. Bhasin
and Santosh Rawat

Contents

List of Tables

List of Figures

Preface

James Russell Lowell 1819–91

This book is written for people engaged in international development cooperation. Its goal is to provide practical and useful information and insights about the professional aspects of their work. It is designed for people who are in *practice* in the international development field. For those who serve in rural places, this book is designed to be useful as they cope with the daily flood of unpredictable problems and opportunities, attempting to enhance the lives of those around them. It should also be a valuable tool for those who train, supervise, and otherwise support these field personnel.

The professionals in international development have grown in numbers and diversity throughout the second half of the 20th century, and will have a significant impact on the first half of the 21st century. They are the staffs of national and local governments, of international public agencies, of non-government organizations, of international development banks, of educational and research institutions, of charitable and religious agencies, and of small private consulting firms and large corporations. They include paid professionals and dedicated volunteers; some are engaged in the international arena for a few months or years, while others find it to be their lifelong careers. Globally, by the close of the 20th century, they number in the tens of thousands.

Rationale

This book is different from others in several respects. Other authors have described international development—there are rapidly growing numbers of both descriptions and analyses by observers of this scene. And practitioners have written books featuring their own personal experiences, and offering them as a guide to others. As believers in the importance of both scholarship and practice, we provide a personal perspective on international development, based on our many years in the field. We have each been field technical workers and administrators in rural parts of Africa, Asia, Latin America, and North America for more than four decades. We have also been researchers, writers, teachers of university students, and trainers of development professionals. To this book we have brought the essence of our learning over the years. But it is more than that.

We reflect upon lessons from *our personal field experience*, coupled with and supported by the scholarship and experience of others reflected in the *literature* on this subject and personal communication. This combines perspectives from such vantage points as:

- local level technicians within projects,
- managers of projects and larger programs,
- trainers of personnel at various levels,
- administrators of organizations providing development inputs,
- managers of agencies conducting national programs, and
- diplomats negotiating international and interagency agreements.

We do this because, in our experience, the most effective practitioners also read about the field; are acquainted with the writings of scholars in the field; participate in courses, seminars, and workshops from time to time; consider themselves to be *professionals* in international development work; and are what we refer to as *professional practitioners*.

This book, therefore, is a mixture of theory—with generalizations based on both our personal experience and literature—and how-to-do-it "handbook-type" tools designed to be a guide to action for field practitioners in international development. It attempts a holistic systems perspective, and includes original analytic tools such as the *development cycle*, the *force field analysis of continuity and change*, the *recycling ratio*, the *means/ends hierarchy* for planning, and the *index of seriousness*. It is designed to help practitioners become more *professional* in their practice. That is why we sample the current published writing in the field, sprinkle a taste of what others have written throughout the book, and offer a bibliography for those who wish to read further.

Over the years, we have each become increasingly concerned with the issues and concerns of GENDER as a crucial variable in international rural development cooperation. In this book, we have resisted pressure from colleagues and friends to include a separate chapter on *gender*. Instead, case examples and analyses of gender issues are included in every chapter of this book. That is done to avoid the neglect of gender considerations which occurs when international development programs and organizations assign a separate office to "cover" gender matters, or have a separate project on gender, and then use that as the excuse for not actually investing sufficiently in these matters to make a significant difference. Instead, the gender dimensions of each topic are addressed, because development in human groups will be more likely to occur when there is also strategic understanding of gender relationships.

Professional Practitioners

We began as field workers in rural America, with home economics extension and research, as well as with agricultural research and extension; later as teachers and administrators of rural development activities in the USA; still later as practitioners in several different countries in Africa, Asia, the Caribbean, and Latin America. Having served at the grass-roots as well as at policy levels, and also as technicians, administrators, grant-givers and grant receivers, our connection with *development* has been grounded in first-hand experience.

Individually, or as a team, we have worked for Michigan State University; the US Agency for International Development; national governments in countries such as Thailand, India, Chile, and Malawi; The Ford Foundation; The Midwest Universities Consortium for

International Activities; the World Bank; the International Fund for Agricultural Development; private consulting firms; non-government organizations; and such United Nations (UN) agencies as the Food and Agriculture Organization (FAO) and the United Nations Children's Fund (UNICEF). This experience has included seven years of continuous work in Nigeria, over six years in Nepal, and several years in India, as well as dozens of shorter assignments in various countries in Africa, Asia, and Latin America.

The two of us have been collaborators in our personal and professional lives for more than fifty years. Besides rearing four children, and sharing the experiences of parenthood and grand-parenthood, we have been students, teachers, practicing development workers, diplomats, and authors. The chapters which follow are partly a narrative of our personal experience, and readers will often find the words *we* and *our* when we refer to ourselves.

Fieldwork has been our first love, occupying most of our professional careers, interspersed with periods of teaching, research, and administration. Our teaching opportunities have included formal classes at universities on three different continents (North America, Africa, and Asia), and non-formal classes in five. Research and writing have included joint authorship as well as work done individually and with other colleagues. The opportunities for a professional couple focusing on international development to work together on so many assignments have been a rare experience, and we feel fortunate.

After many years of being "change agents", of urging others to escape from professional well-carpeted ruts and search for the significant, and of grappling with the forces of *continuity and change* in many parts of the world, the need was felt to bring these thoughts together.

We have been greatly influenced by the potential for exciting changes as people of the world community transition into the 21st century. After a half century of global power polarization and neglect of the weak, the old ways of thinking are changing. Old social, political, and economic structures are fragmenting. Reflections on the conceptualizations and the practices in rural development, in international development, and particularly in international development collaboration, reveal the dramatic evolution of challenging and positive possibilities which are the focus of this book. The goal is to enhance the reader's understanding of this critical phenomenon and empower her/him to contribute significantly in the 21st century.

As the world waits for the new century to unfold, we offer various propositions which experience and research suggest may be principles. That is done not with answers, but with questions; not with recipes, but with intuition. The purpose is to stimulate, to encourage, and to excite. We are seekers of truth; not the keepers of the truth. Thus the goal is to share that quest!

Organization

This book is organized in three major parts, which follow an Introduction. Part 1 contains two chapters which focus on the *field of international rural development*, and identify *current issues and concerns* in this subject. Part 2 turns to the *strategic and policy alternatives*, and the design of programs and projects. The emphasis here is on *the collaborative mode*; and the essence of accountability, participation, decentralization, and devolution. After a general look at policy, strategy, programs, and projects, there are chapters on *program development and evaluation strategies*, and *learning and communication strategies for development*.

The next three chapters which constitute Part 3 address *implementation* and *administration*, and include such aspects as organizing, staffing, directing, and financing international development. The chapters contain various charts, tables, and forms intended to be guides to others as they design aids to management in their own particular projects and programs.

Part 4 offers a challenging but optimistic view of the future of collaboration in international rural development. It reflects our committed interest in the future.

Acknowledgements

We have been enlightened over the years by scores of men, women, and children who live in rural places, who till the soil and tend the livestock, and are the target of many international development programs. Those in the villages of Edam Ani in Nigeria, and Rampur and Lamjung in Nepal are particularly close to our hearts. We have also learned from many, many colleagues, teachers, students, administrators, and friends. In the last few years, dozens have contributed their ideas and suggestions for this book, and we acknowledge their contributions with gratitude.

Our faculty colleagues and students at Michigan State University, Cornell University, the University of Nigeria, and the Institute of Agriculture and Animal Science of Tribhuvan University in Nepal were among our teachers. Professional practitioners of rural development in UNICEF, FAO, The Ford Foundation, and The Midwest Universities Consortium for International Activities also helped prepare us to write this book, as did close associates who were activists in several non-government organizations. We are also indebted to many serious professional practitioners in the governments of India, Nepal, Nigeria, the UK, USA, and many other countries.

CHAPTER 1

Introduction

...the old paradigm can no longer offer control of ongoing social processes. The very powerlessness of the powerful in the face of today's crises is what will in time open the way for the people with the new paradigm well in mind, particularly including women, to play new roles in the world scene.

Elise Boulding 1977: 224

Based on the rationale and setting discussed in the preface, the introduction begins with our working definitions of the key words in the title: international, rural, development, and collaboration. We then concentrate on the term *rural*, and offer readers an analysis of some useful ways to approach rural life from the perspective of international development. Chapter 2 does a similar analysis of *development, international development*, and *collaboration*.

1.1 Definitions

This book focuses on INTERNATIONAL RURAL DEVELOPMENT COLLABORATION. Here is how these key words are defined.

DEVELOPMENT is one of many words in the English language which has many different meanings. The context reveals the meaning, but even in the international context there are several ways in which the term *development* is used. In the professional field, which has been dominated by economists, many books with the word *development* in their titles use the term to mean *economic* development. Books on horticulture use the same term to mean the evolution of a plant through its various stages of maturation and decay. Each discipline is inclined to use the word *development* in its own context.

The seed of a plant which falls to the ground has the potential to *develop*. If the environment is appropriate, it may grow roots, sprout leaves, and eventually blossom and even produce the seed for a new generation. The human infant, similarly, has the potential to *develop*. DEVELOPMENT, viewed in this perspective, is a process by means of which living things evolve in the direction of their potential. This is the meaning that we use in this book when we refer to communities, watersheds, regions, or whole nation states. *Development* is different from growth. At certain times, *development* may involve growth; but at other stages, growth may be dysfunctional to development. There are many different types of development; there are different types of growth. As the United Nations Development Program (UNDP) says in the opening of its *Human Development Report, 1996*, the "series has been dedicated, since its inception in 1990, to ending the mismeasure of human progress by economic growth alone" (UNDP 1996: iii).

However, development in human groups as they evolve over the years and generations is different from INTERNATIONAL DEVELOPMENT. While much of what is written in this book is relevant to domestic development within a particular nation state—its urban, rural or industrial development—the concern here is the *international* arena. Our focus is on the activities of people from one or more countries who travel to a different place, and attempt to enhance development in other people's worlds, or even within their own countries. This book deals with the complex tasks of "outsiders" who are working to improve the situations of others who are the "insiders" in the place where the work is being done. Chapter 3 identifies some of the issues and concerns which characterize *international* development efforts.

Another key word in the title is RURAL. While *rural* and *urban* life are absolutely interrelated, since so much of international development in the last fifty years has been addressed to rural situations, and since most of our personal professional experience has been with rural life, this book gives priority to those who live in remote locations, in smaller and more isolated human groups. They are the *rural* people who produce the food and fiber which nourishes and clothes urban people as well as themselves.

The other key word in the title is COLLABORATION. It refers to the type of partnership among people in a place designated for planned international development activity, in which both *insiders* and *outsiders* have something to gain from the interaction, and something to give to the interaction. There are costs to both groups, and benefits to both groups. Only when each group considers the benefits of collaboration to be greater than its costs does the inter-action continue. For each group, there are high transaction costs; but the benefits are also high.

And in INTERNATIONAL DEVELOPMENT COLLABORATION, outsiders usually are groups of individuals with different levels of competence, from different disciplines, and often different nations and cultures. *Collaboration* among outsiders alone requires large investments of time and money, but these high transaction costs are necessary for success in the complex task of international development.

Each chapter which follows returns to the concept of the PROFES-SIONAL PRACTITIONER, because our field experience has convinced us that this important field of professional work demands personnel who are both *practitioners* and *students*. Researchers continue to produce insightful analyses and describe these in a growing body of literature. But much of it is not implementable. Practitioners, on the other hand, learn much from their experience, but if they fail to keep up with the literature they will tend to see only a narrow specialized angle of the global reality. Therefore, the contributions of people who combine practice with scholarship, and become professional practitioners, are particularly valued and encouraged.

Although the major focus of this book is on rural development, the rural and urban people of the world are linked together in most communities, in nation states, and as a part of a larger global system.

If rural people were allowed by their urban brothers and sisters merely to feed themselves from the lands and waters upon which they toil, rural life would be more pleasant, and the challenges to professional agriculture, forestry, fisheries, and rural development would be much simpler. But that is not the case in today's world. Higher and higher proportions of a growing global population are living in large towns and massive cities. They produce little food for themselves. If rural people do not feed them, urban people might starve to death. But, of course, before they starve they will do everything they can to force rural people to feed them. Those who farm must produce enough not only to feed themselves, but the increasing numbers of those who live in the urban world. The reality is that urban people tend to control the political systems, the economic systems, and the military systems. This has led to conversion, in many places and over hundreds of years, from small-scale, self-sufficient farming systems to large-scale, monocrop commercial haciendas, plantations, and export-oriented estates.

The ideas that small is beautiful, that self-reliance is appropriate for villages, that rural people must organize to achieve power, that the rural rich exist along with the rural poor, have been in the minds and words of those seriously concerned with rural development for many generations. One of the most articulate thinkers about rural life in the beginning of the 20th century was Rabindranath Tagore in India. He was very interested in the revival of the villages of India, but also called for a mutually supportive relationship between the people of the cities and rural people as necessary for the well-being of both (G.H. Axinn, 1977b).

1.2 What is Rural?

The meaning of the word *rural* changes from time to time and place to place. It is used here to refer to places where population is not as dense as in urban places. Rural settlements usually include families scattered over the landscape, with relatively small clusters in occasional villages. This contrasts with urban settlements in which many families live very close to each other, with perhaps no open spaces between living quarters and workplaces. The actual numbers vary tremendously in different locations, but villages tend to have populations in the hundreds, or sometimes in the thousands, whereas urban cities have populations in the tens of thousands and in millions.

Rural people are usually more separated from each other than urban people. The connections of roads, public transportation, telephone, cable television, and shared electrical and water systems, for example, are more numerous in urban places. Rural life tends to be dominated by farming, along with forestry, fisheries, and similar pursuits, rather than manufacturing, commerce, and services typically found in cities. Because rural livelihoods depend so heavily on these biological production systems, and because they, in turn, are influenced by rain and drought and other natural phenomena, rural people tend to rely heavily on their traditions and their gods. While women do play vital roles in urban life, their roles in rural life are usually critical in both production in farming systems and the re-production of future generations. Thus, while gender considerations are important for change and development everywhere, they are absolutely vital in rural places.

The rural–urban relationship is intimately linked to hunger and poverty, in both urban and rural places. Food security is a term which refers to the attempts to solve problems of hunger, usually on a national scale. However, food security is not simply a matter of having a global supply greater than the demand. As Amartya Kumar Sen (1981) has demonstrated so effectively with data on several of the world's famines, it is not merely a matter of having hungry mouths to feed, and therefore demand for food. If you don't have what economists call *effective demand*, you don't get any food. There may be plenty of food available on the streets of Bangalore, Enugu, Tegucigalpa, or Chiang Mai, but if you do not have a coin, you do not get any food! Put another way, food security has at least three dimensions: (*a*) the *production* of food; (*b*) the *marketing* of food so people have access to it (storage, transportation, processing, wholesaling, and retailing); and (*c*) the *entitlement* to food. At the close of the 20th century, we are far from solving the entitlement problem.

While urban dwellers absolutely need the food, fiber, and other raw materials produced by rural people, there are also many benefits to rural life which come from urbanization. Mass production of consumer goods in the cities results in greater availability of the conveniences of contemporary life for rural people. Everything from their vehicles for transportation to appliances for food preparation, to heating and cooling of the human habitat, to radio, television, computers and the other tools of the communication revolution, tends to be manufactured by urban people. In some countries, these manufacturing functions are being deliberately moved to rural areas to enhance rural development. The strengthening and maintenance of the symbiotic rural–urban relationship is essential for the development of both.

The UNDP, in its *Human Development Report, 1995*, has a most useful presentation on *rural–urban gaps.* It demonstrates that in most countries urban people are better placed than rural people as regards health, access to safe drinking water, and sanitation (UNDP 1995: 166–67). Poverty is higher among rural people, and literacy is higher among urban people.

Rural people have a wisdom that is not always appreciated. They understand the *interdependence* between nature and people; between animals and plants; between the need for sunshine and rain. Rural people are often seen as simple people, and they may express simple needs, but they need to understand the complexities of the biological world in order to survive. Increasingly the recognition of what uneducated people *know* is appreciated by agricultural scientists looking for sustainable solutions to agronomic problems. And increasingly, agricultural scientists and farm men and women are demonstrating the value of working together to address production and sustainability issues.

Rural women and men know the need for hard work; the value of family members working together; the reward of bringing new life—plant and animal—into the world; the difficulty of being at the mercy of the weather. They typically have an appreciation for a force of life (however defined in their religion) which is greater than they are.

1.3 Conceptual Perspectives

Because later chapters of this book deal with the strategies and design of international rural development activities, several different ways of thinking, or conceptual perspectives, are presented in this chapter. They have been selected because we have found them to be useful for describing and analyzing various rural situations, and also for designing and evaluating development projects. These concepts provide categories which are useful tools for professional practitioners of development.

Two of the most simple concepts are those of *insiders* and *outsiders*. While people from another nation state would obviously be *outsiders* from the perspective of *insiders* who were born in a village, there are other types of *outsiders* as well. These may include urban people from the same country who come to assist in a rural place, rural people from a different ethnic or language group, and even young people from that same rural village who have received formal education in other places and return to their homes to discover that they are now *outsiders*. And when a delegation of elders from that village travels to the capital city to meet one of their political leaders who may now be the minister of finance, they discover that in the ministry of finance, they are the *outsiders*, and they are surrounded by *insiders* who consider them to be "strange".

In this introductory chapter, there are illustrations of *functional* approaches to categories for analysis and planning, and there is also a discussion of *structural* categories. We also briefly discuss the differences in the *size of farms*, and the extent of differentiation in the *components* within farming systems. Each of these sets of categories is useful to those who try to comprehend rural life, and to plan activities designed to enhance it. But they are not independent of each other. While they are presented separately, they can also be used in combination. In fact, all of the categories, and their many subdivisions, are presented as tools which can be useful to those concerned with the quality and effectiveness of development projects and programs. A useful approach to comprehending rural life is to see the rural world as a unified system in which all components are linked to each other, and all are needed for sustainability.

This brief description only scratches the surface. It is beyond the scope of this book to detail each of the types of production or marketing systems—for livestock, for fruit, for vegetables, for fluid milk, etc. But we do wish to provide an analytical framework for planners and implementers of rural development. Toward that end, a systems perspective has proven useful. This perspective has emerged in many parts of the world in the last third of the 20th century, partly because scholars and practitioners in agriculture have become, like the practitioners of reductionist science, so highly specialized that few of them are willing or able to deal with the whole farm as a system. Simultaneously, a separate group of scientists, with its roots in electrical engineering, has developed methodologies for systems analysis. Building on this, a holistic systems approach is being implemented through the research efforts of many scientists concerned with international development and rural life (see G.H. Axinn 1991b; Bawden 1991; Conway 1990; Flora 1992; Hildebrand 1986; Lightfoot et al. 1991; Shaner et al. 1982; Whyte 1991).

1.4 Functional Approach to Rural Development

Among the alternative strategic approaches to rural development, some focus more on functional matters, and others attempt to change structural matters. Function is used here to refer to the kinds of things people do, both in families and communities. Rural people, for example, are usually engaged in the *production* of food, fiber and other extractive materials. But they are also engaged in *marketing* those products. Whether one family consumes all that it produces, so the same items are *produced* and *marketed* by the same people and to the same people, or one family produces vegetables (as an illustration) in much greater quantity than it can eat, and therefore sells most of its *production* to another family which owns a vehicle and takes the surplus to a city for sale (*marketing*), these two functions are always involved. But these are not the only functions in which rural people are involved. For most production systems, there must be inputs, and thus the *supply* of these inputs is a vital function.

They must also somehow manage their system, and therefore *govern* it. For example, if the family grows a crop like maize or yam, even if they are remote from other families and rather independent, someone must fulfill the function of seeing to it that part of the crop is saved as seed for the next growing season. If they fail to do this, they may not survive. This is called the *governance* function, and it is found in every human group. Figure 1.1 illustrates seven functions found in every rural social system.

Of course, the governance function is also carried out in a much more specialized way by individuals and groups who are not involved in production or marketing, but who devote all of their time and energy to governance. They are an essential part of every society. General Obasanjo, former president of Nigeria and chair of the Africa Leadership Forum, addressed governance functions in an interview. He said,

> food insecurity has been caused by its [Africa's] inability to both produce enough of its own food and by its lack of resources to purchase food. But underlying these issues is another fundamental problem—governance. Whatever else we plan to achieve in Sub-

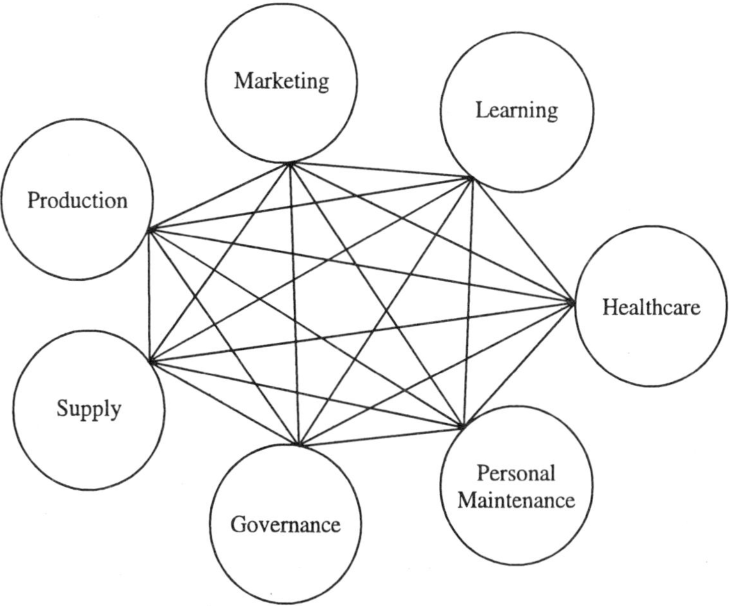

Figure 1.1
Functions in the Rural Social System

Saharan Africa, be it food security or social issues, these must be predicated upon measures in governance that ensure stability and security and the prevention, elimination, and management of conflict. These are the fundamental requirements needed before we can build any other productive activity in Sub-Saharan Africa or build even wholesome human interactions (Obasanjo 1995: 5).

In addition to the four functions mentioned above, every human group carries out the *learning* function. From this perspective, *learning* includes *research* and *education*. If you, as a reader, are more comfortable separating the learning function into these two branches, the figure can easily be drawn with eight circles instead of seven. The point is that every human group does some *research* (where it explores the world and discovers things without the benefit of a teacher), and is usually exposed to some *education* (where certain members of the group help others learn what they need to know). The two are grouped here for convenience and simplicity.

The value of such a diagram is that it demonstrates the relationship of the various components of the system to each other. The lines between and among them are linkages, and all components are linked to all other components. The critical aspect of this is that since all functions are linked, any change in any one of them will have some impact on all of the others.

Before further discussing the functions as a system, a brief explanation of the other two components may be helpful. *Healthcare*, like the other components, is found in every human group. It may be that a remote family provides this function to itself, or, in a larger community there may be a doctor, or a health post, designated to provide healthcare. In an even larger community, there may be several hospitals, clinics, and special emergency services. But this function, like the others, is always a component of the larger system.

Personal maintenance is also a necessary function among all human groups. Sometimes people resent the need to spend time in grooming themselves, or even taking time out for meals. But every human group must invest time and energy in housing, clothing care and maintenance, exercise for those whose lifestyle is sedentary, and matters of that sort. Therefore, one of the functions in the diagram is called *personal maintenance*. This function also includes reproduction of the human group.

This way of looking at the functions in rural life is a useful analytic tool. It can be used by development planners in describing and analyzing particular rural social systems. It is useful in discovering and demonstrating the relationships among the components of a particular system. For example, in a review of the contribution of forests to food security, it was noted that

> in drafting rural development plans, an integrated approach should be adopted to promote appropriate management of forest resources for their contribution to food security. This approach should be developed on the basis of local needs: relevant scientific research by anthropologists or botanists should be reviewed and complemented by community-level research, which retrieves relevant indigenous knowledge and understands its contribution (Ball et al. 1995: 44).

The functional approach is also useful in analyzing, comparing, and understanding gender differences from place to place. In some rural communities, for example, men look after crops in the field, while women care for livestock near the homestead. But within that general framework, the seed for the field crops is a woman's responsibility in many places. She saves it, stores it, and protects it for the next planting season. In some groups it is the woman who actually places seed in the ground; in other places it is the man. Similarly, in some rural communities men will drive cattle with carts or plows, but it is women who milk and feed the cows.

The biological "givens" of women as reproducers of the family define some functions. Beyond the obvious roles of healthcare and personal maintenance of infant family members, women in most societies assume more of the "at home" roles of rural life.

1.5 The Structural Approach to Rural Development

Other international development programs focus on what may be termed a *structural approach*. The structure in a rural social system takes into account differences in wealth and power among its rural families. Some families may control rather large quantities of land, and be comparatively wealthy. Others may control much smaller pieces of land, and be comparatively poor. Still others may be landless. In addition to matters of class and control over productive resources (relative wealth), there are often differences in ethnic groups, castes, language, and networks of relationship (such as families and clans). A combination of these represents the social structure of the rural community, the region, or the whole nation state. An oversimplification of the structural situation in one area is illustrated in Table 1.1.

Table 1.1
Typical Social Structure

(Total = 100%)

	Rich	*Poor*
Urban	8%	12%
Rural	2%	78%

Let us consider, as an example, a place where there is a predominantly rural population. In this place 80 percent of the people may be in rural areas, with the other 20 percent in urban places. Again, in this oversimplification, there might be large numbers of relatively poor people, and small numbers of the rich. But this is only an illustration of the structural phenomenon. In any real situation the percentages would probably be much different than in this illustration.

If such a place were concerned about the rural poor, people in that place might seek international development cooperation to "do something" about the rural poor. If one were serious about doing something regarding the rural poor, it would also be necessary to take into account the rural rich. And, from a systems perspective, the urban rich and poor are also involved.

Much discussion of the structural phenomena in the literature on international development focuses on some of the causes of the inequalities of distribution of wealth. These include social class and caste, ethnic competition, and the disadvantaged position of women in most societies.

Policy solutions which may address inequalities often result in increasing women's labor or reducing their access to common resources. On the other hand, "a gendered approach provides key insights that can enhance sustainability of local resource use" (Sen, 1995b: 65). Women involved in agricultural production are very aware of the need to conserve resources as well as conserve their own energy for their multiple daily tasks.

Efforts to promote industrial development and provide cheap food for the cities (where so many voters live) often "amount to looting the agricultural sector" (Daily et al. 1995: 59) and increasing the inequities between the rural and urban populations. The opportunity to increase crop yields and overall production depends on the amount of credit available and the timespan needed for different production activities; inputs of a type which support sustainable agricultural practices; infrastructure such as farm-to-market roads, market price information, and adequate storage facilities for seasonal crops; and markets which will benefit small landholders as well as larger farmers.

One of the most eloquent writers (and activists) in this area is Paulo Freire, from whom we have been learning for many years. He writes:

The central problem is this: How can the oppressed, as divided, unauthentic beings, participate in developing the pedagogy of their liberation? Only as they discover themselves to be "hosts" of the oppressor can they contribute to the midwifery of their liberating pedagogy. As long as they live in the duality in which *to be* is *to be like*, and *to be like* is *to be like the oppressor*, this contribution is impossible. The pedagogy of the oppressed is an instrument for their critical discovery that both they and their oppressors are manifestations of dehumanization (Freire 1970: 33).

In her advocacy of women, and their rights in agriculture and the environment, Vandana Shiva has pointed out that "The masculinist paradigm of food production which has come to us under the many labels of 'green revolution', 'scientific agriculture', etc. involved the disruption of the essential links between forestry, animal husbandry, and agriculture, which have been the basis for the sustainable model" (Shiva 1989: 97). Shiva recommends an ecological perspective which reflects the interrelationships of the forest, water, and animal systems with food production. She labels scientific agriculture as "anti-nature" since it disrupts natural processes and shifts control of food systems from women and peasants to multinational agribusinesses.

Seeing a local rural community as a unified system, in which all components are linked to each other, and all are needed for sustainability, is a challenge to those who would analyze and attempt to understand rural life. We turn now to a different dimension of analysis which coexists with the functional and structural perspectives just discussed.

1.6 Size and Differentiation in Farming Systems

A critical perspective in rural development has to do with the differences in size and the variety of crops and livestock produced on individual farms. That is because some farms are very small, and others are very large, and there are some of every size in between. Small hill farms of less than one-quarter of a hectare[1] outnumber larger farms in many countries, while massive farms of several thousand hectares dominate agriculture in some others.

[1] A hectare is a metric unit of area equal to 2.471 acres.

While farms may be different from each other in many respects—soil type, rainfall, slope of the land, family size and ages of family members, distance from markets, availability of public services such as electricity and telephone—there are some generalizations which are useful in the planning and implementation of rural development.

For example, there is a tendency for smaller family farms to produce a variety of different grains or tubers at the same time, along with some livestock, and perhaps fruit and vegetables. The small area of land is used quite intensively, with one crop being planted soon after its predecessor is harvested from the same small plot of land, or different plants may be mingled (called intercropping). Conversely, the largest farms may specialize in one crop, or one class of livestock, and be much less diversified than the small ones. Land on the larger farms is usually much less intensively used. Smaller farms tend to utilize human labor; large farms tend to be mechanized.

In general terms, the smaller farms are less specialized. They produce many different types of crops and livestock. They are sometimes described as more *differentiated* than the larger farms. The larger farms, by contrast, may be more specialized, sometimes producing one major crop for a national or international market. These more specialized farms are sometimes referred to as producers of *plantation crops* or *export crops*. They, therefore, are likely to be less *differentiated* than the smaller farms.

There are also great variations in other dimensions of farming. In some places one individual will own the land and have legal title to it. In other places the traditional community may own the land, with allocations among village or lineage members being made from time to time, usually by male elders. Livestock producing farms vary all the way from ranches, where land is owned by the farming family and fenced, to range production where the farming people rent or lease the land, or merely pay for grazing rights, to more traditional pastoral systems where livestock owning families, particularly in semi-arid places, move with their cattle over hundreds of miles seeking adequate grazing and water. Then there are intensive livestock feeding operations, which specialize in adding market weight to animals bred in another farming system. Thus for cattle there are cow and calf herds, pastured on extensive pieces of land, and there are feed-lot operations where cattle are confined to very small pens and fed high energy rations.

Landownership and control can also be examined from the perspective of gender. As mentioned in the preceding paragraph, typically in a patrilineal social structure, it is the males who inherit land, and it would be the *male elders* who make the land allocations. In a few places, inheritance of land is on the female side, and it is women who control land. These strategically vital aspects of rural life, while well known to village residents, are often invisible to outsiders who work there for brief periods of time. Since power and control of various types of decisions are usually gender-related, and women tend to be disadvantaged in many rural places, this type of structural analysis can be highly useful in evolving development project strategies.

1.7 The Recycling Ratio in Farming Systems

When a systems approach is applied to the study of farms, it is typically found that the system includes such components as people and livestock, as well as several types of plants, in an agro-climatic ecosystem with physical, economic, social, and political components as well as biological ones. The high degree of specialization among agricultural scientists has resulted in professional researchers who have been trained *not* to see *all* of the components, but to focus on only one and on those aspects of the ecosystem which interact with that one component. To help specialized agriculturists take into account as many of the components as feasible, we have developed an analytic approach called the *recycling ratio*.

The *recycling ratio* (illustrated in Figure 1.2) is the proportion of the total materials and energy flow into, out of, and within a farm family ecosystem which recycles within that ecosystem. It is calculated from estimates of the materials and energy flow among components of that system such as plants, animals, and people; each of them transforming energy from one form to another. It also takes into account components of the environment such as solar energy, water, forests (for fuelwood), and fodder which may be either cut or grazed by livestock. It can also be estimated by comparison of cash purchases and sales to total consumption within a farming system.

As shown in Figure 1.2, there are some inputs supplied to this farming system from outside the system (the A arrow), some outputs from the

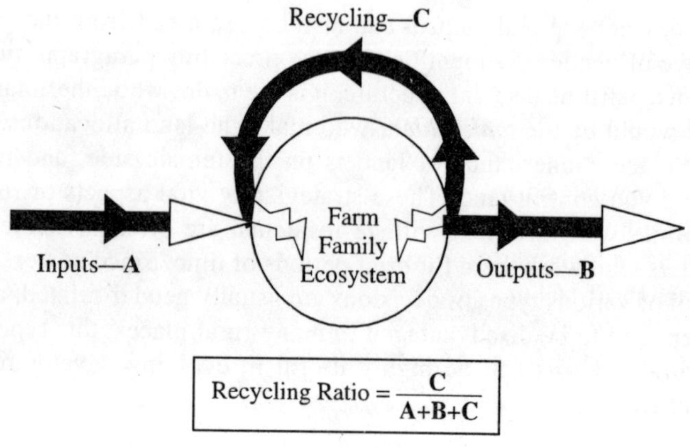

Figure 1.2
The Recycling Ratio

farming system which are marketed outside (the B arrow), and some outputs of the system which are recycled and become inputs to the system (the C arrow). When the three types of flows are measured, it is possible to calculate a *recycling ratio*. The higher the proportion of the total flow on the C arrow, the higher the recycling ratio will be.

We have seen in our own field studies, that even in regions where all farms seem to be small and poor, the larger the landholding of a farm family ecosystem the smaller the recycling ratio is likely to be. Farm size and the recycling ratio are likely to be inversely related. This is also the case among farms which are more commercial, more mechanized, and larger in scale. Any type of farming system can be described in terms of the three variables shown in Figure 1.2. The relationship between the quantities of materials which flow into the farming system as inputs, the quantities of materials which flow out from it as outputs, and the quantities of materials which "recycle" both out of it and back into it is, then, the recycling ratio.

From a systems perspective, any system can be relatively *closed* or *open*. A more closed system has fewer linkages with "outside" systems, and fewer interactions with other systems. A more open system has more interactions with outside systems. Another way of putting it is that an open system may be more *dependent* on other systems. A more closed system will tend to be more *independent* of outside systems. From this perspective, the recycling ratio is a tool for estimating the relative openness or closedness of a particular farming system. (For more details regarding the recycling ratio, see Axinn and Axinn 1987, 1984a, and 1984b.)

The recycling ratio can be a useful indicator of change in individual farming systems, or in whole villages if the systems analysis takes a larger perspective. Whether or not such change is "development" will depend on what the farm families, or the whole rural community, value in terms of their lifestyles. The community where each farming system has a high recycling ratio may not be benefited at all by the introduction of technologies which would reduce this ratio. On the other hand, if that community wants more of the goods available from outside, then it may set goals for a reduction of the recycling ratio.

1.8 Development Implications of Size, Differentiation, and Recycling

International development collaboration which is designed to enhance life and livelihoods among rural people, like other forms of international interactions, relies for its effectiveness upon the understanding each collaborator has about the others. Outsiders to any system, therefore, have a greater probability of becoming acceptable and helpful collaborators, to the extent that they understand the nature of the system. However, if the systems represented by insiders and outsiders have a history of being relatively open to each other, this improves the opportunity for successful interaction. It is in this perspective that outsiders intending to intervene for the purpose of enhancing rural development have much to gain by deepening their understanding of the types of farming systems in the place where they will work.

There are significant implications of the size of farms, the extent of differentiation within farms, and the relative openness of those farming systems for any such outside intervention. For example, *the smaller the farming system, the larger the diversity of crops and livestock involved in the system is likely to be* (**1a**).[2] Similarly, *the*

---

[2] Throughout this book, propositions which the authors believe are key principles and generalizations are placed in italics, and numbered consecutively according to the chapter in which they are presented. They are neither true nor false, but tend to have a certain probability. At best, they are a means to understanding and a guide to action.

smaller the farming system, the more intensely the people on it are likely to utilize the land (**1b**). On the other hand, *the larger the size of a farming system, the more likely that it will be dependent upon outside market forces* (**1c**). And in terms of size, there is some probability that *the smaller the farming system, the less likely that the people in it will be willing and able to consider technical changes in their normal practices which outsiders might introduce* (**1d**).

The greater the diversity of plants and animals involved in a farming system, the greater the need for analysis of the linkages among the components of that system by outsiders desiring to enhance its development (**1e**). Because farming men and women themselves are more concerned with the interactions *among* the components of their farming systems than agricultural scientists, a farming systems research approach can be useful for development interventions. This approach includes a need to involve farmers, along with scientists, in the development of agricultural research agendas. Thus scientists may focus on production of a particular commodity, while farmer–researcher partners will press them to do that in the context of other relevant components of the farming system.

By observing activities on family farm ecosystems it is possible to develop recycling ratios. These, in turn, permit comparison between rural groups of different cultures, different types of agriculture, different religions, etc. *A systems approach enables the separation of "subsistence" or "self-sufficient" agriculture where the recycling ratio is very high from market agriculture where the recycling ratio is usually much lower* (**1f**).

Both from the perspective of insiders who might systematically organize for their own development, and from the perspective of outsiders whose goal is to assist with development, some strategies are likely to be more appropriate for farming systems with high recycling ratios than for farming systems with low recycling ratios. Thus programs of technology development, extension education, market infrastructure development, etc. would be quite different for areas where farms have low recycling ratios than for areas where farming systems have high recycling ratios.

To illustrate, cooperatives which supply credit have been attempted in areas where farms have a high recycling ratio. Since farmers in these areas may not buy and sell on the market, they usually do not need outside production credit of the type which such cooperatives typically provide. As a consequence, these cooperatives have tended to fail in such situations. Rural families might take credit for festivals or weddings, but not for purchase of production inputs. Conversely, places which have farms with low recycling ratios and high-potential saleable market outputs need credit sources so that supplies of inputs can be purchased from the markets. Farmer cooperatives with short-term production credit programs are appropriate for such places.

Those with a lower recycling ratio are likely to be more "open" to new information and services which might be provided by outside systems. Farmers whose low recycling ratios reflect surplus production available to the market tend to be receptive to information on credit, marketing, etc. as well as alternative energy sources such as mechanization and mineral fertilizer. Additionally, this group of farmers is likely to be more specialized, and hence look to outside sources to expedite exchanges among specialized commodity producers. For example, these are the farming families who are most likely to need outside suppliers of "improved" seed and mineral fertilizers, and they will require availability in a timely manner and at a price which encourages high production.

Using the recycling ratio, as illustrated in Figure 1.2, development projects designed to increase the flow on the *B arrow* are appropriate for large-scale, more specialized types of farms. For the smaller, mixed, more self-sufficient farming systems, increasing the flow on the *C arrow* is likely to be more significant to the farming families involved. For the latter group, increases in their *consumption* (sum of A arrow and C arrow) are more likely to be readily accepted goals than increases in their *production* (B arrow) alone.

1.9 Implications for Professional Practitioners

Professional practitioners in international rural development should realize that we have merely skimmed the surface of a few concepts which may be useful in the design of policies, strategies, programs, and projects. There is a large and growing literature in each of the areas touched in this chapter, and practitioners are discovering new and better approaches in the field.

Out of frustration with programs designed to enhance rural development, several years ago we suggested *rural renaissance* as an alternative goal (G.H. Axinn 1975). Renaissance refers to a new birth or revival. From this perspective, renaissance may be defined as a marriage of traditional values, norms, behavior patterns, and technology with innovative values, norms, technology, and behavior patterns, resulting in the birth of changed behavior patterns, technology, norms, and values. With this conceptualization, rural renaissance cannot be *delivered* from outside. It is not something that can be injected, like an antibiotic, into an infected person. It has to be *born from within* any particular social system. In that sense, it is indigenous—it is the child of its older parent. From an international development perspective, renaissance can be encouraged and supported by collaboration between insiders and outsiders.

Concepts such as the functional approach to rural development, the structural approach, variations in size and diversity of farms, and the recycling ratio are presented here because they form a base for the discussion of international development collaboration in the next chapter, and for the later chapters on strategies, design, and implementation.

Planners of international rural development activities who neglect these concepts may make serious strategic errors. Different from those who are less professional in their work in this field, professional practitioners are expected to at least ask the broad general descriptive questions raised in this chapter, and at best be informed by responses to those questions in their practice.

PART 1

The Field of International Rural Development

CHAPTER 2

Development and International Development

We have for over a century been dragged by the prosperous West behind its chariot, choked by the dust, deafened by the noise, humbled by our own helplessness, and overwhelmed by the speed.... If we ever ventured to ask, "progress towards what, and progress for whom", it was considered to be peculiarly and ridiculously oriental to entertain such doubts about the absoluteness of progress.

Rabindranath Tagore 1965/1941

As humanity approaches the close of the 20th century and the opening of the 21st, practitioners of international development might well continue to reflect on *progress towards what and for whom* as Rabindranath Tagore did a century earlier. Better known as a poet and philosopher of Bengal, of South Asia and of the world, Tagore gave much thought to what was then called progress. Unlike others, he did not accept the changes brought by outsiders as naturally good for all.

His challenge may be even more appropriate at the time of transition to a new century than it was a hundred years ago. In the interval, many of those who thought about development and tried to implement development grossly oversimplified the process. As practitioners of development, we made many mistakes. Much of what we tried to do has not been sustainable.

Development has not been sustainable partly because development practitioners made unwarranted assumptions. But the challenge is still there; the hope is still there; and the opportunities for human creativity abound. Among fellow passengers on spaceship

Earth there continue to be many who are concerned about the welfare of others, about the interface between technological development and the natural environment, about inequities in the distribution of the material goods of life, and about the opportunities for professional interventions which will enhance the potential for this planet to sustain humanity as history unfolds.

This chapter opens with an analysis of *continuity and change* among human groups, and moves from there to analyze the concepts of *development* and *international development*. It is increasingly clear that well-meaning people attempting to enhance development in local, national, and international agencies have new lessons to learn. As in other aspects of life, the mixture of scholarship with practice reveals some of those lessons.

In the struggle for development, there have been many successes which have enhanced the human condition, and have been sustainable over time. But many apparent successes at the time of implementation proved later to be unsustainable. Some programs were not sustainable because people assumed that technological transfers alone could bring about development. Some assumed that capital transfers could bring about development. Others thought it was primarily a matter of political independence.

Many people failed to recognize that the development of any country, state, or district must be continuously driven by people from within that place, not by outsiders. Most scholars and practitioners failed to recognize that equity is a necessary condition of development. If the rich get richer and the poor become poorer and more in number, such a development will not be sustainable over time. If development excludes women and children, it is not sustainable. And if development substitutes machines and chemicals for human labor, and thereby threatens to destroy the natural environment, it will not be sustainable.

Susan George, writing from Paris, gets right to the heart of the matter. To answer the question of how to overcome global hunger, she has a six-word response: "strengthen the weak; weaken the strong" (George 1984: 1). That simple and valid recipe is not at all attractive to those who are strong, in power, and control development efforts. Perhaps that is why so much development effort has been sustainable neither from the perspective of its consequences to the ecosystem, nor from the perspective of its own continuity.

George recognized that development is more than an economic, technological, and administrative phenomenon. Its roots are political and diplomatic. "That all governments are concerned for, and representative of, the majority of their people is patent nonsense. Plenty of governments are most concerned with enriching those who keep them in power. Human rights, including the right to food, run a poor second" (George 1984: 12).

Rajni Kothari writes:

We have been looking at some of the signposts of our time. But they are not signposts for a new paradigm, just part of the reality in which we live. What would be their significance for alternative development thinking?... There is a need to rethink the basis of development cooperation and technology transfers, to recapture the real basis of self-reliance and the basic needs perspective—and to do this in the context of the rise of new movements and new actors on the scene (Kothari 1988: 68).

And thinking in a similar direction, from half-way around the world in Peru, Hernando de Soto writes:

This paradigm unifies concern for the poor, and concerns of the poor, with the creation of a modern democracy and market economy. At the same time it clears an area of common ground where left and right can meet. It pushes those on the right to realize that the free market is not enough, that modern political and judicial institutions must accompany liberalization if economic growth is to take place, if it is to be sustained, and if it is to be accompanied by social justice. As full participants, the poor can not only be the beneficiaries of economic growth, receiving the drops as they fall, but the engines of growth. To the left, the paradigm has the reverse message. Capitalism is not incompatible with the elimination of poverty; it is rather the poverty of legal institutions that conspires to create the disparities that preoccupy the left (de Soto 1989: xxi).

As Robert Chambers put it, "What matters most to poor people often differs from what outsiders assume. ... We have failed to understand that participation by them means non-ownership by us. Empowerment for them means disempowerment for us" (Chambers 1995: 14–15).

2.1 Continuity and Change

From our perspective, the human condition includes many different groups of people, surviving in a great variety of ecological niches. From time to time, and from place to place, each is perceived as being almost isolated from the rest. And yet none of our cities, villages, hamlets, or even wandering pastoral clans, is a closed system (G.H. Axinn 1991a: 121). With a systems science approach, all human groups can be viewed as components of one system. All components are linked to each other. Any change in any one component will affect all other components. Any attempt to bring about a change in any component, or any linkage among components, may be resisted by all other components.

Rural life around the globe, and the agriculture which sustains it—older than recorded human history—is a mosaic of the conflict between continuity and change. As each human group has learned the strategies for survival in its own agroecological niche, over generations of trial and error, it has also learned to institutionalize its technologies (Harris 1977). Thus, continuity defends and protects the patterns which exist.

However, change is also constant. As shifts in such natural resources as climate, soil conditions, forests, fish and game, and available energy have occurred, human groups have changed their technologies (Cottrell 1955). The search for appropriate technologies and adaptive practices has fueled the forces of change.

But since no human group remains forever isolated, and since separate systems are not closed, the creative tension between continuity and change is pervasive.

What then is the difference between DEVELOPMENT and CHANGE? For clarity within this book, we use the word *change* to refer to the general phenomenon which pervades all conditions. Some things change much more rapidly than others, but everything is always changing. As will be described below, there are forces which resist change, and there are countervailing forces which encourage change.

But not all change is development. DEVELOPMENT is a *normative* concept, conditioned by the values of those who describe it. Whatever is *normal* for any particular human group will influence what they think of as *good* or *bad*. Therefore, some people, viewing a particular change, will describe it as development. If they perceive it as making the conditions of their lives better, they are more likely to call it development. However, others who experience the same change may label it as a change for the worse, and not development.

For example, if workers in a factory or on a large farm press for an increase in their wages, and receive it, they may think of that as *development*. On the other hand, the managers of that factory, or the owners of the farm, may see the same change—the increase in wages—as a catastrophe, and certainly not development. What is viewed as development by some will usually not be viewed as development by others. The *normative* nature of this concept means that in a diverse population, there is likely to be disagreement on what is development.

Development, like so many other words in the English language, gains its meaning from the context in which it is used. The prior experience of each individual, and her/his sensing of a particular situation, will give meaning to that situation for that individual. From this perspective, development is like the elephant described by John Godfrey Saxe in his poem entitled "The Blind Men and the Elephant". Each blind man touches the elephant in a different place, and each perceives it differently. One blind man touches the elephant's leg, and says, "the elephant is very much like a tree". Another blind man touches the elephant's tusk, and says, "the elephant is very like a spear". And a third, grasping the tail, says, "the elephant is like a snake". In fact, each individual, touching the elephant from a different perspective, conceives of the elephant only from his own experience. Of the six blind men, the poet concludes, each was partly right in his description of what the elephant actually was, "and all were in the wrong".

Similarly, change in human groups is perceived differently by each person who experiences it, depending on her or his own perspective. One could say that if the change makes things better for the people involved, it is development. But others might ask, better for whom? When a river running through a valley is blocked by a dam (or barrage, or weir) to create a reservoir upstream to provide for irrigation and drinking water downstream, and perhaps to generate electric power at the same time, the changes brought about by the designers, the implementers, and the funders of that project will be viewed by them as *development*. The label, *development*, is often used in reference to *planned change*, or *induced change*, especially by the planners of that change.

But to the people living upstream of the dam, whose lands will be flooded, and whose villages may have to be abandoned, the change may not be seen as *development* at all. They may view it as a disaster, caused by outsiders who had no respect for them or their way of life, and who caused the change merely because they had the political, economic, and perhaps military power to cause the change. In South Asia, both the Narmada dam project in India and the Arun hydro-power project in Nepal are illustrative of very large, outside-donor-funded projects with positive development implications for some and negative development implications for others.

Thus *development* is a *normative* concept. Based on its norms (reflecting values, understandings, and behavior patterns), each group decides whether any particular change is development, or is not development. Therefore some change is thought of as development and some change is not considered to be development. And one particular change may be considered to be development by some individuals, and not be thought of as development by other individuals.

Development is often considered to be a *zero-sum game*. When there is a change, things can become better for some and worse for others. And many "successful" development activities fit this pattern. Some benefit from them; others suffer from them. However, it does not necessarily always have to be a zero-sum game with the gains of some equaling the losses of others. Instead of a *plus/minus* game, it could be a *plus/plus* game, or even a *minus/minus* game. Often the goals and objectives of a development project are described as a *plus/plus* situation, particularly by the funders, and sometimes by the designers. And critics of a particular project will often describe it as a *minus/minus* activity.

For instance, Uphoff in his analysis of the experience with the Gal Oya Irrigation Program in Sri Lanka observes, "whenever we include others' welfare in our own calculation of utility, what was a zero-sum situation becomes positive sum ... people's subjective willingness to contribute to each other's improvement produced measurable, objective consequences ... our efforts to analyze, predict and improve situations in 'either–or' terms proved inadequate." He suggests: "greater satisfactions can be created from limited means if value orientations can be realigned in positive-sum directions" (Uphoff 1992: 288–89).

Reflecting on change in the human condition which might be called *development*, ancient Hindu writers were aware of the pains which tend to accompany any such change. They describe how Lord Shiva, known to some as the *Great Destroyer*, actually took the position that unless you destroy the old, it is not likely that you can replace it with the better new. Thus the transition to the "developed" may be accompanied by the pain which is a part of any significant change. Some scholars refer to Shiva as the *Creative Destroyer*, and thus to development as a process of *creative destruction*.

However the development process is conceptualized, there are implications for practitioners. The professional may assume that some people view development as a process of creative destruction, others see it as a zero-sum game, and still others comprehend it as a process of change (positive or negative). Practitioners in the field of international development have a responsibility to grasp this process at greater depth than those who look only at the surface and assume that what is seen on that surface represents reality. Significant development, *planned change which will result in improvement in at least some conditions of life for its intended beneficiaries*, is not a simple process. Neither is it impossible. But successful practice requires analysis of the pluses and the minuses; the successes and the failures; the benefits and the costs; the easy and the difficult; the historic past and the creative future.

Toward that challenge, to the changing perceptions of development, we now turn.

2.2 Changing Perceptions of Development

2.2.1 History

The historical context for recent experience with international development goes back to the earliest of human groups who moved from place to place, taking plants and animals with them. In a new setting or ecological niche, some of the plants and animals (and probably people) did not survive. But other plants and animals adapted to their new environment, grew, and multiplied. This occurred (and is still occurring) over many centuries of international trade, where the technologies of agriculture and rural life were often not the main rationale for the exchanges, but merely incidental appendages. Nevertheless, the artifacts of rural life moved on trade linkages from system to system (G.H. Axinn 1988b: 7).

Military adventures and military conquest also provided a vehicle for technology transfer, as did religious expansion, and the inter-family relationships which linked fiefdom to fiefdom. Organized government efforts to transfer appropriate plants and animals from place to place have been documented throughout written history, from Biblical times to the Dutch/British collections in the botanical gardens at Bogor, Indonesia. When the United States Department of Agriculture (USDA) received its mandate from Congress in 1862, one of its major tasks was to seek and import appropriate new crops from wherever they might be found.

Years later, the United States carried on operations in its own overt strategic interest through the office of Foreign Agricultural Relations of USDA. Agricultural research, carried out in such places as Turrialba, Costa Rica, was designed in the interest of commercial production for the US market. Provision of strategic items was also the goal. That is, it was seen to be in the national interest to produce tropical agricultural products like rubber or banana closer to home to avoid any threat to steady supply in the event of wars or other turbulence.

Earlier, the British operated agricultural research establishments in South Asia (e.g. the famous Cotton Research Institute at Coimbatore in India), in Africa (e.g. the West African Oil Palm Research Institute in Nigeria), and in the West Indies (e.g. the School of Tropical Agriculture in Trinidad). These were designed to increase efficiency and productivity of crops exported to Britain and other markets. Over time, production of items manufactured from these agricultural raw materials (cacao, palm oil, cotton, etc.) and their resale in the same "colonies" which produced them, was seen as "unfair" (if not immoral and unethical) both within the colonies and in Britain, and became one of the compelling arguments for independence after World War II.

The Japanese carried out similar activities in pre-War Formosa and Korea, introducing improved rice varieties for home consumption in Japan. Japan also had earlier experience bringing in technical experts from other countries. They carefully selected them, controlled them while they were in the country, and sent them home when their services were no longer needed.

The botanical gardens in Bogor and other Indonesian research farms were established to serve trade with the Netherlands.

In the last half of the 20th century, a transition has taken place. The nations of the world have turned to a different type of intervention in each other's affairs. Instead of each overtly attempting to exploit the other, the "new style" intervention was designed for the stated purpose of helping the other to *develop*. As this evolved, thoughtful writers, particularly in Latin America, introduced the idea that underdevelopment was politically and diplomatically controlled. Former colonial powers had arranged the world so that they could extract wealth from the poorer nations and keep them in a state of *dependence* even after official independence. Writers on peasantry described center–periphery relationships from a similar perspective, while others focused on women and addressed gender-sensitive issues of inequity (de Janvry 1981; Sen and Grown 1987). This way of looking at international development, known as "dependency theory", was a significant challenge to earlier simplistic views of development, and inspired many practitioners to think more deeply about the process.

Dependency relationships are found everywhere in human interactions. Sensitive parents wrestle with the challenge when they consider how independent they should encourage, or permit, their children to be at various ages. Each culture has its own patterns, but at some stage, it is considered "normal" in many cultures for children to become almost completely independent. Similarly, a large business, or government organization, after establishing a branch or other unit, may stimulate greater independence in the new entity, or may attempt to keep it more dependent. And the same phenomenon is found in the relationships between nation states, whether one is the former "colony" of the other, or former "ally".

The recognition of dependency challenged the assumptions that mere capital and technical assistance would ever really result in development. But alternative strategies for more appropriate interventions which were likely to result in less dependence and more interdependence were not forthcoming (Boulding 1977; George 1984; Newby 1978).

2.2.2 Development Assistance

The recent systematic effort at *international development assistance* springs from the global perspectives generated during World War II. While that "assistance" has typically included capital transfers, military assistance, and technical assistance, the focus of this book is on the technical aspects, which can be called "international technical development cooperation". These have included activities in the fields of health, education, agriculture, forestry, ecology, industry, general infrastructure, etc.

Systematic efforts at international development assistance have been called "*induced* development. This is development purposively pursued, accelerated, and programmed, often guided by policy based on a mix of knowledge and assumptions, and therefore distinct from *spontaneous* development" (Cernea 1995: 342).

This new style of intervention, while similar in many ways to earlier international technical interventions, was different in its overtly stated rationale. While earlier official activities of nation states were carried out blatantly in their own direct interest, international development assistance had the stated purpose of serving the interests of the "recipient" state. Benefits accruing to the "donor" state were indirect, secondary, or incidental—such as "peace in the world" and "an enduring atmosphere for world trade"—or perhaps somewhat more directly, "better trade relationships for the 'donor' in the long run".

In his second inaugural address in 1949, President Harry S. Truman of the United States proclaimed this policy. Perhaps misinterpreting the success of the United States Marshall Plan in assisting the rapid economic recovery of Europe after World War II, the goal was to share US "know how" with the "backward" countries of Africa, Asia, and Latin America.

In response to the fourth point in President Truman's address, the president of the National Association of State Universities and Land Grant Colleges, John A. Hannah, wrote to him in a letter dated February 4, 1949:

> ...being fully aware that sacrifices are involved in a world program such as you have outlined, I am personally convinced, and our member universities are collectively convinced, that the sta-

bility, welfare, and democratic freedom of the world demand the cooperation of all Americans in such a program. We feel that this responsibility is particularly incumbent on us as colleges and universities supported by state and federal funds and carrying on in a long democratic tradition (cited in NASULGC 1969: 6).

Responses over the next several decades included the evolution of a multilateral network of agencies as part of the United Nations system; bilateral government agencies from every continent practicing international development within other nation states; non-government organizations (NGOs, referring also to religious, voluntary, and charitable organizations) working within, between, and among the nation states; universities with global outreach; foundations, and other organizations.

Just as the idea and the implementing organizations have changed over the years, so has the definition of the concept of *development* and the conceptualization of *international development cooperation.*

2.2.3 Modernization

Mid-20th century views of *development* were dominated by the idea of MODERNIZATION. The assumption among the more wealthy nations was that they were more developed than the poorer nations, and the way to help others become developed was to strengthen their economies. From this perspective, development *was* economic development, and writers in the field used the words synonymously. The idea was that, over time, as a place developed, it went from conditions of "less of everything" to conditions of "more of everything".

It was assumed that in the beginning of a development program, a country, state, or district, for example, was poor. As time went by, in a successful development effort, people in the place which was "developing" would have more and more of the goods and services they needed. This was called "economic growth". The assumption was of a linear time line, from an earlier stage to the present, and then on to the future, with things getting better as time moved along. And "better" was generally defined as more of everything that wealth could bring.

With the dominance of an economic perspective, it was relatively easy to measure development. Indicators such as gross national product (GNP) could be used to compare "more developed" countries with "less developed" countries. Figures for average income per capita were often available, and countries or regions could be compared with each other by plotting those figures on a straight line. Economic indicators of development, which completely dominated development thinking in the 1940s and 1950s, are still in use at the close of the 20th century. (The World Bank, UNDP, and other agencies have been publishing annual lists of these indicators, by country and by region, in recent decades.)

A basic assumption of this approach was that if economic indicators were positive, everything else would improve. There has also been a tendency for many measurable, and particularly material, dimensions of the human condition to point in the same direction. Those who have the most money (per capita cash income) also tend to have the best health (longest life expectancy), best education (more years of formal schooling per capita), most miles of paved road per person, highest rates of conversion of energy (fuel consumption per person), and so on.

Although the literature on *development* has been growing vigorously during the past five decades, the definitions have tended to be weak, culture-bound, general, vague, insufficient, or simply ignored. Some of the writers and practitioners in the field began with the term *economic development*. This simplified the matter for many, and made it more straightforward. And the assumption of *trickle down* was accepted as a rationale for providing direct assistance to some, with the expectation that, over time, the benefits would trickle down to all others (Borton 1966; Eicher and Staatz 1984; Islam 1974; Mosher 1969).

This perspective is often referred to as "modernization theory", even though other indicators have been added to the purely economic. Practitioners and scholars have realized that life is both economic and more than economic—as evidenced in the experience of international development.

Barbara Ingham has reviewed development economics, and points out that "economists are also taking more interest in issues of decentralization, participation and grass roots rural development in order to reverse the concentration of power and resources at the center, which is observed in many developing countries" (Ingham 1993: 1804), and "...this is still a goods-oriented view of development. When development is defined as human development, however, what is proposed is a people-oriented view of development" (ibid.: 1813).

Among the problems with the modernization perspective has been the increasingly apparent historical fact that, after years of massive international investments in economic development, the relative positions on the time line haven't changed very much. In fact, by some calculations, the rich countries are becoming comparatively richer, and the poor countries are falling further behind. In some instances, countries which were quite poor began exporting oil, and figures like GNP and per capita income showed them moving much higher on the line. However, in many of these same countries, the bulk of the population still lives in abject poverty and health and education levels are not rising.

Planners and consultants in fields like agriculture, engineering, education, and health have had great confidence in technical indicators. Measurements of such variables as the *tons of mineral fertilizer applied per hectare*, or the *proportion of the arable land which was artificially irrigated*, the *number of telephones per thousand people, consumption of kilowatt hours per annum, numbers of classrooms or trained teachers per population*, and the *numbers of hospital beds or X-ray machines per capita* have been utilized heavily. Increasingly, "quality of life indicators" have been substituted for, or used in conjunction with, both economic indicators and technical indicators. These have featured such numbers as *food calorie consumption per person*; *infant mortality* and the *proportion of mothers who survive childbirth*; *life expectancy*; *relationship of college degrees earned and employment*; and *proportion of jobs which require difficult hard labor*.

Indicators, however imperfect, are needed to guide policy planning. One major problem with these types of indicators is that they are measured in numbers, and then the numbers are grouped. The most common reporting of the grouping is as an *average* of all the figures, or the *mean*. However, with these development indicators, the *mean* is usually misleading. That is because users of the data tend to think about some type of normal, or "bell-shaped" distribution where most of the cases are grouped around the *mean*. For example, when it is reported that farm families in a certain area have an *average* (or *mean*) farm size of one hectare, then planners assume most farms are about one hectare in size. Actually, however, in much of the world, indicators such as size of farm are not distributed in that "normal distribution". Instead, there is a bimodal curve, with many farms (in this example) of around one-fourth hectare, hardly any between one-half hectare and ten hectares, and then a few of over fifty hectares. Thus, misled by the mean, programmers plan development programs for one-hectare farms in a place where there are hardly any of that size.

Let us take an example from the field of education where, for development planning, data is presented on the average years of formal education in a particular place. The data may be reported as an average of 2.5 years of formal education per adult person. That may be a correct, but misleading, *mean*. For example, in a typical village of 2,650 adults, there may be a bimodal distribution. If twenty-five of them had advanced university degrees, with about twenty-five years each of formal education; another group of twenty-five might each have had 20 years of formal education; and fifty of them might have each had two years. That could leave 2,550 other adults who each had only one-half year of formal education. But, mathematically, the *mean* might actually be 2.5 years per adult.

Similarly, when rural and urban data are grouped, development planners may be misled. In many countries, a very low proportion of women have any formal education. But in those same countries, a much higher proportion of urban women than rural women have formal education. When rural and urban data are presented separately, the extreme dearth of formal schooling for women is revealed. When urban and rural data are not disaggregated, the national average figures tend to hide the extreme figures.

It is not that the *mean* itself is in any way at fault. It is merely that so many figures used to describe the development situation are reported only in terms of that *mean*. If the *mode* and *median* were also given, the same data could be used more effectively to describe a situation and develop appropriate programs. This phenomenon has led many to refer to the cruelty of the average, or the *meanness of the mean*.

In addition, as indicated earlier, whether the indicators are economic, technical, or quality of life, they tend to be culture-bound. Practitioners and scholars from the wealthy countries of the North and West tend to assume that the "good" things of life in their own countries are what everybody wants and needs. They assume that to be like them is to be *modern*, and to be anything else is to be something less. Therefore the ideal toward which *development* is directed is referred to as *modernization*. And it is assumed that the reasons why other peoples are not as modern are that they simply lack the technical information or the capital to develop further. Too often, what is called *modernization* by outsiders, is considered, from the perspective of people in Africa, Asia, and Latin America, as "the outsiders just want us to be more like them".

This kind of thinking, coupled with a linear perspective on the development process, has resulted in some observers viewing *international development* as a negative force. They see it as being thrust on the poorer countries by the wealthy. Arturo Escobar discusses "the emergence and consolidation of the discourse and strategy of development in the early post-World War II period, as a result of the problematization of poverty that took place during those years, …the professionalization of development knowledge and the institutionalization of development practices…." He goes on to suggest that "the system defines the hegemonic worldview of development, a worldview that increasingly permeates and transforms the economic, social, and cultural fabric of Third World cities and villages, even if the languages of development are always adapted and reworked significantly at the local level." He includes "a cultural critique of economics by taking on the single most influential force shaping the development field: the discourse of development economics" (Escobar 1995: 16–18).

The Nepalese anthropologist Dor Bahadur Bista took a hard look at outsiders trying to help Nepal "develop" and observed,

As a rule Nepalis do not plan for the future. It is far easier to mentally speculate on the next life in an imaginary hell or heaven than to plan for one's old age or even later years. Peculiarities in temporal orientation, then, interact strongly with the lack of a sense of internal personal control and achievement motivation to frustrate the ability for planning which must surely have important consequences on Nepal's ability to navigate the future (Bista 1991: 85).

2.3 The Development Cycle

Most international development strategies have been built on the assumption that development is a linear phenomenon. Things go from less to more, or from bad to better. Whether it is less money, less technology, or poor quality of life, the *development* line is a straight one, going always in one direction—upward and further upward. A result of this way of thinking about development has been that agencies and organizations conducting international development have assumed that they should deliver *more* to a place with which they are engaged in international development activities.

For example, in programs of "donor" countries, or even specialized agencies of the UN, which were started to "help" governments of other countries improve their effectiveness and efficiency, typically additional departments and bureaus were added. But in some of those places, the problem was that governments were already *overdeveloped*. There were already too many overspecialized bureaus, divisions, and other units in the public administration. When the "outsiders" established new additional government departments, the situation became worse, instead of better.

A similar situation has been common in agricultural marketing. Specialists have entered *less developed* countries when requested to help improve the movement of fruit and vegetables from farmers' fields to consumers' kitchens. With their straight line assumptions, the outsiders recommended building new and larger central marketing facilities in large cities. But some of those places already had large numbers of highly efficient, small-scale "middle-men" who were doing cost-effective marketing of the fruit and vegetables. In spite of large foreign investments in the new system, it was defeated by local people for whom their own system was working very well. Since the system was already *appropriately developed*, people did not want to make it *overdeveloped*.

As a result of these kinds of experiences, some international development practitioners have moved away from the older way of thinking about development as a linear process. We have suggested elsewhere that the linear assumption has misled development strategists (G.H. Axinn 1977a). As an alternative, development can be thought of as a cyclical process. History demonstrates that nations and cities and villages do not continually improve, whatever the criteria may be. Neither do they always grow larger, and larger, and larger. Things do not always get "better" all the time.

Henry David Thoreau wrote, "there are thousands hacking away at the branches of evil for every one who is cutting at the roots"

(Thoreau 1958: 55). For the development process, what are the roots?

The world is changing all the time. Change is more rapid in some places, and slower in others, but change is everywhere. However, human history is not a narrative of continuous change for the better. As mentioned earlier, not all change is development. Development may be defined as those changes which are seen as desirable among the particular group of people who are changing. Such a view of development insists that no outsiders' criteria will be adequate. Neither economic indicators nor political ideals nor simple measures of life and death provide a universal base for development strategy.

Instead, the analysis of human experience suggests that while it is possible to be *underdeveloped*, it is also possible to be *overdeveloped*. Some change is in the direction of more development; some change is in the direction of less development. How, then, can planners cope with the process of development? What assumptions about the development process are likely to yield more appropriate strategies?

An alternative to the traditional way of assessing development as a linear process (moving from less of everything to more and larger), is to consider a DEVELOPMENT CYCLE. Each human group is somewhere on this cycle, and moves at its own pace to the next stage. The human group may be a nation state, a city, a village, or a single family. For convenience, the stages on this cycle can be called *underdeveloped, appropriately developed*, and *overdeveloped*. There are certain characteristics of each stage which seem to be common to all parts of the Earth, and all periods of time.

For example, groups which are called *underdeveloped* tend to underutilize the resources of their environment. They do not strain the resources of their ecosystems in enhancing their own levels and styles of living. In contrast, human groups which are overutilizing the resources of their ecosystem to enhance their own levels and styles of living (given the technologies available to them at the time) may be considered overdeveloped. And somewhere between these two extremes, human groups which are in equilibrium with the resources of their ecosystems may be considered to be appropriately developed (Figure 2.1).

Being human, and having been socialized into a particular culture, each individual tends to view his/her own situation as appropriate. However, since change is universal, underlying strategic issues

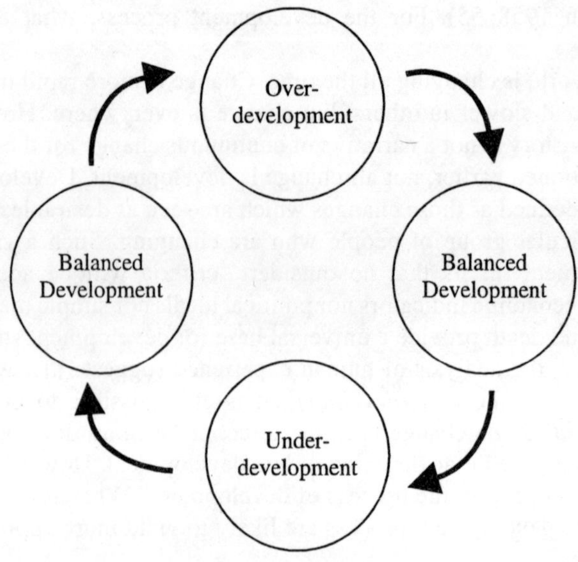

Figure 2.1
The Development Cycle

relate to the direction and rate of change away from the past, through the present, and toward the future. Seen from a time perspective, each human group moves through cycles of underdevelopment, balanced development, overdevelopment, balanced development, underdevelopment, and onward. The rate of change on the development cycle varies from group to group. Some are apparently static. Others seem to move quite rapidly. A given group may also go through periods of rapid change, periods of very gradual change, and periods when change may not be visible at all.

The idea of a cycle of development is useful to international development practitioners in that, prior to making any kind of intervention, the following questions could be asked: Is this situation really *underdeveloped*, needing more of something? Is it *overdeveloped*, requiring less of what it is already doing? Or is it presently *appropriately developed*, and would it be in the best interest of those who live there to try to conduct programs to maintain their current conditions?

The idea of a development cycle does not imply that no interventions are necessary, since eventually everything will move around the cycle. It does imply that any intervention strategy is likely to be more successful if prior analysis is made of the position of things in a *development cycle*.

This idea that the human experience follows a cycle is certainly not new. Ancient Hindu scholars postulated such cycles on their Sanskrit scrolls. Buddhist thinkers visualized humanity as constantly following a cycle. It may be the Biblical view of a Creation, coupled with Darwinian evolution, which gave rise to the single straight-line assumptions of growth and development.

Stages along the cycle may be identified by characteristics other than the use of resources. One way to assess the relative appropriateness, or balance with the environment of development of any particular human group, is in terms of its conversion of energy (petroleum, electricity, sunlight and heat, wood, etc.). If a group is utilizing relatively little energy per capita in enhancing its own level and style of living, then it may be considered to be underdeveloped.

If a group is converting relatively high amounts of energy in enhancing its own levels and styles of living, it may be considered to be overdeveloped, particularly if its ecosystem cannot sustain the high levels of energy conversion. And if a group has balanced its utilization of energy with its level and style of life (what its ecosystem can sustain over time), it may be considered to be appropriately developed.

As the sociologist Fred Cottrell wrote nearly half a century ago, "the amounts and types of energy employed condition man's way of life materially, and set somewhat predictable limits on what he can do and on how society will be organized" (Cottrell 1955: vii).

Development can also be measured in terms of the specialization of human performance of functions. Certain functions (italicized below) are performed in every social system. However, in more developed groups, individuals are more differentiated—are more specialized—and perform fewer different functions. In less developed groups, there is a tendency for each person to perform a greater variety of different functions. For example, a rural family living alone on a steep hillside in Peru will *produce* food, *supply* itself with inputs of seed and fertilizer, *market* its produce through consumption and storage, and *govern* the rates at which it does such things. It will also see to it that its members *learn* what they need to know, provide for their *personal maintenance*, and arrange for their own *healthcare*.

A rural family in Canada, by contrast, may specialize in *producing* food. Other persons living in a nearby town may *supply* the inputs, and still others from a faraway city might *market* the outputs. Similarly, such functions as *governance*, *learning* (including both research and education), and *healthcare* are also partly "delegated" to other specialists who live in other places. The Peruvian hill family may be said to be less differentiated, and hence less developed. The Canadian family could be labeled as more differentiated, or more specialized. (For more details, more examples, and other factors which tend to vary along a development cycle, see G.H. Axinn 1977a.)

The proposition is that human groups which are underutilizing the resources of their ecosystem, given the technologies at their disposal, are usually less specialized in their social organizations. Those organizations also tend to be smaller, and have characteristics common among groups generally referred to as less developed. By contrast, overdeveloped human groups not only convert their resources at a faster rate than their ecosystems can sustain over time, they are also usually organized in much larger groups, and are much more specialized in their functions.

Thus, the idea of a *development cycle* can be highly useful in the design of development policies and strategies. It is offered here as a way of analysis and understanding of the development idea. Like other conceptualizations offered in this book, it is a deliberate over-simplification of reality, and merely indicates a general tendency. There are other useful ways of thinking, as well. For example, one can consider a *pendulum* which swings back and forth. One extreme of that pendulum swing might be thought of as *underdevelopment*. The opposite extreme of the pendulum swing could be envisioned as *overdevelopment*. In this illustration, the middle of the swing would represent a state of *balanced development*. This conceptualization suggests that while human groups pass through a situation of balanced development from time to time, they do not remain there. Instead, the momentum of the swing propels them in their movement toward the opposite extreme.

Both the pendulum and the cycle illustrations have the advantage of visualizing development as constantly changing. But neither is unidirectional—that is, they do not imply that development goes in one direction: from less developed to more developed, to more developed, to more…. It is this unidirectional perception which we believe has misled much thinking and planning in international development.

2.4 Forces of Continuity and Change

Another strategic way to view the opportunity for development intervention is to take a systems approach. In addition to the ideas mentioned above for building a development strategy, systemic thinking groups many types of issues. It accepts that significant changes in the human condition do have *economic* dimensions; but also *political, social, technological, biological, physical,* and *cultural* dimensions, as well as *administrative, political,* and *diplomatic* dimensions.

One can further assume that each of these types of factors is *linked* to each of the others, like *components* in a system. And a change in any component may have an impact on any and all other components. Similarly, the system is never completely closed; there are linkages to other outside systems. And each component identified within the system could also be viewed as a system in itself, as it actually has smaller components within it.

If one thinks about planned change, or development, as a task in which the goal is to systematically change a situation as it appears at one point in time to something different at another point in time, then it is helpful to use a *force field* perspective. We can assume that the present situation does not exist by chance. There are forces which are pressing the situation toward change, *but* there are also forces pressing against any change. These may be called the *forces of continuity* and the *forces of change*. At any particular point in time, things are as they are because the forces in one direction balance the forces in the other direction. Figure 2.2 illustrates the forces of continuity and change in a development situation.

From a development perspective, no outside intervention occurs in a vacuum. Change results from introduction of additional force on the change side, or from reduction of some force on the continuity side.

For example, in agriculture, change to a new variety of wheat or rice usually means abandonment of an old variety. Using a new

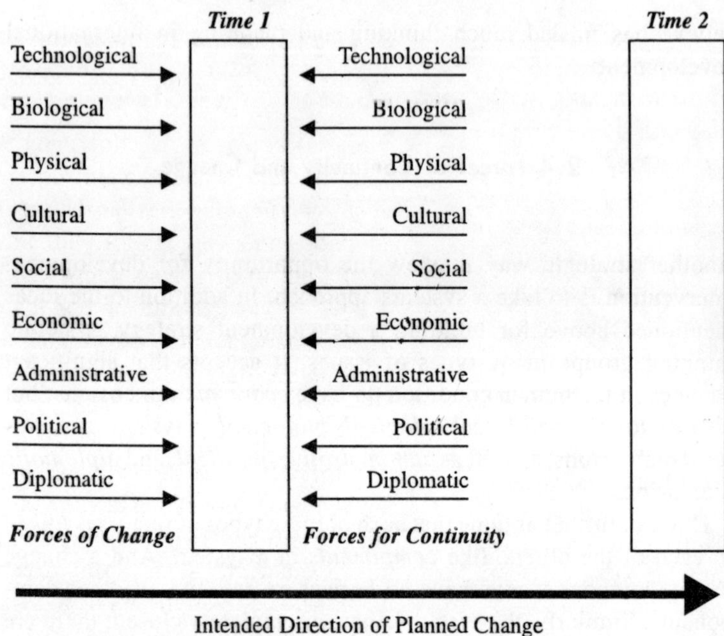

Source: G.H. Axinn 1988b; Lewin 1951.

Figure 2.2
Forces of Continuity and Change

form of draft power (i.e., a tractor) requires a shift away from an old form of draft power (and the ox or the horse becomes just another mouth to feed). Using fertile land to produce a new cash crop may require not using that land for family food production.

In the context of continuity and change, what components of any particular human ecosystem are involved in international technical cooperation? Or, for any technical change, what are the non-technological forces also impinging upon it? To what extent are they, as the diagram suggests, biological? physical? cultural? social? economic? administrative? political? diplomatic? Even the simplest technical change may interact with this whole range of forces.

To illustrate this, in a South Asian farm family ecosystem, the shift to an improved buffalo might enable the women of that system to increase the production of fluid buffalo milk. However, that will be successful only if there is enough fodder to feed the new buffalo through the year. The fodder may come from the straw of grains produced on the farm; it may come from cuttings along the sides of the road; it may come from common village pasture areas; or it may come from cutting leaves from fodder trees. But it must come from somewhere.

Without meeting the *biological* and *physical* requirements, no technological change is likely to persist over time.

But those are not the only forces impinging on the situation. There are *cultural* dimensions. The buffalo may outproduce the cow, but some groups need the cow for religious purposes, and that need is as real as your need to be wearing clothes today. Unless the buffalo can earn enough to pay for keeping the cow as well, the technical shift to a milking buffalo may not be acceptable.

And there will also be *social* considerations. If the woman of the farm family ecosystem owns the buffalo, her relative power in the household will increase. If her husband owns the buffalo, and particularly if the cash income from any sale of surplus milk goes to him, her workload will be increased, and his power may be greater.

Similar social phenomena will relate to the relative social position of that family among other families in the village. In some villages the social status of a family is directly related to the number of livestock it owns. In some, however, while owning cattle is considered to confer a high status, owning buffalo is considered to denote a lower status. And in other places, buffalo ownership may be valued higher. These considerations could account for a high proportion of the variance in the probability of acceptance of the improved buffalo.

On the *economic* side, many relevant forces have been analyzed in farming systems research. Will the benefits to the family exceed the costs to the family? Can some kitchen garden land be converted to fodder production for the buffalo? If it can, will the cash income from the sale of buffalo milk be sufficient to purchase fruit and vegetables no longer produced? Could it provide more income than that? If less, why make the change?

And, of course, there are always *administrative* forces. If a cooling tank is installed in this district, it will be possible to take milk to the tank any day of the year, and be paid for it in cash. Collection will be made there, and the milk transported to a large dairy processing plant in the city. But administration of a series of milk collection points at various distances from the city may be impossible with an absolutely centralized administrative system. All dairy plant personnel will wish to be posted in the central city. No one would take a job at a remote milk collection point if all promotions of personnel are in the central dairy plant. Administrative decentralization may be a necessary condition to achieve expansion of the dairy collection system. And that may, in turn, be necessary for year-round effective demand for fluid milk.

But if the cooling tank is installed in another district on the other side of the river, then the market will only be available during the dry season when one can walk across the river with a container of milk. However, if the *political* power of the representative of the other district is stronger, it may not be politically feasible to have the collection point in this district. Political participation, perhaps by an organization of women who own milking buffalo, may be necessary. It could be a precondition for improved buffalo to be an acceptable change in the farming system.

And the political forces are not the end of the line. In the *diplomatic* arena, it could be that in faraway Europe and North America, there is a surplus of dairy products. The ministry of agriculture in the country of our example has perhaps requested some food grains from the World Food Program. Now they have negotiated an arrangement to accept 70,000 tons of dry milk powder in addition to the grain. When this is reconstituted at the city dairy plant, there will be no need to collect from any of the new cooling stations for over six months.

When the area's politician confronts the minister of agriculture to ask how they could have done such a thing, the minister explains that he tried not to take the milk powder. He even traveled to Rome or Washington to beg that only food grain be shipped, showing evidence that neither milk powder nor cooking oil were needed at all. In fact, imports of either would depress local prices, discourage local production, and worsen the food security situation for the entire country. But diplomatic power is like political and economic power. It belongs to the strong, not the weak. And the powerful "donor" nations may have forced the "gifts" of dry milk powder, because local politicians in the "wealthy" countries have their own problems with surplus dairy products.

Thus a simple technological innovation can be defeated at any level: by biological, physical, economic, cultural, social, administrative, political, and even diplomatic forces. And conversely, its acceptance might be enhanced at any level (Axinn 1988b: 12–13).

Summarizing this position from his vantage point in the World Bank, Michael Cernea writes:

> The intellectual argument that I regard as the main entry point for social scientists into the environmental debate is that an improved and sustainable use of natural resources depends decisively on improving the patterns of social organization for their management by the users themselves. Who are these users? Primarily the world's enormous mass of small farmers. My basic proposition is that *effective environmental policy must promote and rest on appropriate social organization.* Neither technology unnumbered in social organizational structures nor free-market fundamentalism unable to control externalities can alone tackle runaway resource abuses (Cernea 1995: 346).

2.5 Looking Ahead

If development is a normative concept not all that easily identified in the 20th century, it may be a much more complex concept in the 21st century. In 1995, at the close of the first UN World Summit for Social Development, Juan Somavia, Chile's delegate to the UN, said "the unfinished business of the 20th century is the eradication of poverty. The century that multiplied wealth, technology, trade, and freedoms in the most incredible way also multiplied poverty, and that's completely unacceptable" (*New York Times* 1995b).

The end of the Cold War era has changed the actors as well as the scene for development assistance. Simple black and white issues are now all shades of gray. Lessons learned in development efforts in the 20th century may have diminished influence on development as new movements evolve. Hernando de Soto suggested the need for identifying programs where left and right can meet. The UN "Social Summit" conference set goals and directions for reducing the debt of the poorest countries, protecting the rights of workers, including children, and establishing levels of assistance for disadvantaged people.

This suggests the need for new approaches to collaboration; growing appreciation for, and knowledge about, the subtle nuances of sustainability; shifting from zero-sum to positive-sum directions; and building on the knowledge of indigenous populations to strengthen the inputs of new technology.

In a provocative paper, Robert Chambers suggests that

development professionals have for too long been ruining [the procession of development] by allowing themselves to be deceived. If all power deceives, then it is in stepping down and empowering others that new and more practical realities can be expressed and shared; and it is through empowering the poor, vulnerable and weak, that their reality will count more and equity will be better served (Chambers 1994: 26).

2.6 Implications for Professional Practitioners

There are many implications for practitioners of the various perspectives on the concept of development, and current issues and concerns in the field. Awareness of the multiplicity of definitions in itself is a mark of the professional. Further, genuine doubt of any simplistic solutions to development is a necessity.

In a thoughtful analysis, Jan Knippers Black came to this conclusion:

Real development, of the sort we are calling empowerment, will never be neat and orderly and predictable. For better or worse, consequences do not derive directly from any identifiable constellation of motives. But the same uncertainty that makes development work so frustrating also makes it intriguing, challenging, and promising.

Likewise, such development cannot be unthreatening. No matter that change be sought by peaceful means or that initial goals be modest and nonpolitical. The empowerment of "have-nots" is by definition threatening to "haves". [The most insecure people and nations are those that have the most to lose.] Its very success will continue to attract donors and agencies whose motives are hidden and less than benign. But poor people are often rich in ingenuity and spirit. Any program that pretends to promote organization and self-help on the part of the have-nots runs the risk of being successful (Black 1991: 200–201).

Each person who is actually involved in the practice of development should be able to live with, and even thrive on, uncertainty. Professional practitioners may have a deep commitment to empowering the marginalized who are participants in development activities. However, this requires understanding the historical factors which exist in any social setting. It is our hope that the practitioner would find the idea of a development cycle useful, enabling him/her to gauge the pace of change of any particular group, as well as recognize that in any nation or social system different groups of people may be in different positions on the development cycle.

Practitioners are likely to be more effective when they can perceive the interplay between the weak and the strong, the rural and the urban, the high status and low status of any particular community. Practitioners are advantaged when they are enough of *scholars* to know other people's experiences and understanding, and use them to strengthen their own efforts. Each human group, even subcultures within a particular cultural group, will have its own unique *normal* ways of thinking, feeling and doing—the norms of that group. The professional practitioner needs to be able to recognize his/her own normative concept of development in order to understand the forces of continuity and change which exist in a different culture or society.

CHAPTER 3

Current Issues and Concerns in Development

A world in which 20 per cent of the population enjoys 84 per cent of the annual income, while another 20 per cent struggles for survival on a mere 1.4 per cent of the world's income, as stressed in UNDP's 1994 Human Development Report, can never provide a secure and sustainable way of life for humankind.

M.S. Swaminathan 1994: 11

International development is the field of planned change across national and regional borders. In international development change is both the goal of a particular activity and a feature of the larger environment in which everything happens. Therefore, those who practice development are subject to continuous change in the larger stage on which development is played. Thus the issues and concerns current at any point in time are likely to be different than at earlier times, and certainly will change in the future. The issues identified within this chapter are described by the words which became "popular" as the issues surfaced. Over time, even the word used for the issue has acquired many meanings. This challenges the practitioner to ensure there is a common understanding of what is being discussed. The issues which are current at any one time are very much interrelated, although they have been separated for analysis in this chapter. The focus here is on the current issues and concerns from the perspective of the last decade of the 20th century, and perhaps the first decade of the 21st century.

3.1 Sustainability

By the 1970s it had become apparent to many development professionals that things could not get "bigger and better" forever; that there were limits to development in the size of things; that there were limits to growth (Meadows et al. 1972). Miguel Altieri pointed out that the Green Revolution model had not led to improvement for small farmers or slowed the vicious cycle of rural poverty and environmental degradation in the Third World. And, he suggests, the problem is more than just technology and production. It is the "social, cultural and economic issues responsible for underdevelopment that require attention" (Altieri 1995: 15).

Human history is a demonstration that nothing continues forever. Plants, animals, human beings, and the physical dimensions of our planet—they all go through cycles of youth, growth, maturity, aging, decay, and replacement by the next generation. But at least for most of the last thousand years it was considered safe for each human group to assume that the earth was more than sufficient for unlimited creative application of new technologies to enhance the human condition. When careful selection of food plants led to discovery of varieties which produced more food, people planted them, and both plant and human populations grew. When new technologies were available, like the invention of the sailing ship, or, later, the invention of the steam engine to power sea-going vessels, human groups traveled greater distances. This enabled them to expand trade, to conquer other places, and to build large empires. Until the 20th century, there always seemed to be new frontiers, and thus new opportunities for "more and better" for those who would venture forth.

A major shock of the 20th century was the awareness that there were no more "new worlds" left on this planet. Wherever one might venture, others were already there. And the natural resources which fueled human consumption were not unlimited. In the last twenty years of the century, serious official international development efforts have been required to consider the *sustainability* of development activities being planned and implemented.

Much of what has been planned and implemented in recent international development cooperation has been focused on AGRICULTURE AND RURAL DEVELOPMENT, the main focus of this book. Like other important contemporary issues worthy of the attention of serious scholars and practitioners, these are complex questions, and not simple problems. RURAL DEVELOPMENT includes everything happening in the countryside: the people, the land, the forests, the mines, the lakes and rivers, and all other aspects of the environment.

It relates those who live on the land to the larger environment of the community, region, and nation, as well as to technological, social, cultural, political, administrative, and diplomatic considerations. AGRICULTURE is a major, but not the only, component of rural life. Broadly defined, agriculture includes production and marketing of crops of all kinds (grain, fruit, vegetables, fodder, etc.) and all types of livestock. Agriculture includes the components of the farming system—plants, animals, and people in their near environment of soil, water, weather (or climate)—and the ecosystem in which the farms are located (Axinn and Axinn 1987). The *sustainability* of the ecosystem is challenged by both rural development and agriculture.

In such a complex system, how is sustainability to be assessed, understood, and enhanced? Here the current literature is inconsistent. At one level, there is concern over sustainability of a particular project, program, or technological arrangement. Thus projects are considered sustainable if they are likely to be funded for the second five years; farming strategies are considered sustainable if investors can quickly increase their financial position in them and withdraw with profits, rather than losses; and new production technologies may be considered sustainable if they succeed in increasing production on a research farm. Much international development strategy falls within this definition.

By the last decade of the 20th century, with increasing concern for the damage to the ecosystem which was often related to various types of development activities, practitioners in development turned to the interface between human development and the environment. Tracing the history of development assistance and pointing toward a more *sustainable* development, Ruddle and Rondinelli (1983) suggested strategies for "transforming natural resources for human development" through a "resource systems framework for development policy", including balanced development with social equity.

According to William M. Adams:

The history of thinking about sustainable development is closely linked to the history of environmental concern and peoples' attitudes to nature. Both represent responses to changing scientific understanding, changing knowledge about the world and ideas about society. Where they differ, and more particularly where their histories differ, is in their geographical scope. Histories of environmentalism have tended to focus on Europe or America.

However the history of sustainable development thinking must embrace the way these essentially metropolitan ideas were expressed on the periphery in the present century, initially on the colonial periphery and latterly within the countries of the independent Third World (Adams 1990: 14).

Sustainability, in current usage, is different from continuity (discussed in Chapter 2). *Sustainability is a temporal, holistic concept.* It represents an attempt to combine optimistic with realistic conceptualizations. It can also be seen from a global perspective: there may be negative consequences of any change—some kinds of short-term improvement in the conditions of some people may result in a serious worsening of the conditions of others, or those same people, over time. In a changing world, no condition is permanent. Some things are more sustainable than others. From our perspective, *the serious issue is the sustainability of Earth as a planet where humanity may survive over generations.*

Addressing this concern, Gro Harlem Bruntland, as prime minister of Norway and chair of the World Commission on Environment and Development, defined sustainability to include "paths to human progress that meet the needs and aspirations of the present generation without compromising the ability of future generations to meet their needs. It requires political reforms, and a more just and equitable distribution within and among nations" (Bruntland 1989: 14).

Many contemporary definitions of sustainability focus on the holistic approach to planned change which takes into account the consequences for future generations (see Collins 1991; Edens et al. 1985; Ropetto 1985). Examining policy perspectives on social, agricultural, and rural sustainability, Wimberley suggested that

> To be sustainable is to provide for food, fiber, and other natural and social resources needed for survival of a group—such as a national or international society, an economic sector, or residential category—and to provide it in a manner that maintains the essential resources for present and future generations (Wimberley 1993: 1).

Characteristics of sustainable systems and the complications in achieving them have been identified by scholars working in development programs throughout the world (Conway 1990; Lynam

1992; Lynam and Herdt 1992; Thrupp 1993). Lynam points out that "the sustainability problem demands such collaboration between crop and natural resource management programs, sometimes within the same institution, but often between institutions" (Lynam 1992: 128). As Lynam and Herdt suggest,

> This is the challenge for impact assessment of international agricultural research: to ask how the output of such research contributes to meeting today's needs (i.e. its contribution to income), and how it may affect the capacity of future generations to meet their needs (i.e. its contribution to sustainability) (Lynam and Herdt 1992: 3).

Scholars have identified two major types of sustainability problems in agriculture. One arises from overuse of such inputs as fertilizer and irrigation water in large-scale commercial agriculture. The other relates to the marginal lands and fragile ecosystems where small mixed farming systems are characterized by high populations of poor people who are trying to survive from day to day and prosper by producing whatever they can.

In a larger sense, the sustainability which is most significant is that of "spaceship Earth" as a place where future generations of human beings can survive and thrive. From that perspective, the question for any particular approach to agriculture and rural development is the long-run consequences of that approach for future generations which might attempt to survive in that particular environment.

Some natural resources, like coal and petroleum deposits in the earth, are not considered renewable. If a mine has 10 million tons of coal in it, and if all 10 million tons are removed by mining operations, there will be no more coal in the mine. Similarly, if an oil field has a fixed amount of petroleum in it, and half of that petroleum is removed, then only half of that petroleum remains for future use.

Alternatively, some natural resources are considered renewable. But even they are not unlimited. Forests are an example. Since trees, growing on fertile soil with moisture from rain, are able to convert solar energy into the fiber of wood, forests have expanded and grown wherever the soil and moisture on this planet have permitted. But they do not grow in an instant. Some reach a diameter of 10 cm in less than a decade; others take two decades, and others take still longer. If people cut trees faster than the trees grow, forests disappear. If people develop an industry which uses forest products as its raw material—making paper, plywood, furniture, or houses, for example, from the wood—and these industries are near very large forests, it will appear in the beginning that there is plenty of the resource to be exploited. When the nearby trees have all been cut, it may be necessary to travel further to find new trees, and perhaps pay more to transport logs to the factory. Factory owners and operators will assume there are economies of scale, and the more trees they process per year the more profitable the venture will be. And for some time, that may be an appropriate strategy.

Some sustainablity problems arise from too many inputs such as fertilizer and insecticide, rather than too much output. In the Punjab states of India and Pakistan, thanks to heavy investment in surface irrigation (canals, etc.) by the British in the first half of the 20th century, and an even greater growth in the proportion of irrigated land in the second half from dams, canals, river diversions and shallow tube-wells, the area has become one of the world's outstanding examples of increased grain production. When the high inputs of water were accompanied by high inputs of mineral fertilizer and seed, the result was significantly increased yields of wheat, rice, and maize (known as the Green Revolution).

However, if irrigation water is brought to land where there had been very little water before, it is necessary to provide drainage which will remove excess water. An old saying among agriculturists is that irrigation without drainage is like production without marketing. If intervention through development efforts brings one, it is necessary to also bring the other. In the Punjab, unfortunately, the land is relatively flat, and arranging for drainage is expensive and difficult. Over the years, vast areas of land have been irrigated without sufficient drainage. And at the same time, high levels of mineral fertilizers, particularly nitrate fertilizers, have been added to the land to achieve high (and financially profitable) yields. The price of that development effort has been a whole series of "second generation" problems. Among them are waterlogging of some fields, which makes them unsuitable for production of grain. Another problem is the salinization of the soil, where salts from irrigation water have built up to such an extent that low soil pH (the measure of acidity or alkalinity) has made it unsuitable for grain production. In this example, the technologies were sustainable for a decade or two, but without further major adjustments were not sustainable for a longer period.

Sustainability is a serious issue because when any change makes things better for a while, it may make conditions worse later on. Similarly, when a change makes conditions better for some, it may result in a worsening of conditions elsewhere. The growth of cities, for example, may offer higher levels of living to some people. Like a magnet, rural people are drawn to their fringes, and urban populations grow. But then pressures increase for urban people to extract food and other goods from rural people, and economic and political consequences may lead to turbulence.

Lori Ann Thrupp has written that "pervasive social-ecological predicaments continue and are poorly understood in most countries of the world. The pernicious erosion of both human livelihoods and natural resource conditions are all too familiar" (Thrupp 1993: 47).

Altieri suggests that "the failure to address the ecological causes of environmental problems in modern agriculture" has diverted scientists from appreciating the context and complexity of agro-ecological processes. "The need to increase food security while conserving the resource base requires not only profound changes in strategic research agendas, but also in the fundamental approaches to rural development that involve true farmer participation" (Altieri 1995: 16).

3.2 Participation

The issue of *participation* is not new to the development field. By the middle of the 20th century, it was recognized in both agricultural extension and in community development that those affected by any development activity must participate in it if it was to satisfy their needs and endure over time. But the idea of participation was not widely accepted, particularly by those in power in systems where top-down authority was the cultural and political norm.

The meaning of *participation* as a concept has been clarified by many writers in different ways, but like other social science concepts, there are variations. If people in a village are forced by the village leaders to serve as laborers in the construction of a motor road, the leaders may report that there was much *participation* in the project. But who would benefit from such a road? Who asked for the road? Who decided when, and where, and how to build it? If one discovers that the need for a motor road was felt only by those having motor vehicles, and in this village everyone walked and only the leader had a motor vehicle, it is difficult to recognize genuine *participation* in the project. The people did participate in the work, but they did not participate in deciding what should be done, and they may not benefit from the product of their work.

A favorite illustration of ours is the work of a man and a team of oxen in a field. From one perspective, the man and the oxen are all participating in the work. But the oxen do not decide when to work and when to rest. The oxen do not decide when to start, how much work to do, when to drink some water. The man makes all of the decisions, but the oxen share the work. This view of participation is common among the powerful who control social/political/economic systems. But it is not a type of *participation* which is fruitful in the design and implementation of development activities.

A special issue of the *Journal of Agriculture and Human Values* titled 'Participation and Empowerment in Sustainable Rural Development' addressed the question of participation and observed that "the increasing recognition of the weaknesses and high social costs of conventional 'top-down' models of agricultural R&D has contributed to the rising interest in innovative participatory and 'bottom-up' approaches" (Thrupp and Haynes 1994: 1).

A good example of different interpretations of *participation* can be found in agricultural extension. The assumption is that those who till the soil and tend the livestock will learn relevant information from agricultural extension to increase their production of food and fiber, and also be better off financially and in other ways. Throughout the world, most governments have a branch which is designed to provide technical information to farming people. Non-governmental organizations (NGOs), private farmers' associations, and other types of organizations also conduct agricultural extension.

There have been some great successes in this field, as well as many failures (Gamser et al. 1990; Khan 1996; Korten 1986; Niehoff 1966; Uphoff 1986). One of the most critical differences between success and failure is the extent to which the people who are supposed to benefit from the program have a voice in deciding the content, the objectives, and the methods used by the system. In other words, *the extent to which the clientele participate in all aspects of planning and implementing the program is directly related to its success* (**3a**). The people who are the recipients of the program benefits are often called the clients. They are the local rural residents—men, women, and children. Elsewhere words like audience, target groups, or participants are used to describe this group.

But, in spite of the well documented evidence for this proposition, many agricultural extension organizations, particularly those controlled by governments, make a different basic assumption. They tend to assume that farmers are really not competent to decide what should be the objectives or the content of agricultural extension programs, simply because many farming people often have very little formal schooling and no advanced science degrees. These professionals take the position that scientists at government agricultural research establishments or in universities should make those decisions.

This is an example of substituting the knowledge of outside experts for that of the clientele. The organization takes on a "top-down" delivery system approach in which others decide what farmers need to know, and attempt to deliver it to them. And while this sometimes works very well in specialized situations, for agricultural extension in general, and especially with the small mixed farming systems in which most rural people live and work, it is almost invariably a failure. (For an analysis of these different approaches to agricultural extension, see G.H. Axinn 1988a.)

Scholars and practitioners of development, observing agricultural extension in the so-called developing countries and elsewhere, have come to a general consensus that "top-down" approaches tend to be much less effective than participatory, farmer-centered approaches. The "top-down" approaches feature technology transfer—such as that of the typical ministry of agriculture delivery system—from central research organizations to extension specialists to field extension personnel to farmers. In contrast, in the participatory, farmer-centered approaches the clientele participate in determining the agenda, the content, the communication channels to be used, and even the personnel to staff the system (Antholt 1991; Brokensha and Little 1988; Chambers 1993; Chambers 1983; Clark 1991; Esman and Uphoff 1984; Farrington and Martin 1987; Korten 1986; Korten and Klauss 1984; Uphoff 1992; Uphoff 1986).

Thus, some of the most effective agricultural extension systems have been those organized by groups of farmers, such as the Farmers Associations of Taiwan or the County Farm Bureaus in the USA in early 20th century. The clientele participated in everything, because they *owned and operated* the extension systems. Both the United Kingdom Overseas Development Agency (ODA) and the International Service for National Agricultural Research (ISNAR) of the Netherlands have been supporting research on farmers' organizations in technology change, and have produced a useful annotated bibliography on the subject (Arnaiz 1995).

In forestry, toward the close of the 20th century, a similar approach became popular. In many places, government forest wardens or rangers were not effective in protecting government forest lands from exploitation by people who needed fuel, fodder, and other forest products. There were many reasons, but among them, forest officers were paid very little, and local people discovered that for a small gratuity (bribe) the forest protectors would be happy to allow them to enter and cut all they wanted. However, over the years, in many places community managed forest lands continued to be productive. Professional foresters began to introduce PARTICIPATION in their programs. If the people living in the area were *given* the forest, then they could become responsible for protecting the forests. Beyond that, they could take over responsibility for managing tree nurseries, planting replacement trees, protecting new plantations, etc. Social forestry and community forestry emerged as better strategies for maintaining forest environments than the old style policing-type, top-down administration of the forests. This was a participatory approach to forest management, and it spread in many countries by the close of the 20th century.

However, some social and cultural systems do not have a tradition of participatory decision-making. Our personal field notes from several years ago contain this experience:

I was at the offices of the planning commission in one state of India at the opening session of a national workshop on community forestry. The head of the state planning commission gave the welcoming address, describing some of his state's achievements and plans for future development. I followed with a talk on community forestry, claiming that it was an idea whose time had come.

After this session tea and refreshments were served, and it was announced that the group would move to a forestry training center for the next session. Not having a vehicle for transport, and learning that my fellow speaker was going to attend the second session as well, I asked if I could ride with him to the training center. He generously welcomed me to his vehicle, and we set off.

During the trip of about one half hour, he raised a serious question with me. "The community forestry business you are advocating", he asked, "has it been tried in other places? And has it been successful?"

When I described community forestry and social forestry projects in several other countries, he was troubled. Then he said, "If it would really work here, that would be great. If people would take responsibility for their own forests just because we let them *participate* in making the decisions as well as doing the work, we would be much better off than we are now. In fact", he continued, "if that strategy could work here, we need it in many other programs besides forestry. We need it in education, and in health, and in developing our transportation system!"

My enthusiasm was growing, and I became excited by the prospect. But then he said, "However, you must first understand us. For centuries the people of my country have not been asked to participate—not in deciding what to do and controlling our own decisions. For centuries we have always looked up to a king or a god, who told us what to do. Can this type of people's participation really work here?"

Not only in the country in the example, but in many parts of the world, it is easy for outsiders to recommend *participation*, but it may not be implementable. The nature of *participation* itself may be different from place to place, from culture to culture. Participation is one of the current concerns for professionals in international development work. Like other major issues, it is practiced quite differently from group to group, and there is not one simple formula which can be implemented everywhere. In some places, the assumption is that all people have a right to be treated with equity, and that equity is an essential component of sustainable development. In other places, equity among human beings is unknown, and difficult to imagine. But from a strategic perspective, it is increasingly clear that change without the *participation* of those people most affected by the change is not likely to be viewed as development.

3.3 Decentralization

One strategy which governments and large organizations can use to achieve participation is known as *decentralization*. For large, far-flung organizations, instead of making all decisions at central headquarters, scattered local field units are given authority to make some of their own decisions. Like sustainability and participation, there are many different meanings of decentralization.

Carney summarizes the distinctions in the definitions of decentralization to include the following:

Decentralization is a process, a shift in the locus of power from the center towards the periphery. Beyond this there is little consensus as to the meaning of the word…. We focus on restructuring and changes in power relations *within* government. Decentralization does not, however, imply that all power resides at the periphery. The center still sets broad policy guidelines and goals and is responsible for coordination between decentralized units in addition to supplying certain key goods and services.

DECENTRALIZATION WITHIN THE LAW-MAKING, LEGISLATIVE BRANCH IS REFERRED TO AS *devolution*. This involves the creation or revitalization of elected bodies at a lower level.

DECENTRALIZATION WITHIN THE APPOINTED BUREAUCRACY, OR EXECUTIVE BRANCH, IS KNOWN AS *deconcentration*. This involves a shift in operational power away from the central ministry to sub-units outside the capital. It may coincide with a redefinition of the scope of a ministry but such a change is not, in itself, an example of deconcentration.

HOW DO DEVOLUTION AND DECONCENTRATION RELATE? Logically the two processes are independent; although they often take place concurrently this is not necessarily the case. However, since legislative agencies depend upon executive agencies to put their decisions into action, devolution is unlikely to be effective without some accompanying deconcentration (Carney 1995: 1).

There are great differences between physical decentralization and financial decentralization, or decentralization of control. A national government roads department, for example, can physically decentralize, and have an office in each district in the nation. If all decisions about which roads are to be built, when, and how, as well as road maintenance decisions are made in the central office in the capital city, and district offices merely implement decisions made in the center, that is a case of physical decentralization without decentralization of planning, decision-making, or *control*. On the other hand, if the central office, for example, sets standards for construction of certain types of roads, and perhaps makes annual reports on the situation in the entire country, but leaves it up to each district to decide and implement its own construction and maintenance projects, that is a higher level of decentralization.

On the financial side, if the central government collects all the money through taxes, etc., and allocates some funds to each district for road construction, that is one level of decentralization. If, instead, each district raises its own funds for road construction, and also makes its own decisions as to which roads to build, and how much maintenance to do, that is a greater level of decentralization.

Private and non-governmental organizations also have various levels of decentralization. The extent of decentralization is a major factor in development activities. An NGO, for example, working in one part of a particular country, may be conducting women's income generating activities in twenty nearby villages. From a decentralization perspective, must all twenty villages do the same kinds of projects? Will members in each village decide what to do, or will the leaders for the whole NGO specify what to do? Sometimes such an NGO will demonstrate genuine participation in facilitating different decisions made in each village. And in other situations, central leaders will try to control everything themselves. However, some international NGOs, and also multilateral agencies, make program decisions at their headquarters, and then implement them through the national, regional, or community offices of their organizations in many different parts of the world.

Figure 3.1 illustrates some of the alternatives for decentralization which have been useful to practitioners of international development in designing and implementing activities.

In Figure 3.1, the circle on the left, named rural social system, represents a village, or a cluster of individuals, usually organized in

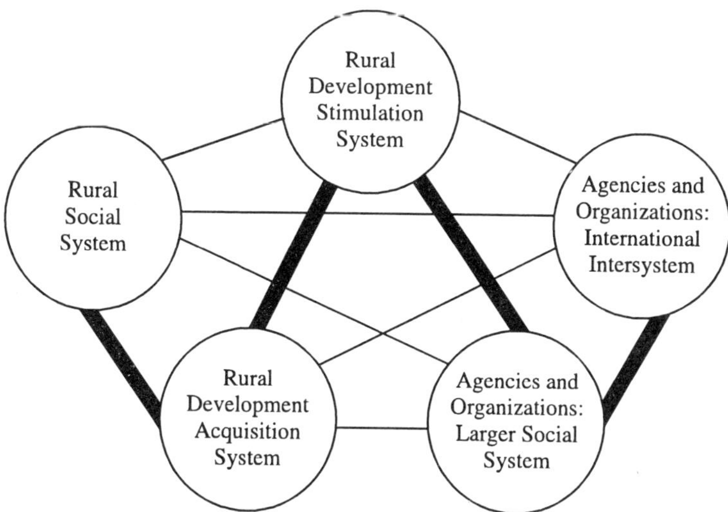

Source: G.H. Axinn 1978, Ch. 3

Figure 3.1
Critical Linkages in Rural Social Systems

families. Typically, they are found in one physical location, and remain there for many generations. There are exceptions, however, such as transhumant pastoralist clans, which move from place to place, but still may be considered as the basic unit in a rural social system. This is the grouping which is usually the client, or the "target system" of both national and international development programs. From the perspective of agriculture, this circle represents the men and women and children—the farming families—who till the soil and tend the livestock.

The next circle, moving toward the right, is labeled acquisition system. This represents organizations of people from within the village who have taken on the function of *acquiring* from the outside world what the insiders believe they want and need. It might be just one individual, or an informal grouping which emerges when needed and then disappears, or a rather formal organized group. It is distinguished from other circles (further to the right in Figure 3.1) because it is controlled by the people of the village. They own it and operate it.

In the center of the diagram is a circle labeled stimulation system. We have also referred to it as delivery system. Like the acquisition system, its function is to provide stimulation to the village, or to *deliver* ideas, information, or sometimes physical inputs. Unlike the acquisition system, it is owned and operated by outsiders, and controlled by outsiders (people from cities or other centers away from the rural village). Rather than to *acquire* for the village what its members request, it is designed to *deliver* to the village what some outsiders think should be delivered.

For a development practitioner becoming acquainted with an unfamiliar social system, it is rather easy to distinguish an *acquisition* system from a *delivery* system. One can ask an individual representing the system (a paid worker on its staff, or a volunteer doing its work) how they were selected or employed in that assignment. If the person says that they live in the village, and were selected or appointed by a friend or relative or local committee, it is probably an *acquisition system*. If the person says that she or he was selected or appointed by an agency of government, or an NGO or private firm in the outside world, and then assigned to this particular position, it is almost certainly a *delivery system*. This is an important distinction from the perspective of development programs, and is discussed further in Chapter 5 of this book.

The distinction between an *acquisition system* and a *delivery system* is not necessarily static or permanent. Sometimes a group of village people, organized by an outside development agency, may begin as a delivery system. After some time, if the group works well together, it may build confidence in its own ability to get things done. As the members become more "empowered", they tend to take control of their own agenda—perhaps taking on tasks which were not in the original plan of the development agency. When that happens, the group is changing from a delivery system into an acquisition system.

Similarly, an acquisition system, over time, may become dominated by one or more of its members. When those individuals press their personal agendas, at the expense of group interests, the organization may become more of a delivery system than an acquisition system. At any one point in time, any group may tend to be more like an acquisition system than a delivery system, but it also could exhibit characteristics of both.

To complete the diagram in Figure 3.1, the next circle represents agencies and organizations of the larger social system. These can be national organizations like a ministry of agriculture, or ministry of local government; an educational institution; a private business or commercial firm; or a national NGO, perhaps functioning with a religious base. It is linked to the rural village in order to provide goods or services to it, to extract products or information from it, or for other purposes. And finally, on the far right side of the diagram, is the circle representing international agencies. These are organizations from outside the nation state, either belonging to another nation state or to a multilateral international organization or international NGO. These are described in detail in Chapter 8 of this volume.

In terms of decentralization, national agencies often decentralize functions, and sometimes decentralize decision-making to local delivery systems. Those which are even further decentralized will share functions with acquisition systems. In the middle of the 20th century, Taiwan had demonstrated the effectiveness of Farmers' Associations as instruments of village development. Malaysia followed by converting some of its delivery systems, particularly in agricultural extension, into acquisition systems. By the end of the 20th century, both the Philippines and Indonesia had launched programs of decentralization, or devolution, by attempting to convert several different types of local delivery systems into acquisition systems.

Like other strategies, *decentralization* is utilized in a great variety of ways for different purposes. For example, a central government may decentralize certain functions (like primary education, or local healthcare) to local governments. But there are many ways in which control and financial support may be handled. If the "center" delegates the authority to run activities to local people, and also supplies the financial support for those activities, that is very different from delegating program management and telling local people to find their own funds. Sometimes funds are provided by a central government to "local friends" for political support purposes, and no program implementation is expected. And in other situations, central governments will cost-share with local governments, sometimes also sharing program control, and sometimes keeping program control at the center. *Decentralization*, then, is manifest in many, many different ways in different places.

3.4 Human Greed and Corruption

Human greed and corruption are concepts which development literature did not address during most of the 20th century. But these are factors which can defeat the best of development strategies when they are ignored. By the close of the century, professionals, especially in international banking and business, began to address this problem with systematic study.

Self-interest may be viewed as a basic, intrinsic human characteristic. Most human groups develop norms of appropriate interpersonal behavior, in which greed (uncontrolled personal interest) is socialized into "enlightened" self-interest. Normal individuals learn that it is actually in their self-interest to also be concerned about the well-being of others, to share, etc. However, a breakdown in "normal" social and cultural behavior patterns, which might be labeled as overt greed, and which leads to corrupt manipulation of international development programs for individuals' personal benefit, is part of the international development cooperation scene.

A research and advocacy group called Transparency International, based in Berlin, published its first Corruption Index in 1995. It attempts to rank the most corrupt and least corrupt countries in the world. While this first index was based on a variety of impressionistic surveys done by risk analysts and government organizations, the organization will be doing its own surveys in the future. It is suggested that sometimes corruption is not measured only in payoffs or kickbacks but also in the way personal, family or ethnic relationships are used. These behavior patterns may not be considered unethical by many. The surveys showed a correlated pattern of ranking despite cultural differences (Crossette 1995: 8).

As early as 1966, Ferrel Heady addressed the issue of corruption in developing countries:

> Corruption, on a scale ranging from payments to petty officials for speeding, a minor transaction, to bribes of impressive dimensions for equally impressive services, is a phenomenon so prevalent as to be expected almost as a matter of course. Sanctioned by social mores, semi-institutionalized corruption may serve a useful function, but it is at best an indirect and undependable way to carry out governmental programs (Heady 1966: 71–72).

Increasingly, the literature in development practice uses the word "greed" to account for some of the failures of international development activities. For example, the *Human Development Report, 1993*, focuses on peoples' participation. Its section on OBSTACLES states: "Participation is a plant that does not grow easily in the human environment. Powerful vested interests, driven by personal greed, erect numerous obstacles to block off the roots to people's political and economic power" (UNDP 1993: 28). These obstacles include: legal systems, bureaucratic constraints, social norms, and maldistribution of assets.

Human greed is an issue because, while philosophers and some social scientists have addressed it, the literature does not relate it to the problems of design and implementation of development activities. The issue is whether or not development projects which take greed into account in the planning stage are more likely to achieve their objectives. Greed and corruption are areas where well-meaning planners, scholars, experts, and administrators are typically defeated politically by powerful commercial, industrial, and agricultural forces.

An example is river water pollution by industries. Planners and government officials may support schemes which can clean the water, or at least make it relatively safe for drinking by people and their livestock. In India, when factories dumped toxic waste into rivers in one location, the minister of environment threatened to close the plants. But wealthy industrial investors had more political clout than she did, and were able to defeat her environmentally sound effort. Heavily polluted streams have been a concern of activists and some government officers in South Asia over the years, but the pollution remains.

The issue of human greed and the resulting corruption as a countervailing force to planned sustainability have been a central aspect of the human condition throughout history. There have been studies of class, status, and social power structures, and a whole body of literature has featured "dependency" with respect to development. However, greed (narrow, short-term self-interest) has been neglected as a significant variable in the analysis of the successes and failures of development projects.

In his case study of the Gal Oya irrigation scheme in Sri Lanka, Uphoff observes that, "Allegations of corrupt practices are worrisome in Sri Lanka because most are credible" (Uphoff 1992: 138). A recent statement quoting Barnesh Rana in a local newspaper notes that "in earlier floods in Nepal the bulk of the aid packages had not made its way out of the four walls of our missions in the Indian capital...the powers that be must guard against and minimize the recurrence of the possibilities of the wails and woes inflicted being further compounded by human greed" (*The Independent* 1993: 6). And the bi-weekly *India Today* reported, "the Tripura voter has decisively voted against a coalition which had assumed the trappings of a criminally corrupt syndicate" (*India Today* 1993: 14).

Lest readers from a wealthy nation feel that these problems are characteristic only of poorer countries, the *New York Times* carried a story on the front page of its Money and Business section on April 2, 1995 which was titled "This is the House that Greed Built", with a subheading "Texas Developers Profit From Squalor". It included this statement: "The existence of those developments owes to two factors", said Dan Morales, the Attorney General of Texas. "The first is greed. The second is corruption" (*New York Times* 1995a).

In the international development assistance community worldwide, the evidence of human greed by powerful individuals who siphon off large proportions of the funds for development projects is well known. Referred to sometimes as "leakage", practitioners attempt to keep the proportion of total money used for this purpose to a minimum. Sample cases have been well documented by such writers as Susan George (1992, 1988) and Graham Hancock (1989).

The policy issue, concerning both scholars and practitioners, is that of the legitimacy of greed as a variable to be studied and better understood and utilized in the design of development strategies. If this variable is considered either too slippery and illusive for serious scholarship, or always the province of some other discipline, then it may remain an "untouchable" blind spot in the field. Serious professional practice of development will be strengthened when this variable is taken into account.

Our personal field experience suggests that data on these dimensions of international development cooperation tend to be deliberately hidden, especially from "outsiders". Thus scholars and practitioners may need to acquire greater skills in use of the local language, as well as local social and cultural patterns, in order to obtain valid and reliable data, and to make appropriate operating decisions. And to protect themselves against potentially corrupt outsiders, insiders need to maintain control. Sometimes, serious professional practitioners who are insiders are able to utilize collaboration with outsiders to strengthen their position in defending themselves from more powerful people within their own countries.

3.5 Gender Considerations

In the latter part of the 20th century another critical issue has been gender considerations. Contemporary scholarship on sustainable agriculture and rural development places increasing emphasis on gender issues, the necessity of disaggregating data by gender, and on designing programs which take into account the different functions of women and men in any development activity.

Danforth points out that through the lens of gender, women are viewed as members of societies in which men and women are intrinsically bound. "Instead of reinforcing discrimination against women, gender-sensitive planners have developed strategies in which women and men work together toward shared goals: in part separately and in part together—much as they function in daily life" (Danforth 1995: 33).

In Africa, Asia, and Latin America the evidence that a high proportion of the actual work of farming is done by women is well documented (N.W. Axinn 1990b; Axinn and Axinn 1969; Cloud 1989; Shiva 1989). At the same time, the professional personnel who work on agriculture and rural development are mostly men. In some countries where this phenomenon has been analyzed, figures show that as much as 85 percent of all farm work is being done by women, while 99 percent of the professional agricultural extension personnel are men. Men also dominate the professional staffs of universities, government agencies, and NGOs which deal with farming (Kardam 1991; Sen and Grown 1987; Shiva 1991; UNDP 1995). While excellent research, teaching, and development practice are being done by some men who are sensitive to the impact of gender on agricultural productivity, marketing, and food and fiber distribution, there is a global tendency for gender issues not to be integrated into mainstream development plans. This is a major strategic error.

In designing international development activities, the critical variable of *gender* refers to both men and women. The need is to build a better understanding and "balance" of how men and women relate to each other in the many tasks and responsibilities of life in any particular location. *The Human Development Report, 1995*, observes, "Development, if not engendered is endangered" (UNDP 1995: 23).

The Beijing Declaration and Platform for Action drafted at the United Nations Fourth World Conference on Women in 1995 points out that

> ...women are key contributors to the economy and to combating poverty through both remunerated and unremunerated work at home, in the community and in the workplace. Growing numbers of women have achieved economic independence through gainful employment (#23). One fourth of all households world wide are headed by women and many other households are dependent on female income even where men are present. Female-maintained households are very often among the poorest because of wage discrimination, occupational segregation patterns in the labor market and other gender-based barriers. Family disintegration, population movements between urban and rural areas within countries, international migration, war and internal displacements are factors contributing to the rise of female-headed households (#24) (UN 1995: 11).

With more women—particularly anthropologists, economists, and historians—becoming involved in documenting the roles of women in the development of their families and communities, there has been increasing awareness of the ways that gender issues affect the development of society. Colonization of countries in Asia, Africa, and Latin America centuries ago introduced European male attitudes which contributed to the marginalization of women. Women's traditional roles in each society were ignored as European patterns for governance and production were established.

Jodi L. Jacobson notes that:

> ...gender bias is especially pervasive in the poorest areas of Africa, Asia, and Latin America. It ranges from the exclusion of women from development programs to wage discrimination and systematic violence against females. In its most generic form, such bias boils down to grossly unequal allocation of resources— whether of food, credit, education, jobs, information, or training (Jacobson 1992: 9).

The Human Development Report, 1995, points out that "poverty has a woman's face—of 1.3 billion people in poverty, 70% are women. The increasing poverty among women has been linked to their unequal situation in the labour market, their treatment under social welfare systems and their status and power in the family" (UNDP 1995: 4).

Towards the end of the 20th century too much of the international development effort is still dominated by the linear "economic only" perceptions of development referred to in Chapter 2. Janice Jiggins summarized it this way: "It is a world governed by the public decisions of men who choose to solve problems by force. It is a world in which women and children form the majority of the poor, the displaced, and the hungry. Such a world is not sustainable" (Jiggins 1994: 41).

In his analysis of women in poverty, Wignaraja notes that:

Disunity among the poor (women and men) arises from asymmetrical dependency relationships that tie the poor individually to the rich. This, then, generates dependency attitudes and a vicious circle is initiated with disunity built into it. In the case of poor women, the patriarchal system creates dependency on men…before the poor women can benefit, their dependency on the rich has to be reduced by giving them independent staying power in a conflict-ridden social environment (Wignaraja 1990: 116–17).

The UNDP reports on the situation with respect to agricultural extension:

Agricultural extension services for women also are limited. Even where women constitute a larger share of agricultural producers or where there are cultural constraints to easy communication between men and women, almost all extension workers are men. In the late 1980s, only 13% of agricultural field agents in the developing world were women—only 7% in Africa and 0.5% in India. Most Indian states do not include female farmers among extension beneficiaries—even though 48% of India's self-employed cultivators in 1983 were women. In Africa, even among the innovative farmers who were early to adopt high-yielding varieties, only 69% of female farmers received extension visits, compared with 97% of male farmers (UNDP 1995: 38).

Much of the fieldwork in agriculture, as well as livestock production, has been done by women in all parts of the world. This is only beginning to be recognized by development practitioners, many of whom have yet to appreciate the knowledge which women have of production activities. Here are two excerpts from our field notes which illustrate this situation. The first was made in 1990; the second about fifteen years earlier:

While driving through rural Bangladesh, accompanied by a Ministry employee, a local woman with a B.Sc. degree in field crop production, I asked about the farm-field tasks of women. The answer was that "women here work within the home. They do not work out in the fields." This response, influenced by culture and religion, was normal. But when I then asked if those were not women in the field alongside which we were driving (about thirty of them) she said, "Oh, they are not our women. They are strangers who just came here to do that work."

I had just completed several weeks of field observations in Tamil Nadu state of India. In a wrap-up session in the office of the Director of Agriculture for state government, I noticed a very large painting on the wall behind the Director. It was a typical farm scene: rice planting time with many fields in sight, and people in the midst of their work. It included about fifty women and four or five men. When asked about men's and women's work in agriculture, the response was that men work in the fields, and women stay in the household (which does include livestock sheds). With some discomfort, I pointed to the picture behind him and asked the Director whether that picture came from another state in India. He glanced at the picture, and explained that artists don't understand agriculture, and what I was seeing was merely the artist's conception.

Studies of the status of women in several different areas of Nepal in the 1970s were supported by the US Agency for International Development (USAID) (Acharya and Bennett 1981). These reports were published in English, and then UNICEF supported a summary in the Nepali language. After that, neither the professional agriculturists nor their government agencies could deny the significant role of women in Nepal's agriculture. Unfortunately, many could still ignore it. However, a direct result was a program of Production Credit for Rural Women (PCRW), which has since flourished and expanded throughout Nepal.

Ponna Wignaraja, a keen observer and scholar, writing from his base in Sri Lanka, has described the achievements of the Women's Development Section of Nepal's ministry of panchayat and local development.

This department deployed a great deal of flexibility in organizing poor women and was also able to address a large variety of issues, such as health, education, credit, and economic activities, in response to the needs of the poor. This was possible because the Women's Development Section was headed by a woman deeply committed to the cause of poor women. Also, by creating a new administrative unit and training new kinds of women catalysts it was possible to overcome many of the difficulties encountered by the more conventional bureaucracies reaching the poor (Wignaraja 1990: 57).

This was done by identifying the needs particularly of poor women, finding resources and services to respond to these needs, and to use these innovatively for the benefit of poor women. The PCRW project was to address the poorest sections of women...with preference given to disadvantaged ethnic and caste groups, landless and female headed households.... In five years of experimentation the program was operating on a limited scale in thirty-two out of the seventy-five districts in the country. The program...was, in effect, operated by the poor women's groups. The groups ensured participation and formed the basis of a new type of village level development organization, with the ministry and the WDS providing a promotional role and a support system (Wignaraja 1990: 62).

Some years ago, Elise Boulding observed:

The issue is whether by institutionalizing opportunities for the education, training and participation of women in every sector of society at every level of decision-making in every dimension of human activity, we will now set in motion a dialogic teaching-learning process between women and men that will enhance the human potential of both (Boulding 1977: 231).

The gender issue pervades all aspects of international development cooperation, and will be illustrated many times in the pages which follow.

3.6 Accountability

Another issue which is increasingly being recognized as crucial in the development process is *accountability*. This is not merely the accountability for money: to see to it that all spending is for properly authorized expenditures; that budgets are not overspent; and that funds are not misused. Financial accounting is a field by itself—an important profession, discussed briefly in Chapter 9 of this book. The accountability which is the focus of this particular section could be labeled *professional accountability; that is, to whom is the development professional responsible?* That a person, group or organization should "be accountable" is a phrase frequently used today, but there is limited understanding of what being accountable implies.

Susan George put it quite bluntly:

> ...people working in the field of "development" are wholly disqualified from claiming "professional" status. Unlike other, genuine professionals, they are accountable to no one (except in the ordinary hierarchical way). If they make a mess of a development project, they can walk away from their victims, towards the next disaster (George 1992: 168).

Since development activities so often involve outsiders who are invited to participate because of their technical or economic knowledge or financial inputs, but who have no long-range stake in the consequences of whatever "advice" they might give, the field is deserving of the type of criticism George offers. The very "short-termness" of their involvement contributes to this problem. And in international development cooperation, this problem is exacerbated by the fact that the activity typically was enabled by a formal document, a project document, officially signed by the representatives of two different governments; or of one government and an intergovernmental agency. The nature of diplomacy makes it difficult for either side to blame failures on the other, and the nature of politics makes it even more difficult for either side (elected or appointed government or NGO officers) to admit that they made a mistake.

Of course, while science learns from "trial and error", if everyone hides the errors, it is extremely difficult to learn.

Robert Chambers takes an analytic perspective on this problem.

> The new beliefs which are today's orthodoxies are held by some with no less conviction than those of the past. But any historical view would suggest that, if we have been wrong on much before, we are likely still to be wrong. It would suggest that error is endemic and cannot be completely avoided (Chambers 1994: 14).

After making an analysis of the errors typically made by development professionals, he makes these positive suggestions:

> Three lessons stand out. Each entails an upending or reversal of the normal condition which generated and sustained the error.... The first lesson is to replace dominance with deference and respect, and to reverse positions and roles.... The second lesson is to reduce social and physical distance.... The lesson is to spend time close to people in the field.... The third lesson is to redefine professional ego.... The redefinition of professional ego implies change, to eclectic pluralism, embracing error, acknowledging complexity and diversity, and learning through successive approximation. The lesson is to link professional prestige and ego with doubt, critical self-awareness, and enabling others (ibid.: 24–25).

He concludes:

> If all power deceives, then it is in stepping down and empowering others that new and more practical realities can be expressed and shared; and it is through empowering the poor, vulnerable and weak, that their reality will count more, and equity will be better served (ibid.: 26).

The problems of *accountability*, however, are not found only with "professional" outsiders. In her analysis of several self-employed women's associations (SEWA) in India, Poonam Smith-Sreen found that there were significant differences among four different groups in two different states. She defined and measured "member-accountability" among the officers and staff of these groups.

> Accountability to the members may be reflected by the degree to which the intended beneficiaries can hold the decision makers

responsible for the outcomes of their decisions. It may be measured through: i) extent to which members contribute in the decision making process; ii) extent to which decisions are reported to the members; and, iii) extent to which the members control the decision making process within the organization (Smith-Sreen 1992: 3).

Then she made measurements of the extent of client accountability in each group, which revealed that some of the groups had staff who were seriously dedicated to their clientele and held themselves professionally accountable to their women members. In other groups, the main directions of accountability were toward higher status leaders or to outside "donor" agencies which provided financial support (Smith-Sreen 1995).

Lack of client-accountability is found in all types of agencies and organizations in the development field, within particular countries or internationally. Another example was documented by Jairo Cano when he studied agricultural researchers in several different countries of Central and South America. His study was designed to compare the personal professional feelings of accountability among these researchers, to three different groups. One group comprised administrators and senior officials of their organization and its government. The second comprised rural people, farmers, who were the designated beneficiaries of agricultural research in official documents about their organizations. The third group included other professionals doing agricultural research in their own country or abroad.

When the analysis of accountability was completed, most professional researchers in this study gave top priority to accountability to the profession. Their goals were to impress other agricultural researchers regarding the quality of their work and the significance of their findings. Publication in international professional journals was a principal means to that end. The second largest group, in terms of priority, was accountable to administrators and senior officials above them in their own bureaucracies. Their goals were to become director of the agricultural research organization in which they worked, and perhaps rise even higher in the bureaucracy. In this particular study, none of the agricultural researchers considered farming people as sufficiently significant and deserving of accountability! (Cano 1981)

In research organizations, accountability to the clients includes returning the results of research to the persons who provide the data. In agricultural research scientists need to find ways to share their findings with farmers who participate in the research, as well as with appropriate central government organizations. For example, when experimental plots are conducted on a farmer's field, the farmer has a right to understand the rationale for such research, and the results. Similarly, when individuals or groups of people respond to questionnaires or focus group interviews, they have a right to know why the research is being conducted and what are the findings.

Again, this lack of accountability to clientele is not unique in the agricultural research field. It is found in other branches of agriculture, in the health field (where accountability is often to others rather than to patients), in forestry, in education (where some teachers do not feel accountable to their students for what students learn or do not learn), and in other fields. The phenomenon is found throughout the development professions, and is a serious issue.

Robert Chambers has addressed this concern in international development:

> The early project process is dominated by engineers and economists, and preoccupations with infrastructure, budgets, schedules, and quantification. The way professionals and organizations think and operate biases the process against poor people. A new professionalism and a new paradigm start with people rather than things, and adaptive processes rather than blueprints. Practical implications for this approach include the need for caliber, commitment and continuity in field staff, restraint in funding, use of methods of rapid rural appraisal, and support for "learning projects" without deadlines or targets (Chambers 1993: 76).

Without using the word *accountability*, but with deep concern and insight into the same basic issue, Chambers further writes,

> Finally, a step for all concerned, whatever the profession, discipline or nationality, is to recognize and offset the imprint in their minds of normal professionalism and normal project identification. When people are put first, and the poorer rural people first of all, it is more they who do the identifying and who set the priorities. At this frontier of the early project process, the question

is not just identification *for* whom, but identification *by* whom. Some big projects will always be worthwhile, but one lesson of experience with rural development is that many successes start small and slowly and evolve through participation and mutual learning, with and by committed new professionals. Structures, policies, and procedures can and should be modified to release them from pressures to spend and to give them freedom to explore and learn. The challenge is also to find, train, and support many more of them. For the key to improving the early project process is not just changes in management, needed though they are, but more pointedly, better people in the field (Chambers 1993: 88).

Thus *accountability* is related to all of the other issues and concerns described in this chapter. It is a "built-in" feature of the next major issue discussed below, *the collaborative mode.*

3.7 Collaboration

Essential to *client-accountability*, *decentralization*, *gender sensitivity*, *participation*, and, therefore *sustainability*, is a different mode of interaction for all those involved in international development. It is a shift from development assistance programs in which the outsiders' assumptions that they know best what insiders need are replaced by a new type of genuine *collaboration* (*interaction*) among insiders and outsiders. It is also a mode in which specialized professionals from any one field or discipline acknowledge that they need to work with and support specialized professionals from other fields. Thus the *collaborative mode* involves collaboration among insiders and outsiders at all levels, and also collaboration among individuals from various different specialized fields at every level.

While international development activities have featured some level of collaboration throughout history, the need at the turn to the 21st century is for a certain *genuineness* in the collaboration that has usually been hitherto absent. There has typically been a tendency for those who finance development efforts to assume it was their right to determine what kinds of activities could be considered to be *development*. Whoever pays the bill has the right to decide what should be done. This kind of thinking hasn't changed over the years. However, the experience in the last half-century has identified a number of issues and concerns discussed in this chapter. An analysis of them, in turn, reveals that from the crass perspective of getting the most from the investment, a different style of relationship is required. More efficient, more effective, and more appropriate for the 21st century style is what is here termed the *collaborative mode.*

Collaboration, by definition, requires a different approach. While it is defined as "to labor together" and "to work jointly with others, especially in an intellectual endeavor", *planning together* is also essential for collaboration. The phrase came into common usage during World War II when it described those who *collaborated* with or willingly assisted an enemy of one's country. But it also has other meanings. Professional collaboration is built on each collaborator (person, organization, or nation) having something to give to the relationship, and something to gain from it. In the 21st century the more positive interpretation of collaboration may be *an effort built on trust and a sense of equity which enables people with different backgrounds to work together to achieve common goals.*

Collaboration does not occur without cost. The *transaction costs* of achieving collaboration are a factor for which development agency administration, host country organizations, professional insiders and outsiders, and rural villagers may not be prepared. And that cost includes the investment of time and energy, as well as travel and cash costs. It may involve long hours of patient listening to each other by specialists from different professions; by individuals from both the outsider organizations and those who will need to live with the project after completion; by those whose expertise is in planning with those whose work is to implement what has been planned. It often requires days, weeks, or more of outsiders' time while they sit with local village people, walk their lands with them, attend their festivals, and gain appreciation not only of what they think and how wise they are, but *how* they think; and equal quantities of the time of those village people are needed as they learn to appreciate the outsiders' skills and knowledge, and perhaps begin to share aspirations with them.

After all, if *development* is actually a process of *subversion* of old ways so that new ways can replace them, and if the grand strategy is to do this in such a way that most of those involved will see themselves as better off, not only in the short run but over many years, it requires a genuineness of collaboration. And that takes time and energy from all involved. Just as the timing of some biological processes cannot be abbreviated, time is required for the establishment of truly collaborative relationships with a commonly agreed upon agenda.

As an intellectual endeavor, collaboration is not achieved overnight. It takes hard work as people with diverse personalities, professional training, and allegiances, as well as a diverse cultural heritage and frequently diverse languages, attempt to establish a common framework and operational mode to solve problems. Collaboration is an act of sharing, of trust, of mutual support. A group attempting international development cooperation in the next century will need to discover the obstacles to collaboration, recognize and address the many barriers which can threaten success in collaboration, and work systematically to overcome them.

Jiggins identified some of these barriers as having a gender base. If scientists are mostly male in areas where many farmers are women, it may be socially and culturally difficult to establish collaboration. And yet, women farmers often have very specialized knowledge which scientists need in order to support sustainable agricultural practices (Jiggins 1994: 225).

Collaboration is more than a quantitative process; it is also a qualitative process. There are many types of collaboration, but those most likely to enhance international development will require the type of interpersonal trust and appreciation which also requires an investment of quality time. The formation of a genuine collaborative relationship which will involve individuals or their institutions over an extended period requires a great deal of time to be invested in the early years. It is necessary to establish shared project and program goals, common language and meaning, an operational framework, and a schedule which recognizes differing perspectives and attempts to satisfy all collaborators.

Collaborative development efforts have an incremental growth potential, and cannot be measured in the short term. However, in designing and implementing international development cooperation, it has become increasingly evident that collaboration is a necessity between insiders in any location where development is to take place and outsiders participating in that design and implementation. And that must be GENUINE COLLABORATION.

3.8 Implications for Professional Practitioners

Professional practitioners have opportunities and responsibilities with regard to current issues and concerns which go beyond those of people who see themselves as *only transitory* practitioners. A serious practitioner cannot, professionally, claim responsibility only for particular specific dimensions of development programs and projects. As a professional, an individual is expected to be aware of *all* the factors which might impinge on the professionalism of her/his work. Issues can be conceptual tools for describing and analyzing development activities. If practitioners remain sensitive to new issues that appear, they can bring them to the attention of development programs and colleagues.

Issues can become more or less serious in any social system at any time, since they are always changing. Practitioners need to be alert to the changes in issues, as well as additional ones not described in this chapter. And since international development cooperation is played out on a constantly changing stage, practitioners are expected to update themselves continuously regarding the changing issues and concerns which are particularly relevant to their work. Even an issue which may appear trivial could become significant for development programs, and should not be disregarded.

The practitioner also has a professional obligation to know his or her own racial, ethnic, gender, and other cultural biases. That self-knowledge may be necessary for the valid description and analysis of the nature of other peoples' situations. Professionalism in practitioners can be measured by the way these issues impinge on their own performance.

Thus the capability for *client-accountable* practice among professionals in international development cooperation may be directly related to their willingness and ability to keep themselves informed about these and other issues and concerns.

PART 2

Strategic and Policy Alternatives

CHAPTER 4

Strategies and Design of International Development Collaboration

The sense of unease about the inadequacy of reductionist science in agriculture (as well as in many other areas of human endeavor) comes precisely because of increasing evidence that in dealing with complexity by simplifying it to "manageable bits", we fail to come to terms with the "real issues" facing humankind. Among these lie basic questions about the way we interrelate with our environment.

Richard J. Bawden 1990: 2363

A critical consideration in any effort at international development cooperation is the strategy and design of the activities to be implemented. Many different approaches are now in use for the basic design of development activity, and they make a significant difference in the extent to which the activity can actually be implemented. The approach is also critical in relation to the consequences of the implementation of the development effort.

Before turning to specific approaches to *international* development cooperation, however, any nation state (or region, or other grouping) has the possible option of attempting to develop itself entirely from within. There are two grand strategies of development which are polar opposites. In one, the developing place attempts to close the boundaries, shut off all interaction with outsiders, and assume full control of the nature of development and the direction it takes. The opposite strategy is to encourage as much interaction with outside places as feasible, assuming it will learn from the others, and enhance its own development. While these extremes are rare, and perhaps impossible to attain in the contemporary world of satellite communication and global transportation, certain degrees of "openness" and "closedness" are found in every human group.

In general, *the willingness and ability of any group to accept change tends to be directly related to the quantity of its communication with the outside world* (**4a**). Therefore, in an effort to maintain continuity in a particular place, and to prevent unwanted change, those in control may adopt policies of isolation, and attempt to prevent international (or intersystem) exchange. Several nation states have gone through periods of such policies during the 20th century. More often, one state, or part of a state, has been forced into isolation by military blockade caused by other parts, sometimes related to an attempt of that portion to secede from the larger political system of which it is considered a part. During these periods of isolation, people within the relatively "closed" enclave have demonstrated uncommon creativity in coping with their situation.

For example, when one portion of Nigeria seceded from the rest in 1967, and called itself Biafra, it found itself quite isolated from the rest of the world. It had been under military blockade for several months prior to secession, and remained enclosed for more than another year and a half. Surprisingly within that enclave people invented ways to supply their needs which had not been used before. Among these innovations, wooden matches were manufactured within Biafra while they had traditionally been imported from Europe to all of West Africa. Crude oil was transformed into diesel fuel and petrol with home-made distilleries made from old oil drums and bamboo. In that time of crisis and hardship, individual human beings learned how to do many things they had never done before.

The strategy of isolation has many disadvantages, but it does promote self-sufficiency, independence, and a type of empowerment which human groups tend to lose when they become dominated by other groups from "outside" their own system. Therefore without complete closing, or opening, any particular place to transactions with the outside world, there are development options which selectively attempt to control the extent of "outside" relationships. Thus it is common in trade policy for groups to restrict the quantities of various goods they will import from or export to other places. The attempt to control intellectual property through copyrights is similar. In all of these types of situations, strategies for intersystem interchange, or international interchange, can be classified by the extent to which, from an insider's perspective, interaction with the outside world is encouraged or discouraged.

In this chapter various different approaches to interaction are considered from the perspective of international development co-operation. An organization designed to further such cooperation may be a government organization, a private business, or a non-governmental (non-profit) organization. Whether it is an organization belonging to only one nation state (bilateral) or one belonging to a group of nation states (multilateral, as in the specialized agencies of the UN), it may choose from among many different approaches to the task of international development.

4.1 Approaches

Different approaches to international development cooperation vary with the nature of the agencies and organizations which design and implement the activities. They are also related to the social, economic, cultural, political, and technological systems which are found in the countries they represent. Since some are agencies of one nation state, and others are multilateral or international agencies, there are great differences among them. And to the extent that the international intervention is designed to enhance the effectiveness of a local organization in the "host" country, the approach will be influenced by the host country's social, cultural, economic, political, and technological systems.

As discussed in Chapter 2, there have been general changes in the way the international development process has been perceived over the years during the last half of the 20th century. The agencies and organizations trying to implement international development, including scholars and practitioners working in the field, religious leaders, and politicians and other policy-makers, have differed in their thinking. But there has been a gradual moving away from the perception that outsiders from wealthy industrialized countries know best; that they should try to convince people in the poorer, more rural and agricultural countries to change and become more like those outsiders. Increasingly, professionals are becoming convinced that the local setting is important; it has its own real values, and those must be taken into account in order to enhance development.

Some suggest that the local situation must be changed first. For example, in his analysis of the sociopolitical effects of new biotechnologies in developing countries, Klaus Leisinger notes:

> ...people must first be mobilized to amend static traditional modes of thinking and behaving; adoption of economic and technical innovations must follow. Since food shortages in the Third World stem from the interplay of poverty, inequity, low yields, and declining environmental quality, the most promising strategies will be those that address all four problems simultaneously. This approach can be described as the comprehensive and sustained improvement of economic capability and of the conditions shaping rural society: in other words, advancement of those who live on and off the land in rural areas, with particular attention to the female population (Leisinger 1995: 3).

From a similar, and perhaps somewhat more sensitive perspective, Altieri suggests that

> approaches should deal with technological issues in such a way that they assume their corresponding role within an agenda that incorporates social and economic issues in its development strategy. Only policies and actions derived from such a strategy can confront the agricultural–environmental crisis and rural poverty throughout the developing world (Altieri 1995: 17).

From his perspective,

> by understanding ecological features of traditional agriculture, such as the ability to bear risk, production efficiencies of symbiotic crop mixtures, recycling of materials, reliance on local resources and germ plasm, exploitation of the full range of microenvironments, etc. it is possible to obtain important information that may be used for developing appropriate agricultural strategies tailored to the needs, preferences and resource bases of specific peasant groups and regional agro-ecosystems (Altieri 1995: 18).

The *approach* is the essence of an international development activity. Each activity will also have an *organizational structure*; it will have *leadership*; it will have *resources* of personnel, equipment, and facilities; it will have *programs* with goals and objectives as well as methods and techniques of implementation; and it will have *linkages* with other activities, the public as well as its particular clientele.

The *approach* has been described as the style of action within an activity. The *approach* embodies the philosophy of the activity. It is like the beat of a drummer which sets the pace for all of the dimensions of that activity. But it is not merely one of the components of the system conducting the activity. It is more like a *doctrine* for the activity, which informs, stimulates, and guides such aspects of the activity as its structure, its leadership, its programs, its resources, and its relationships with other activities (G.H. Axinn 1988a: 3).

Different approaches to international development cooperation can be illustrated, in part, by Figure 3.1 in Chapter 3. The approaches vary from full control of the program and personnel of the activity by the acquisition system on the left of the diagram, to full control of program and personnel by the organizations and agencies of the international intersystem at the right side of the diagram.

Using this perspective, approaches may be classified as highly clientele-centered, or clientele-dominated at the one extreme, to outside-agency-centered, or outside-agency-dominated at the other extreme. In comparative studies of irrigation systems, some practitioners describe clientele as users. We use these words interchangeably. Publications on management of irrigation systems demonstrate that user-controlled systems are much more likely to deliver water when the users need it, than are non-user controlled systems. The same difference in approach is found in many different types of rural development activities.

In 1988, in order to better counsel various ministers of agriculture about their options with respect to agricultural extension systems, the FAO published a booklet entitled, *Guide on Alternative Extension Approaches*. In it, eight different approaches to agricultural extension were described which illustrate the alternatives mentioned above. They range from *the general agricultural extension approach*, typically used by central government ministries of agriculture to "deliver" technical information from agricultural research establishments to a target audience of farmers at the one extreme, to the *agricultural extension participatory approach* and the *cost-sharing approach* at the other extreme (G.H. Axinn 1988a: 6–10).

The general proposition which is relevant is: *the more that local people control the program and the personnel of an agricultural extension system, the more successful that system will tend to be* (**4b**). The same statement could be made for most other types of international development programs and projects.

In recognition of the complexity of issues facing program development,

> simple nation-wide recommendations are no longer sufficient for extension. Extension will have to create a capacity for targeting recommendations and develop transfer and diffusion strategies which will depend on an in-house socioeconomic research capacity. The sustainability challenge will hopefully open up a badly needed debate over extension design and strategy in the Third World (Lynam 1992: 134).

4.2 The Collaborative Mode

The collaborative mode of international development has emerged at the close of the 20th century as a promising strategic design. It requires a style of genuine full "partnership" between the "outsiders" in international development and the "insiders". International development collaboration is a recurrent theme in this book, as we believe it will replace both *international development assistance* and *international development cooperation* in the early years of the 21st century.

The rationale for this has been summarized in the following statement included in a letter from a president of the Society for Applied Anthropology to its members: "We recognize that human, social, cultural and political problems are now so complex that they cannot be solved by individuals or disciplines in isolation, but require committed joint study and action" (Schensul 1995: 1).

4.2.1 Collaboration in Program Development

International development assistance, as it was known in the early 1950s, tended not to feature a collaborative mode. Those in North

America and Europe who were involved with programs designed to *help* enhance development in Asia, Africa, and Latin America often assumed that they had the *answers* to problems which needed attention, and the major strategy was one of *delivery*. Projects were designed to *deliver* economic assistance and technical assistance.

Technical people in the field of agriculture assumed that if they *delivered* their technologies to people in "less developed" places, those technologies could be fitted into the farming systems which were already there, and would lead to increases in production. They further assumed that these increases in production would benefit rural people, and lead to increases in their consumption of the good things in life. Similarly in the field of education attempts were made to *deliver* the curricula which had been successful elsewhere, along with teaching and learning strategies, and details such as the system of "student credit hours" in higher education, and the chalk boards and overhead projectors in various types of classrooms. Technical assistance in the health field was usually built on advanced technology as well as professional assistance. Staff health workers were sometimes trained in the use of electronic microscopes and other equipment which was not available or functioning outside the capital cities.

It was only after such projects failed to achieve their goals that it became obvious that those from the wealthier countries did not have the *answers* to questions being asked in Africa, Asia, and Latin America. Typically, they did not even know what the questions were. And as outsiders began to try to understand the situations better, to seek more detailed information on various aspects of the situation which impinged upon the problem, they gradually discovered that there were *insiders* who had much better knowledge of those problems than *outsiders*, even those with the best of intentions. While this was often the case with actual technical details, like the local rationale for intercropping different crops in one field instead of planting each crop in rows in a field by itself, it was even more apparent with respect to background information such as the influence of local culture, religion, language, social structure and politics on the problem.

Thus scholars and practitioners of international development began to move away from *technical assistance*, and toward *technical cooperation*, as a basic type of program design strategy. And the need for *collaboration*, between *insiders* and *outsiders* in all aspects of project planning and implementing and evaluating was increasingly recognized.

This did not change the major strategies and design of international development activities very rapidly. Throughout the second half of the 20th century practical field experience has provided growing evidence that collaboration is necessary for international development efforts to achieve their goals and objectives. But those involved in providing financial support for these activities—legislative and executive bodies in the more wealthy countries, in the UN system of specialized agencies, in the international development banks, and in NGOs—have continued to assume that their *experts* actually knew what was needed, and it was more cost-effective to merely send an *expert* who had the answers than to pay for *insiders* to meet with *outsiders*, get to know each other, exchange information and ideas, and jointly try to decide what needed to be done.

It is only after much trial and error that the high *transaction costs* of the collaborative mode are being recognized as worth the investment of time and money. And by the close of the 20th century, many scholars and practitioners are increasingly convinced of the value of these investments in intensive, serious communication, where each respects the position of the other and attempts to understand them. However, the major portion of international development projects is not yet investing in collaboration. Such collaboration is increasingly possible with improved communication which is faster and less expensive. Improved technology in communication, such as fax and electronic mail, facilitates collaboration by reducing the time for and cost of interaction among collaborators. But these improved communication channels do not substitute the need for face-to-face interaction between *outsiders* and *insiders*, particularly in the early stages of the evolution of an appropriate strategy and design for development programs and projects.

Jiggins, addressing program needs for women, points out that "increasing men's access to sustainable livelihoods is a necessary part of the environmental agenda" (Jiggins 1994: 245), and goes on to list the shared characteristics of successful programs:

- Women are fully involved in defining the problem, designing and trying out solutions, evaluating and sharing the results.
- Involvement goes beyond consultation and collaboration; women play roles as managers, owners, leaders, partners and allies.

- The details of programs are respectful of and respond to local context and priorities.
- The programs stay on course because they are founded on principles that incorporate values and ethical concerns, which are negotiated rather than imposed, and which serve as the touchstone for decision-making.
- The programs are designed as frameworks for learning; the details can be adapted over time and space as competencies grow, the environment changes and new opportunities emerge (Jiggins 1994: 246).

Collaboration strategies vary greatly, from some which call themselves collaborative, but are actually dominated by one group to the exclusion of others, to programs where all the persons and organizations involved share a genuine partnership with each other. Examples of the whole range of approaches may be found in different fields, and sometimes within the same country. In some places, in some types of work, there has been a trend in recent decades to move from the strategy where "experts" from outside were expected to enter a place with answers, to a more appropriate approach which recognizes the value of local experience, and "real" collaboration occurs. However, at the end of the 20th century, all kinds of variations between these two positions are still in evidence.

4.2.2 Essential Factors in Collaboration

There are many possible combinations and permutations in international collaboration. The essential factors are: (*a*) trust and respect for the competence of individuals and organizations involved; (*b*) each participant having something to offer to the others for which the others have a need; and (*c*) willingness on all sides to invest time and money in sufficient communication. The evidence is increasing that investments in the relatively high transaction costs of the collaborative mode are excellent investments.

When two or more individuals enter into a *genuine collaborative relationship*, each develops a respect for the knowledge and competence of the other. This is rarely evident at the beginning of a collaborative relationship. It takes time together to address the serious difficulties of a problem, or a development challenge; for people with different world-views, different life experiences, and different levels of competence to appreciate the value of what others bring to a situation. As each offers something different, and others learn to appreciate the contributions those differences can make to a common goal, the productivity of the collaboration tends to gradually become evident to all.

While individual participants in an international development activity—insiders and outsiders, women and men, representatives of different disciplines and perspectives—work together in genuine collaboration, each becomes partially dependent upon the others. This can become a *threatening* phenomenon, and may press the less qualified and less committed to leave the relationship. But when the individuals realize that the *excellence* of what they are doing together depends on the differences they bring to the task, they become willing to accept this type of dependency. In a collaborative team of practitioners who have been working together for some time, individuals may comment freely on the extent to which they depend upon each other, and the quality of what they can achieve together because of the complementarity of those differences.

In the sections which follow, we illustrate some of the advantages of collaborative approaches to international development.

4.2.3 Collaboration with Buildings and Equipment

In international development in the health field, using a technical assistance approach, outside agencies often find it more convenient to provide equipment rather than personnel or training. The assumption is that complex technical equipment may not be manufactured within the host country, and therefore it is an appropriate "gift" from outsiders. However, when project activity is controlled and planned from outside, the particular equipment which is provided may not be appropriate. We have found impressive X-ray machines which had been donated by outsiders to remote rural health posts, still protected by the plastic dust covers in which they were shipped. They have never been used because there is no electricity in the village. The equipment may be kept and preserved for its "prestige value", rather than for the diagnostic purposes for which it was given.

The provision of equipment in projects where there has been greater collaboration, and insiders and outsiders have planned together, is usually quite different. This category includes plastic pipe for use by villagers in constructing their own gravity-flow drinking water and irrigation projects, after it was determined that the equipment was not available in the host location, but could be utilized and maintained within. Also included are windmills for pumping water where there is no electricity, locally made chalkboards for displaying school instructions where there is no electricity, and supply of simple diarrhea-control pills which can be stored without refrigeration in local health posts.

Sometimes, if an international development agency is controlled centrally, it is not feasible to share appropriate activities, even though its local staff is aware of local needs. For example, in the construction of dormitories at a college in one country, the architects and engineers employed by an international construction organization insisted on providing indoor bathrooms with toilets, sinks, and showers, along with provision of both hot and cold running water. This position was supported by program officers of the international development agency as being consistent with its policies. Although local administrators of the college and the ministry of education complained, the outsiders had their way. However, the facilities were installed but never used, since it was not the normal procedure to have indoor toilets in that area, and since only cold water was typically used for both showers and washing at the sink. In the years which followed construction, no local funds were requested or provided to heat the water; and after a few months of use without maintenance, the indoor toilets were abandoned.

In contrast, however, a few of the international development agencies are willing to support new buildings with funds, but leave the actual design and construction entirely to local collaborators. In one case, a bilateral assistance agency specified that it did not wish to be involved at all until the building was complete. At that time, its ambassador was to be invited to a ribbon-cutting ceremony with appropriate publicity.

4.2.4 Collaboration in Technical Training

Where local personnel are to be trained abroad for specific technical careers, collaboration is important. From our field notes:

A young man from (a small Asian country) was sent to the USA for training in dairy cattle management. Although there was general agreement between host country officials and the international agency personnel regarding the need and the field, the faculty in the US university to which the individual was sent had an entirely different conception of what dairy herd management was than did their trainee. He was acquainted with his home country, where the dairy herd average size was one or two animals, sometimes cattle and sometimes buffalo. Fluid milk was partly consumed at home, and partly carried in hand-held containers to a collection point for shipment to a nearby dairy. In contrast, in the place where he studied, all dairy herds had over one hundred cattle, and several of them had over one thousand cattle. On these farms, fluid milk was pumped through a complex cooling and storage system, and then pumped daily into larger milk tank trucks. After six months, in a long distance telephone call, he literally cried to his dean at home to bring him back, as nothing he was learning about dairy cattle management was relevant to his home situation. In the end, he changed his major study so the dairy expertise was not developed (and was still badly needed). He found it difficult to adapt to the living situations (culture, class, etc.) on his return home, so he returned to the USA and his trained manpower was lost to his country.

In contrast, a similar program in India sent technical people abroad for training, but employed a more collaborative mode. First, personnel from a UN international development agency supporting the training met with personnel of the local institutes involved. Together they explored possible institutions abroad as potential training sites. Then a small group from the local institute and the agency traveled abroad for brief visits to the potential "collaborating" institutions. Then one or more overseas institutions were nominated for long-range collaboration. The agency then supported travel of one or two key collaborators to visit the Indian institute. At a certain point, an agreement was made between the collaborating Indian institute and the collaborating overseas institute, and key collaborators (individuals) were designated for five-year terms. Each person continued residence at her/his home institution, but made short visits to the collaborating institution from time to time. When an individual from the Indian institute was identified for overseas training, negotiations between the two key collaborators resulted in training which fit the needs of both the institutions and the individual involved.

Collaboration is important *among* team members from "outside", just as it is *between* "insiders" and "outsiders". Here is an illustrative example from our field notes:

> The animal scientist had come to my office to complain because "headquarters" had assigned an anthropologist to the team. There were funds for only three positions, and the other was filled by a pasture agronomist. But the animal scientist said he needed others who knew more about livestock, and particularly their feeding and breeding. A social scientist would be useless, and they had only three months in Kenya to complete the assignment. I tried to be helpful, explaining some of the possible contributions which a social scientist might make, but was not convincing. The animal scientist left my office muttering about how an important project was going to be defeated by some administrator who didn't really understand, and had made this foolish staff assignment.
>
> (Six months later) Bob (the animal scientist) took time out from his busy first day back to stop in my office today. He said it was necessary, because he had to apologize for what he had said about assigning an anthropologist to the international team. He went on to say that without the anthropologist, the team would have been lost. This social scientist had spent enough time visiting with the pastoralist people to discover that they maintained a higher than recommended herd size because the herd functioned as more than merely a production unit. It served as a mark of wealth and status; certain animals were individually related to gifts given at the time of marriages, and since the people could not take a bank with them as they traveled from one grazing land to another (sometimes over 500 miles in a year) the herd served as a savings account for its owners. Bob went on with other examples, and then pointed out that he hoped future assignments like this would have such balanced, inter-disciplinary teams.

4.2.5 Collaboration in Research Activities

Research collaboration between individual scholars in different countries has been supplemented by institutional efforts at developing collaborative research programs in the last decades of the 20th century. These have been supported by bilateral agencies and multilateral organizations. Examples are the Collaborative Research Support Programs (CRSP), funded by USAID; the efforts of the Cornell International Institute for Food, Agriculture and Development (CIIFAD) to develop collaborative research including universities, government ministries and non-government organizations in a number of countries; and the Centers of Excellence programs supported by the FAO, which bring together professionals from a variety of countries.

Many of these research efforts were initiated to build upon the relationships and scholarly interests developed between scientists who were professors at established universities, and scientists from other countries who came to study with them. This often began with dissertation research which used the particular problems and issues of the student's home country to enlarge the professor's understanding of the scientific situation. In these cases, the collaborating scientists established a common reference base, and often personal and family relationships which enabled them to continue this collaboration when they were apart. The major disadvantages in this kind of collaboration were sometimes the continued professor/student relationship (long after the student was a professor in his/her own institution) and the dominance of the professor and funding coming from the resource base rather than the country where the research was being done.

Ideally, the scientists in country A have special knowledge and technology and some resources which are needed in country B, while country B has special problems to be studied (and perhaps unique biological and physical materials) and the scientists in country B have insights into the history and culture which are important to the research process. To be successful in the 21st century, collaboration will rely on scientists of Africa, Asia, and Latin America to identify the problems to be researched in their worlds and also identify the skills and technology needed from the collaborating institutions elsewhere in the world. And scientists in Europe and North America will appreciate the cultural and philosophical approaches to understanding the problems from other continents. This calls for a *genuineness of collaboration* mentioned in Section 4.2.2, and sometimes a *status reversal* which may be difficult for some established scientists.

The complexity of cross-national collaborative research increases as multiple disciplines are involved in addressing the problem. In a case where concerned scientists at one institution recognize the need for a scientist from another discipline but are unable to identify one in their own institution ready to be involved, they may look to the collaborating country to provide that scientist. This is becoming increasingly possible by the end of the 20th century as there are adequately trained scientists in nearly every country.

4.2.6 Advantages of and Necessity for Collaboration

A collaborative approach may avoid the introduction of inappropriate technology when equipment is involved in international development cooperation. It could also reduce inappropriate building construction, inappropriate training curricula, and inappropriate overseas travel.

Collaboration has costs. It is unlikely to be achieved without considerable investment. However, investment in genuine collaboration can contribute more to appropriate strategies, and project and program design than most other types of investment. Since a deep appreciation by each collaborator of the potential contributions of all other collaborators is necessary, time and travel costs may be involved. Sometimes sufficient patience is required for one member of a collaborating group to simply ask another member what s/he means by a certain word. A horticulturist may use the English word "culture" to mean something very different from what the collaborating anthropologist means by the word "culture". When each understands what the other means by a particular word, the opportunity for useful collaboration is greatly enhanced.

This example is from our field notes:

The Bolivia team was the most impressive we met on this campus. It was led by a female anthropologist, but most members were male. It included agronomists, soil specialists, historians, a linguist, and a horticulturist. They had each been at both high altitude and low altitude project sites, but not as one group. Over time, several small groups of them had traveled together. One told us he could not do his work without two of the others.

Another pointed out that the insight of a person from a different discipline had helped her understand one phenomenon in her own field. Several pointed to significant contributions to their work which came from local, indigenous people.

4.3 Systems for Planned International Development

Different words are used for planned international development in different languages and by different agencies, but it is useful to analyze the systems for planned international development at four different levels. The most general and highest level may be termed the *policy* level. In a national government, or in the headquarters of a global organization, policies are determined by those in control. It may be a corporate board of directors, a legislative body, a board of governors, the chief executive officers, or some other type of grouping. But those responsible for the entire operation of an organization will explore alternative policies, and make decisions from time to time which relate to all aspects of the government's or the organization's activities. And although policies are influenced by individuals at every level in an organization, policies also set the pace and provide the guidelines for planning at every other level.

Once general *policies* are established, an organization can consider alternative strategies for achieving those policies. *Strategies* tend to be more specific than policies, and involve ways and means to implement the policies. Then, closer to actual operations, are *programs*. *Programs* identify the major thrusts of activity within the strategy. And finally, individual *projects* are the specific units which most of the agencies and organizations involved in international development use to conduct their work. Figure 4.1 illustrates this relationship in its simplest form.

Each organization may have its own names for these levels of activity, and the lines between them are often less than clear and sharp, but different aspects of a total development activity can be identified and analyzed with this type of classification. An example which illustrates the different levels of a government's involvement can be found in the area of food security.

Many governments will have specific *policies* relating to food security. These have political and diplomatic dimensions, of course,

Figure 4.1
Levels of Planned Change

but are also related to practical matters of food production, distribution, and entitlement. The policies of several governments may be summarized and oversimplified by the phrase, "cheap food in the cities". That is, at the policy level, they decide that it is of top importance to make sure that the urban population has a sufficient supply of food, always available when needed, and at a price which is low enough that most people will be able to procure the food they need.

At the *strategy* level, for example, several governments have strategies which are designed to provide sufficient total quantities of foodgrain to feed the population. Many relate these to the current population in each state or district. With estimates, either based on the calorie value or the number of kilograms needed for the average person for a year, targets are established for the total number of tons of rice, wheat, maize, sorghum, etc. needed for the country for each year. The strategy is summarized in the target number of tons of grains needed. Another aspect of the strategy might deal with the price at which it is to be sold at retail to consumers. And a third aspect of the strategy might relate to international trade designed to exchange some items in surplus for grains if they should be in deficit.

Then, for each strategic thrust, there might be several *programs* designed to achieve the strategic goals. For example, to achieve the required quantities of grain, the country might have an irrigation *program.* This program might be managed by a water resources ministry, and have targets each year for the quantity of both surface irrigation (through canals fed from reservoirs) and ground water irrigation (fed from tube-wells tapping the underground aquifer). Other *programs* might focus on manufacture, import, and distribution of mineral fertilizer (perhaps managed by a ministry of commerce), provision of high-yielding seed (perhaps supported by a ministry of agriculture), and perhaps extension education for farmers (which could also be handled by the ministry of agriculture).

Finally, at the field operational level, there would be many *projects*. For example, within the fertilizer program, there might be one project focusing on large farms which have irrigation. It might offer them credit for purchase of mineral fertilizer. For small mixed farms which are rain-fed, there might be a different project, in which demonstrations of fertilizer use are implemented on each farm, at no cost to the farmer. And a third project might involve the opening of soil testing laboratories in several locations, with staff available to make soil tests and offer farmers recommendations regarding the appropriate mixtures of fertilizers for them, and the best timing for their particular crops.

But those would not be the only projects at the field level. For example, the irrigation program might have several small projects, each of which has well drilling equipment. Those might go from community to community drilling wells for groups of farmers. Other projects might deal with pumps for the wells. And still other projects might operate only with surface water; not drilling wells, but helping local people make dams or barrages across rivers, which then provide irrigation water to farmers' fields by gravity through hand dug canals.

In general, the *strategy* is usually more specific than the *policy*, which covers a broad topic. Particular strategies are selected after considering many alternatives, often with the technical, economic, administrative, and political dimensions of each being compared. For each strategy, those designing the overall effort (on the basis of past experience, experience in other places, and their best guesses) may weigh the anticipated costs (money and other costs), as well as the anticipated benefits, and then make a decision. Within the framework of a particular strategy, various programs are planned, and within each program, projects are also planned. In combination, as in the illustration above relating to food security, the designers of the total effort evolve strategies based on the policy, and then programs based on the strategy, and, finally, projects based on the program. Specificity in terms of time, location, and financial support tends to be most broad at the policy level, and most narrow at the project level.

Projects are the unit most commonly used, globally, in international development cooperation. There are both advantages and disadvantages in a project approach. On the positive side, the project is specific enough that it can be clearly explained to those who finance it, to those who administer it, and to those who work in it. Most projects have a fixed time frame (as in a five-year project, or a six-month project). They also usually have a specified, and thus limited, geographic area. There might be a program with six projects, each in a different district. Those who attempt to implement the project know which area is inside the project territory, and which area is outside. (Local people also usually know this.) And there is usually a fixed budget, with a specified amount of money set aside for each aspect of the project. A six-year project, for example, might have a budget for the first three years, and some plan for acquiring funds for the second three-year period. For the first three years, a specific amount of the total might be designated for year one, another amount for year two, and the rest for year three.

Professionals in development work can look at the specifications for a project (the time, the place, and the budget) and have a good idea of what is to be done. And planners can add the cost of all of the separate projects, and determine a total cost of the program.

However, there are disadvantages of the project as a design tool. Planning is normally less than perfect. The project might be designed for three years, but in implementation it might take more than three years. Under some circumstances the incomplete project might need to be abandoned without completion after the three years. More flexible organizations might revise the project in the third year, and add another year to make completion feasible.

Similarly, since there is a fixed amount of money, personnel, equipment, and other resources, during implementation it might be discovered that the funds are insufficient. Depending on the flexibility of the financial sources, this can be a major problem. Conversely, sometimes projects are started with an excess of money. When it is not needed for the project, implementers may adjust the project goals, or, it might be siphoned off to other projects or to individuals for personal use.

Thus the project is not a perfect mechanism, as it has the above-mentioned weaknesses. However, it is commonly used by governments, by NGOs, by local cooperatives, by development banks, and by international agencies of all types.

4.4 Alternative Strategic Rural Development Designs

Among the alternative strategies for rural development are those which focus on functions, and those which focus on structure. Each of these was described in general in Chapter 1. This section reviews some of the ways in which these broad types of strategies can be made more effective.

From the perspective of the strategies and design of development activities, many programs and projects are created to encourage a change in one or more of the functions. Most often, the strategies have been focused on *production*. Since all of the functions which are part of every rural social system are linked to each other, this strategy is most effective when it takes into account such other functions as marketing, learning, governance, personal maintenance, and health. *Any attempt to make a change in any one of the functional components of this system is likely to be resisted by all of the other components* (**4c**). Further, *any change which actually takes place in any one of these functions may require some kind of change in each of the other components* (**4d**).

A classic example from the field of agriculture relates to increases in food production in any particular locality without taking into consideration the necessary changes in marketing which will be required. In one district, guided by an enthusiastic agricultural extensionist, farmers discovered that they could easily grow fresh tomatoes. The next year many farmers planted an even larger area of tomatoes. Unfortunately the local market could consume only about 10 percent of the expanded local production in that area, and since no arrangements had been made for outside buyers to purchase the surplus, most tomatoes rotted on their vines.

The relationship between production and marketing in agriculture has been demonstrated many times in many parts of the world. These are both components of the same system. As already stated, any change in any one component will result in changes in other linked components. Many international development programs are designed to change something about one of these *functions*, or the relationships among *functions*.

From a strategic perspective, it is much like the medical process of human organ transplantion, where physicians and surgeons attempt to find an organ which matches the one being replaced as closely as possible. This is also a sound strategy for the introduction of any new technology into a rural social system. The more the new technology is like the old technology, in terms of its relationships to other components, the better. In organ transplantation, the receiving body is prepared with various medications to make it as receptive as possible to the transplant. A similar practice is that of carrying on education or extension programs for a new agricultural technology, so that people who gain access to it will understand how to make it work under their circumstances. After the surgery, it is typical for physicians to see the patient frequently in the following hours and days, to make sure that the patient's body does not reject the transplant, and to make minor adjustments as necessary. In the agricultural technology case, a similar follow-up can be an effective and necessary part of the strategy. Finally, human patients with a new organ transplant usually have regular communication with their surgeons for months, even years, after the surgery. Similarly, a continuing follow-up into the future is an appropriate strategy for international development projects.

Thus, the functional analysis is useful for international development planning in two respects. First, it demonstrates the need for planners to take into account the relationship between the functional component of a rural social system being directly addressed and other components of that same system. Second, it often suggests to planners that their chance of success will be greater if they attach to their main project, project activities directed toward another component.

In addition to the function-based strategies, there are strategies based on the structural differences as described in Chapter 1. Structural strategies often begin with the rural poor and attempt to improve their situation. Many of the large programs of the World Bank, and of bilateral agencies like USAID and the British Overseas Development Administration have specified the "rural poor" as a principal target. And many of the very small local programs of NGOs have also aimed at making things better for the rural poor. Realistically, however, all of those organizations have resisted even acknowledging that there is such a group as the "rural rich".

These programs may be criticized for not taking the rural rich into account, since they are part of the same system, and the two groups are linked. Any change in the rural poor will be accompanied by change among the rural rich. Since the rural rich tend to be associated with those who have political, economic, social, and sometimes military power, both inside rural development agencies and outside, organizations find it "safer" to be silent about the rural rich.

For example, if farm operators in a particular place agree to raise the wages of farm laborers, the laborers will earn more, and the operators will earn less. However, in situations like this, farm operators may take steps to reduce the number of laborers they use. If weeding in the fields was formerly done by the laborers, farm operators may begin using more chemical herbicides for weed control, and therefore less labor. In some cases where tenant farmers were poor because landowners required too high a proportion of the crop as rent, there have been adjustments so that tenants are required to pay less. However this has encouraged landowners in some places to refuse to rent their land to others. Instead, they may purchase a tractor, and farm a larger proportion of the land they own by themselves.

Strategies designed to improve the livelihoods of the rural poor, without being defeated by the rural rich, require especially careful and insightful planning. The risks to the rich must be kept to a minimum, well hidden, or carefully disguised. Normally this requires small, slow, simple projects which are endorsed by at least some members of the rural elite groups, whether they are physically present or living somewhere else. Also, this type of project may be most effective with a minimum of publicity, with leadership which is quiet and does not overtly seek recognition for achievements.

Much international development cooperation has *both* functional aspects and structural aspects, and these are related to each other. Strategies have been manifest in a great variety of programs and projects, most of which are designed in order to make life better for disadvantaged groups. They include programs and specific projects intended to increase the efficiency and effectiveness of such activities as:

- agricultural extension systems
- small farmers' development projects
- community forestry
- women's group income-generating projects
- farming systems research/extension
- production credit for rural women
- integrated rural development
- pond aquaculture
- rural people's associations
- hydroelectric plus irrigation projects
- watershed management projects
- food security programs
- resettlement schemes

Outsiders designing a strategy for implementing programs or projects of any of these types, or others not listed here, are *not* likely to be bringing in an entirely new idea. It is most unusual to ever be working on a "clean slate". For example, many rural development projects have assumed that local people had no organized credit system, since no banks were visible. This unwarranted assumption has led to unexpected competition from local moneylenders (almost always present), as well as rotating credit associations, which are quite common in Asia and Africa.

Ram B. Chhetri points out that.

> ...rotating credit associations are distributed all over the world. Surprisingly, in many societies, they are serving more or less the same kind of purpose—as saving and credit institutions...they seem to exist as competitors or perhaps challenges to the modern day institutions of banking and credit. The element of mutual trust among *Dhikuri* [Nepali name] members seems to be the factor responsible for the wide distribution and popularity of this institution (Chhetri 1995: 452–53).

This type of situation where local people already have some means of achieving, in their own way, what outsiders think to be a new and useful function, is quite common. It is an important strategic consideration. Outsiders can learn much from insiders when they take such aspects of the local reality into account.

The particulars of each type of activity in the list above are different from those of the others. But there are generalizations, general design strategies, and implementation and administrative strategies which relate to them all.

4.5 Implications for Professional Practitioners

A major implication for practitioners in the field of international development is that a *systems perspective*, or *systemic view*, is crucial for the strategy and design of effective performance. As Richard Bawden implies in the opening quotation of this chapter, development, and particularly international development, involves very high levels of complexity. A serious analysis of what is actually going on, what the potential consequences of any change might be, and what types of interventions, if any, are likely to result in positive consequences, is a slippery task. Everything is related to everything else. Thus solutions to specific problems are not possible merely by understanding any one component of the larger systems involved.

For professional practitioners it is appropriate to be familiar with the alternative approaches which have been used in various parts of the world, and the advantages and disadvantages of each in particular situations. Typically agencies and organizations on the local scene, prior to any international development activity, will already be using the approaches which are known to them. Also outsiders who are members of an international development cooperation team will each know, understand, and perhaps expect the types of approaches with which they worked at home. Much flexibility may be required at the field level to avoid the attempt to implement something which does not fit the system. The experience of scholarship and practice can both contribute to this process. The professional may draw lessons from both in the attempt to design programs and projects which are actually implementable, and which promise success.

It is also useful to be able to relate particular projects to the larger programs of which they are a part, as well as to still larger strategies and policies. There is need for "grass-roots" local level ideas to be introduced at broader policy and strategy levels. In addition to ideas, local needs, local ways of thinking and feeling, and other local perspectives have a place in all levels of design. The effective practitioner needs to be able to represent these local perspectives to policy-makers and donors.

It is also important for the practitioner of international development to be able to analyze *both functional and structural* implications of any project design, and to make appropriate adjustments as may from time to time be necessary. Integrating *functional* strategies with *structural* conditions and potential consequences requires a systems approach. Just as one function is related to other functions (increasing production of fruit in an area may require construction of roads for marketing), both are usually related to social and economic structures. Will those who benefit from the increased production also benefit from the change in transportation? If not, what kinds of strategies are likely to be implementable?

Oversimplified categories, such as those discussed in this book—like *structural* and *functional*, or, within *structure*, rich and poor—can be misleading. It is dangerous to assume that people or communities fit within the simple boundaries of such categories. For example, there are not simply rich people and poor people. The poor, even in one rural village, may fit many other subcategories (male and female, employed poor and unemployed poor, poor and landless or poor but holding some land, the poor of one ethnic group and the poor of a different ethnic group, etc.). The professional practitioner may need to push the analysis to appropriate levels to identify the nature of project design which fits particular circumstances.

Without genuine collaboration between *insiders* and *outsiders*, such analysis may not be feasible. It usually requires mutual respect between the two groups, as well as among individuals from different academic disciplines and different bureaucratic affiliations. Sharing the same language may be necessary, but it is more than being able to speak to each other in a common tongue. Words used are unlikely to have the same meaning for insiders as they have to outsiders, the same meaning for government officers as to village people, to agronomists as to sociologists, to bankers and to artists. The investment of time and money in evolving genuine collaboration may be one of the most important investments practitioners can make when the objective is the design of appropriate development strategies.

Collaboration is easy for writers to advocate; but often difficult for practitioners to achieve.

CHAPTER 5

Program Development and Evaluation Strategies

> *Q: In what sense do you think outside help is useful?*
>
> *A: We need help for analyzing and for a better understanding of our situation and experience, but not for telling us what we should do.*
>
> *An outsider who comes with ready-made solutions and advice is worse than useless. He must first understand from us what our questions are and help us articulate the questions better, and then help us find solutions. Outsiders also have to change. He alone is a friend who helps us think about our problems on our own.*
>
> *From a dialogue with activists of the*
> *Bhoomi Sena Movement in India, 1977.*
> *(Reproduced from Wignaraja 1990.)*

Program development is essentially a planning process. Program evaluation is a process of testing, measuring, and making judgments. Although the two are inseparable and related aspects of the same larger development activity, for analytic purposes we deal with planning first, and then evaluation.

Planning is a decision-making activity in which an individual or a group decides what to do and what not to do. In international development cooperation, it is usually a group of persons, not one, which is involved in the decision-making. That makes it important to clarify the process, so that all persons involved can know what the group is trying to do, and where each is in that process on any particular day. Actually, it is more than deciding *what* to do. After the program developers decide what not to do, then it is also a process of deciding *how* to do what they have chosen to do, and *when*, *where*, and by *whom* it is to be done. When two or more groups are collaborating, this joint decision-making is crucial to the process.

Planning is a natural human process. In the course of daily life, we tend to go through planning processes quite often. But they may be very informal, and not even identified as planning.

For example, if you enter a restaurant to purchase dinner, you may be handed a menu. This will tell you what your choices of items may be, and also may provide you with information on the cost of each. Then, of course, you must make a decision among the choices, so that the restaurant staff can provide you with what you request. You have participated in a planning exercise—studied the alternatives, analyzed the costs of each, perhaps made a prediction of the future based on your personal tastes and your estimate of what the chef will actually prepare, and then made a decision. People do that every day.

Put more formally, there are definitions like this: *To PLAN means to study the past and the present in order to forecast the future, and in the light of that forecast, to determine the goals to be achieved, what needs to be done to achieve them, why those things need to be done, who shall do them, and how and when and where they shall be done* (**5a**).

Thus one important aspect of planning is guessing about the future. There are formal ways of describing the process of forecasting, and it is a normal and necessary part of all planning. Sometimes habits and traditional behavior replace conscious forecasting, but that aspect of planning is always present. In the normal course of a day, most of us guess about the future, and then make decisions about what to do and what not to do. When we do that, we are planning.

Elise Boulding has observed

...now we face a world society so complex that centralized planning can no longer work, yet even supposedly free enterprise, non-planned societies like the US are in fact highly planned. Furthermore, all the people who are trained in policy making and administration, whether of political, economic or social structures, are trained to plan and administer coordinated systems (Boulding 1977: 226).

The point is that planning is not a highly specialized process in which only trained specialists can participate. It is a normal human function. Some activities require much more of it than other activities. And some kinds of planning are much more effective than others. *The effectiveness of planning is related directly to the extent to which planning includes the following five aspects: (a) recognition of the need for action; (b) investigation and analysis; (c) proposal for action; (d) decision-making; and (e) resource allocation consistent with the decisions* (**5b**).

All of these aspects of planning are important, and each contributes to the others. One key quality feature in the process is the *investigation and analysis* listed above, which is essential for *forecasting*, an integral part of planning. But all forecasts of the future have their limitations. Human beings simply do not know the future. There are many ways that guesses about the future can be improved in their quality, but all such predictions are less than perfect. For example, the better the quality of the information about the past and the present, the higher the quality of the forecast of the future is likely to be. However, some kinds of planning invest too much of the available resources (time and money) in gathering data in order to make better forecasts, and not enough in the difficult decision-making processes which are also critical aspects of planning. Unfortunately, in the extreme, planners accumulate a mountain of data about everything they can, and fail to assess the feasibility and potential consequences of alternative courses of action. Without that stage, the quality of decisions about who will do what, when, and how tends to suffer. Balance in the planning process is important.

An example of one extreme was the efforts of "outsiders" in several African and Asian countries in the 1970s to assemble a large quantity of data about the agricultural sector of the national economy, and to build it into a computer simulation model. While that in itself may have been a useful exercise, it was justified for its ultimate value to "policy makers" in their planning. Unfortunately the raw data tended to be neither valid nor reliable, and was usually limited to economic factors. Since it did not include political, diplomatic, and social variables, planners found it of limited value.

There are even more examples on the opposite side, where planners did not bother to collect and analyze the facts, but merely went ahead. Sometimes a project which seemed to be working well in one country was brought directly to a second or third country.

Planners changed the names on project papers, sometimes put in a little national population data, and then "sold" the project where it simply did not fit. A specific example was a poultry project featuring caged hens for egg production. The technical aspects of the project were quite successful, but it happened to be attempted in a vegetarian Asian country where a hen's egg is not usually eaten. This project produced a surplus of eggs which could find no market, and the project was abandoned.

Balance in the planning process is important, and all aspects need to be included.

Another quality feature in the planning process is the extent to which those to be affected by a planned activity participate in actually making the plan. In all development activity this is crucial, since if the people affected by the process do not see it as development, they are not likely to make it really work. Some have put this issue in terms of the simple question, what is the problem? It is in the planning process that the problem is defined. If all relevant individuals and groups agree on what the problem is, the probability of gaining consensus on a plan is much greater than if they have different ideas about "what the problem really is".

This has been a major concern in international development, since outside funding agencies usually have a different world-view than local people. Korten and Carner make the case for collaborative planning:

The central concept of people-centered development is quite simple. It is an approach to development that looks to the creative initiative of people as the primary development resource and to their material and spiritual well-being as the end that the development process serves.... Recognition of dehumanizing, inequitable, and environmentally unsustainable consequences of conventional development models has stimulated a serious search for alternatives. These alternatives must surely provide substantial increases in productive output to meet the needs of a vast and growing world population, but they must do so in ways that are both consistent with the basic principles of participation and are equitable and sustainable (Korten and Carner 1984: 201).

Writing about the need for more effective linkages between agricultural extension, agricultural research, and farming people, David Kaimowitz notes:

Looking towards the 21st century, there are a number of new technological challenges on the horizon that will affect the links between extension and research…. The new biotechnologies have made agricultural research much more directly dependent on disciplines such as molecular biology, and in the process, the lines between basic and applied research have been severely blurred. Increasingly, the major breakthroughs take place in sophisticated laboratories, far from farmers' fields. Nevertheless, there will still be a need for adaptive research and feedback on how these technologies perform. New links will have to be designed between the laboratories, extension, and private marketing divisions to make this possible (Kaimowitz 1991: 112).

Beyond that, new links will have to be designed between farming people, local agencies of their own governments and NGOs, and national and international development organizations. New links will have to be formed between planners and implementers at all levels. And new links will have to be developed among national governments, NGOs and specialized agencies of the UN, as well as regional and global development banks.

According to Ludwig F. Stiller and Ram Prakash Yadav, writing in and about Nepal,

Convergent planning will place a different type of burden on the technical departments of the administration. Once plans have matured that include both the interests of local Small Farmers' Groups and the overall national objectives, it is important that the departments carry out their programs with the receiving mechanism in mind. In education, health, veterinary services, forest development, water use, agriculture extension, and the allied services, an effort must be made to respond to the needs actually expressed. These needs are no longer the whims or wishes of local communities, but the results of combining local interests and initiative with desired planning efforts. This is a very strong input that has to be considered.

Planning on the basis of such an input, is more demanding than planning in the abstract. This does not suggest that standardization, uniformity, and administrative management are set aside. Far from it. It does, however, mean that the system must have sufficient flexibility to match planned delivery targets with locally expressed needs. It also implies the need for members of the central administration to go out to the districts on a regular basis to assess local needs (Stiller and Yadav 1979: 305–6).

5.1 Aspects of the Planning Process

Planning consists of a variety of functions which occur in many different orders. Thus, while this section presents a list of many of these functional aspects, and they are shown in order, from A to E, and by number within each group, readers are encouraged not to see this as a list of steps to be followed. Sometimes, the process may be followed in the order presented here. More often, however, the various aspects are not conducted in that order. They are best understood as parts of the process, each occurring when it is feasible in the process, rather than in the order presented here. Some have used lists like this as a *checklist*, merely to remind planners of items which may have been neglected.

The process of planning may involve the following:

A. *Collecting and assembling facts*
1. Develop hypotheses as a basis of determining what facts to get.
2. Decide what kinds of facts to get.
3. Plan ways and means of getting those facts.
4. Go out and get the facts.
5. Assemble facts in a variety of analytic patterns; search for the significant!
6. Decide what the facts mean.

B. *Evaluating the facts*
1. Analyze relationships between facts and existing programs.

C. *Forecasting*
1. Prepare alternative plans.
2. Estimate consequences of each alternative.
3. Estimate cost of each alternative.

D. *Decision-making*
1. Select plan for future action.

2. Secure acceptance of the plan.
3. Make time-phased activity plans.
4. Anticipate future relationships with sources of support.

E. *Allocating resources*
1. Allocate funds in accordance with activities.
2. Allocate personnel as appropriate.
3. Synchronize budget with time-phased plan.

5.2 Program Planning Cycles

The relationship between planning and implementation is often thought of as a cycle. It can be stated that: *Planning may be viewed as a continuous process. As planning guides implementation, implementation informs further planning, which leads to adjustments in implementation, ... and the process continues* (**5c**). The program planning cycle is shown in Figure 5.1.

This approach is taken formally by many large organizations. But it is also practiced informally, even by a farming family, for example. The family plans to plant rice, so seed which has been saved is put

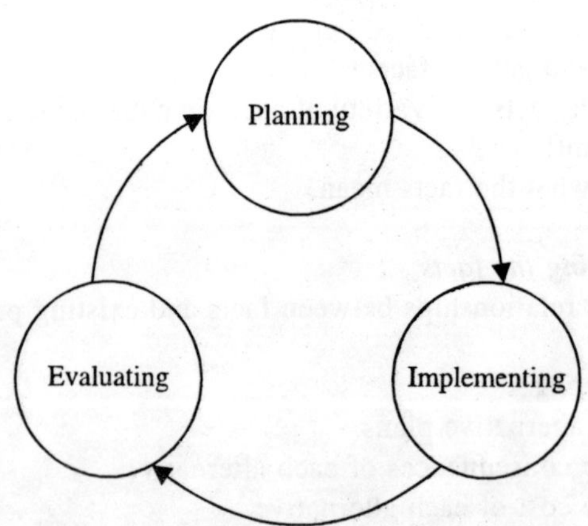

Figure 5.1
The Program Planning Cycle

in a small, well-watered seedbed. The informal planning, of course, began months earlier, when certain rice grain from the last harvest was set aside and stored as seed. While the seedlings are growing, land may be prepared for transplanting the seedlings into a larger field. But the family evaluates the growth process of the seedlings, so they can plan a date for transplanting into the larger field. A tentative date is planned for the transplanting, and arrangements are made with neighboring women to assist with that task. The weather is continuously evaluated. If the rains do not arrive as early as anticipated, the plan is modified to a later date. At a certain date, transplanting is implemented, and then evaluated. If there is sufficient supply of seedlings, a little more land may be planted. If the water for irrigation is limited, less land may be planted. So plans are made, they are implemented, the results are evaluated, new plans are made, and new implementation takes place...and the cycle goes on.

In large formal organizations, separate units may be assigned the responsibility for planning. Even here, however, since others may be assigned the responsibility for implementation, there is need for continuous communication and adjustment of plans. And when a third group is responsible for monitoring and evaluating progress of implementation, the need for collaboration is even greater.

In large organizations, the effectiveness of planning is directly related to the extent to which it is guided by policies stated at the top, but then flow to the bottom for specific plans, which then go up and down again several times. (Like a bouncing ball, it is an iterative process between higher and lower levels.) (**5d**).

In collaborative planning, where several organizations are involved, the idea of a bouncing ball is useful. The ball, in this case, bounces back and forth among the collaborating organizations. Usually representatives of these organizations who see the draft planning ideas, suggest modifications and improvements, "bounce" the plan back to others in the other organizations, and then receive it again. This series of iterations continues to mold and modify the tentative plan, and improve its chances for later implementation. The transaction costs of this series of iterations among the various collaborators can be high, but, as a wise investment in successful collaboration, they are necessary.

5.3 Program Development Strategies

Over the years, certain program development strategies have evolved which are particularly helpful in such activities as community development or agricultural extension. For example, *the cycle of community development programming may include such aspects as:*

a. SITUATIONAL ANALYSIS;
b. identification of the problems (OPPORTUNITIES);
c. establishment of goals (TARGETS);
d. analysis of BARRIERS (why haven't the goals been achieved already?);
e. finding appropriate MESSAGES;
f. designating AUDIENCES for each message;
g. selecting the best combination of CHANNELS to carry messages to audiences;
h. designing TREATMENTS for each message which will achieve the greatest impact;
i. IMPLEMENTATION (sending appropriately treated messages via selected channels to designated audiences);
j. recurrent MONITORING of the extent to which project inputs have actually been made;
k. EVALUATING the extent to which goals have been achieved;
l. (a) SITUATIONAL ANALYSIS;
m. (b) identification of the problems (OPPORTUNITIES);
n. (c) ... etc. since THE PROCESS IS CONTINUOUS!

In the definitions of planning, one of the key aspects is WHAT NEEDS TO BE DONE. This WHAT to do is also known as a *goal*. The *goal* is the *objective* toward which effort will be invested. Some organizations use the word *target* to mean the same thing. In sports games, the goal is usually very clear. In an ice hockey game, or a soccer/football game, one area at each end of the playing field is designated as the *goal*. The players on the field attempt to put the ball (football) or the puck (ice hockey) in the goal. In archery, the *target* is a circular object with a large dot in its center; the object of the archer is to shoot an arrow and hit the target in its center.

In a development activity, one of the major reasons for *planning* is to establish goals, targets, or objectives. These words are used differently by various organizations. Each organization may have its own special meaning for these words. For example, one organization may have a *goal* to dig wells in order to achieve a higher *objective* of providing safe drinking water to the people of a village. But another development organization may use these words the other way around. That is, they may have an *objective* of having the wells in order to achieve their higher *goal* of having safe drinking water.

From a strategic perspective, here are some propositions about the selection of goals or objectives:

The extent to which the goals of any development program will be achieved tends to be directly related to the extent to which those toward whom the program is directed have COLLABORATED (PARTICIPATED), *possibly through representatives, in establishing the goals* (**5e**).

Participation and collaboration, two major issues discussed in this book, are related to many aspects of international development. There is no better way to increase the probability of goal achievement than to be sure that the intended beneficiaries of the program have a major voice in deciding what the goals should be.

Another way is to reduce the number of goals a project is trying to achieve. For example, if a project is started in order to supply drinking water to a village which formerly did not have a safe year-around supply, that will be a challenge. If the planning group decides to also provide irrigation water, that will add to the complexity. While in some cases adding multiple goals may enhance a project's viability, in general each new goal reduces the probability of achieving any goal. Thus, in this example, if the groups decide that they could also start a day care center for small children, and then add a family planning dimension, the probability of successfully completing the drinking water project is reduced.

The extent to which the goals of any development program will be achieved is inversely related to the NUMBER *of those goals* (**5f**).

However, this proposition relates to one particular time. If a group succeeds in improving the drinking water system for the village, that same group probably has a better chance of also improving the village irrigation. And village groups which have been willing and able to work together to manage two such water schemes probably have a better chance of achieving other goals they might identify, such as the child-care or family-size projects.

A similar strategic proposition is that *local people are likely to adopt changes recommended by a development organization directly to the extent that the* TECHNOLOGY IS APPROPRIATE *from the perspective of those people* (**5g**). In the north-east of Kenya, for example, locally controlled windmills were a great success in several villages where deeper, diesel engine driven pumps had failed. For the diesel pumps depended on technology, fuel, and spare parts which were simply not available locally. The windmills, however, could be managed by local people with very little outside help (annual lubrication and some metal parts). Where the technology fits local needs and conditions, people will use it.

Focusing on agricultural extension-type programs, the same idea may be stated as follows: *The success of an agricultural extension program tends to be directly related to the extent to which:*

a. *the benefit of the recommendations to farmers is high;*
b. *the costs of recommended practices to farmers are low;*
c. *recommended practices are relatively simple;*
d. *the benefits to farmers are immediate;*
e. *the recommended practices may be tested by individual farmers on a trial basis prior to complete commitment; and*
f. *the recommendations fit the type of farming system* (**5h**).

Other generalizations about goal achievement, related to the planning process, include: *The extent to which the goals of any development program will be achieved is directly related to the extent to which the planners of the program are* ACCOUNTABLE *to the people who are the intended beneficiaries of the program* (**5i**).

Plans also need to reflect an awareness of the roles of women and men within any community. If women are not permitted to have title to the land they cultivate, credit programs for women cannot be based on landownership. If men market the milk which women collect from cows, any new plans to improve women's participation in dairy programs need to find a way for women to receive the benefits of their work.

Another strategic factor which may be taken into account by development planners is the extent of cooperation within the village or community. If there are competing groups from different social classes, different ethnic or linguistic groups, or other differences, it is sometimes strategically better to arrange separate projects with the different groups than to include them all in one project. For example, some rural credit cooperatives have failed when people with larger landholdings, or larger fish ponds, wanted larger loans. Others with small holdings, or small ponds, needing smaller loans may drop out of the credit program. In some communities this problem has been solved by having two different credit cooperatives, each with members with more uniform needs. In this situation, when limits are set for the size of loans, the group makes them fit the needs of members.

In general, *the more competing groups there may be within a community, the more difficult community development may be* (**5j**).

5.4 Means/Ends Hierarchies

The words *ends* and *means* are useful to clarify the essence of planning. *Means* and *ends* are often ambiguous in life, and in the planning process. Here, *end* is used to refer to a *goal*, or *objective*, or *target*, and *means* is used to refer to the implementation activities designed to achieve the *end*. If the *end* is clean, safe drinking water in the village, one *means* to that end may be the digging of wells. Usually, a specific activity could be viewed as either a *means* or an *end*, depending on the perspective from which it is viewed. The digging of the well, for example, is the *means* to clean water, but viewed from the perspective of planners, or workers, before the well has been dug, it is seen as an *end*. Their *means* to that *end* (the well) might be ten hours of work by five people using digging tools. If you are one of the workers doing the digging, you might ask "why are we digging the well?" Leaders might answer that the well is a necessary goal, or means to achieve the higher goal, or end, of having clean drinking water. But if you ask why we need clean drinking water, they may answer with an even "higher" level goal, like "the people of our village will be healthier if we have clean drinking water".

Thus *means* and *ends* are typically strung from lower to higher levels in a plan, just like a hierarchy. In some development planning activities, it is usual to have a simple linear hierarchy, in which one means leads to one end, which in turn becomes the means to a higher end, which in turn is the means to a still higher end, and so on. In the real world of development, there are often several means used to achieve a particular end, and that end, in turn, may be just one of several means to an even higher end. And often one activity may be a means to several different ends. The hierarchy is not neat and symmetrical. But it is at the core of the planning exercise.

Figure 5.2 illustrates a typical means/ends hierarchy. Each activity on it is BOTH a *means* to the activity above it, and an *end* from the perspective of the activity below it. To planners, setting out to design a development project or program, the concept of a means/ends hierarchy is a useful tool. To evaluators or analysts trying to understand an on-going development activity, the means/ends hierarchy is also a highly useful tool.

For example, in Figure 5.2, if the star at the top represents some general goal like "improved conditions among the people of the country", the next level down in the means/ends hierarchy could have means/ends features like improved supply of nutritious food, improved educational system, improved healthcare delivery, improved transportation system, etc. Then, continuing this illustration, at the next level down, under supply of food, there might be one means/ends on food production, a second means/ends on food distribution and marketing, and a third one on entitlement to food,

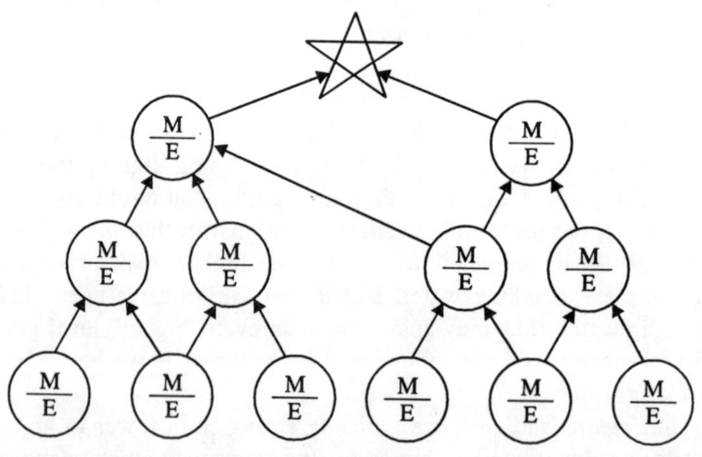

Figure 5.2
Means/Ends Hierarchy

particularly among less advantaged groups. Following down the hierarchy, under food production, there might be a means/ends on increasing production of grains, a second one on increasing production of fluid milk, a third on meat production, and perhaps one on fruit and vegetables. Lower down the hierarchy, under grain, there could be a means/ends on increasing the proportion of irrigated land, a second means/ends on increasing availability of mineral fertilizers, and perhaps a third one on improved seed. If one followed that hierarchy down low enough, under the fertilizer items, for example, there might be a means/ends on purchasing a bicycle for a field worker so that she could visit more farms in less time as a means of collecting soil samples: toward the end of making soil tests; toward the end of helping farmers decide how much fertilizer is needed in particular fields for particular crops; toward encouraging them to put more fertilizer on those crops; toward the end of increased production of grain.

One may start with any activity in a development project or program, and build the means/ends hierarchy. For a particular item, if you ask "why" that is being done, the means/ends hierarchy will tell you what the next item up the hierarchy is. If you ask "how" that is being done, it will tell you what the next items down the hierarchy may be. For any means/ends, the question of "how" should provide information about the *means* to that as an *end*. For any means/ends, the question of "why" should provide information about the higher *end* toward which the first means/ends is seen as a *means*.

Any development program can be analyzed with the means/ends hierarchy. And for planners, it is a useful way of identifying missing components in a plan as it evolves.

5.5 The Project as a Tool for Implementation

The words *project* and *program* have both been used in Section 5.4, and these words are used interchangeably by some practitioners. For purposes of clarification within this book, *project* is used to refer to the smaller, discrete cluster of activities which is often part of a larger combination of activities. The word *program* is used to refer to the larger cluster of different projects. At higher, more general levels of planning and implementing development activities, one could move from the *project* level to the *program* level, and then up to a *strategy* level, and then to the most general, or *policy* level. From a government perspective, there will usually be some *policies* which set forth the highest level of general goals for a country. Then, a government may also have a *strategy*, by means of which it intends to convert that general statement of policy into tangible action. Moving toward the particular, that same government may have several different *programs* which are segments of the overall strategy. And, in turn, each *program* may have many different *projects* within it. (For a discussion of these different levels of planned change see Chapter 4, particularly Figure 4.1.)

Non-governmental organizations, educational institutions, private corporations, and other large organizations may also do their planning at these four levels of specificity. They, too, may have policies, strategies, programs, and projects. In a way, these are merely names for different portions of the means/ends hierarchy discussed in Section 5.4. The upper parts of the hierarchy are policy matters; lower down are statements of strategy; then there are various programs; and within each program, there may be projects.

The project level is the smallest unit of operation, although an individual project will have several components within it. Projects are a convenient administrative arrangement, and have both advantages and disadvantages. Usually, a particular project will have a fixed area in which it operates (one village, or one district), a fixed time (like three years, or five years), and a fixed quantity of financial and personnel resources. An advantage of a project is that those working on it, and those whom it is designed to serve, may know just how long it will last, which places are included in the project and which are not, and how much money is available for investment in it. A disadvantage of projects is the same specificity. Even if it is a five-year project, the world does not end after those five years; what becomes of the activities after that? And if the project is for only three villages in a district, what about the other villages in that same district?

Nevertheless, while the project mode has many weaknesses, it is administratively convenient, and is used globally. There is a tendency for planners and their employers to be optimistic. Therefore, projects are likely to overestimate their potential achievements, and the time allocated for completion of most projects may be too short. Thus, project extensions are very common in international development. Quite often, there are too few people assigned to a project to accomplish its goals. And errors in the financial side are often found. Many projects simply do not have sufficient funds allocated to accomplish their goals, while others have much too much money assigned to them.

These problems are not merely caused by mistakes in the planning process by incompetent planners. The process of development itself, as discussed earlier, is so complex that precise forecasting of the future is not feasible. Some things are relatively easy to plan for; others are impossible. For example, if you are building a road from village A to village B, it is possible to measure, in advance, how many kilometers it is from A to B. It is also possible (sometimes) to get accurate maps of the topography, so that the slope of hillsides, the numbers of rivers and streams which must be crossed, and other such factors can be anticipated. If some experienced road construction engineers are part of the planning team, it may be feasible to estimate the amount of time and labor as well as materials needed for each kilometer of road. If, for example, it takes an average of two months to build one kilometer of road, and if the distance from village A to village B is 10 km, one could estimate that approximately twenty months will be required to complete the construction of that road.

But even with so many tangibles, planners are only using estimates. Most development projects are even more complex and less predictable. If, for example, a program calls for establishing a rural health post in each of the twenty districts of one country, how long will it take? That program, in turn, might have several projects within it. Twenty of those projects might each be the construction of a building to house the health post. Assuming that construction in some sites may move more rapidly than in others, planners would still have to question how many could be constructed at the same time. If there are sufficient skilled builders and building construction supervisors, they might try to build all twenty simultaneously. Or, they might decide to try three different designs of health posts; complete them all; compare the three; and then choose a design for the remaining seventeen health post buildings. And that is just the beginning of the complexity of planning this program. From where will building supplies, like cement, be acquired? How much will it cost? How will it be transported to the building sites? How much time will it take to go through the purchasing, shipment, and delivery process for each building to be constructed? And what about the weather? In a normal year, in that location, can construction be done on most days, or will there be some days in which rain or other weather conditions can slow down, or even stop, construction?

Then there is the matter of personnel to staff the health posts. How many will be needed for each, and what type of training will they need? Are they already available within that country, or will they need to be recruited, employed, and trained before the health posts can open? If some need high-level training, will that be available within the country, or will people need to be sent abroad? If the training takes an average of two years, for example, what proportion of those recruited are likely to successfully complete their training? Of those, how many will then agree to take the assignment, and will really stay and do the job?

Planning a development program is not an exact science. It is fraught with complexity, difficulty, and uncertainty. And the precise costs in time, money, and personnel are not usually predictable. But while it is far from simple and predictable, it is possible, and provides an opportunity for great creativity, and the excitement of successfully completing significant work. And there are some tools (like the means/ends hierarchy) and some generalizations which can help.

For example, on the matter of goals, *the extent to which the goals of any development program will be achieved is likely to be directly related to the extent to which various cultural factors are taken into consideration in planning the program* (**5k**).

To illustrate, if a new drinking water system is installed in a village, it is likely that prior to that development activity, there were already established patterns by which families got their drinking water supplies. If this had been the work assignment of older daughters in the households, they lost their "jobs". Since there were rewards and punishments associated with those old assignments, the very installation of the new system was a threat to those young women, and caused them to be against the new system. In one village it was the mothers who themselves walked down a hill to the well, and carried the family water supply back up in jugs of different types. The practice was to queue the jugs in the order in which the women had arrived, and then sit together under a shade tree while each took her turn at lowering a bucket into the well to draw water. This was a friendly conversational "work-break" which was greatly missed when piped drinking water was made available close to each house.

The goal of having a safe drinking water supply near each home was appropriate. But if project planners had taken these cultural patterns into account, there might have been less resistance to project implementation. If a collaborative mode had been used, in which those who are normally responsible for household water supplies were part of the team designing the project, such matters could have been resolved early in the process.

Another generalization has to do with the *importance* of any particular aspect of a project. For example, interpersonal relationships are very important, and make a tremendous difference in planning and implementing development projects. But these are difficult to identify, especially for outsiders. If two members of the local planning committee happen to be brothers, that could influence the way other members of the committee react to each of them. But if one brother is also married to the mayor's daughter, it could give both brothers more influence in the planning meeting. On the other hand, if the other brother happens to be married to the sister of the mayor's political opponent, those two brothers may not be speaking to each other at all. However, none of this type of information is likely to be included among the data collected for project planning or implementation.

The more important a variable is, the less the probability that it can be measured objectively (**5l**). This is particularly relevant in the analysis of past and present experience.

For planning purposes, the areas where the facts are not available are often more important than the areas where facts are available (**5m**). This is similar to proposition (**5l**). For example, in planning a new project on fresh vegetable production for the market in a nearby city, it is possible to get information on the soil types and soil fertility in the area, along with rainfall, temperatures, and other weather data. But information on prices of the fresh vegetables at harvest time may not be available. Even if historical information were available, it is difficult, if not impossible, to forecast what prices will be if locally produced vegetables arrive on the market in quantity. Thus, information on a very important set of facts may simply not be available. But the usual professional practice is to study similar situations elsewhere, and then make the best guess regarding the missing facts.

Some projects start at the "perfect time" when people in the area really need the project, and are willing and able to do whatever is necessary to ensure project success. Other projects just happen to start at the wrong time. In some cases there may have been a similar project in the area before, but the project implementers promised much more than they could deliver. Sometimes a new technology was introduced which simply failed to perform under local conditions. And sometimes the project design was appropriate, but a revolution, civil insurrection, or a foreign military invasion occurs, and everyone concerned loses interest in the development project. In such cases, it may not be possible to predict the appropriate timing. But in other cases, particularly just after a natural disaster such as a flood or a drought, or a period of severe economic depression, it is feasible to forecast the appropriate timing. *Timing is critical. The effectiveness of a development program tends to vary inversely with the economic wellbeing of its clientele at the beginning of the program* (**5n**).

A group of people are likely to adopt changes recommended by a development organization directly to the extent that the technology is appropriate from the perspective of that group of people (**5o**). This generalization reflects what has already been mentioned in this chapter. It supports what has been said about the collaborative mode of planning. When representatives of *that group of people* are full partners in deciding what technology should be introduced, the probability is higher that they will adopt that technology when it is made available.

5.6 Other Tools for Planning

Logical frameworks, time-phased action plans, responsibility charts, and impact and sustainability analysis are among other tools for planning. For each of these, there are many variations, but the general ideas are used widely in development organizations and other types of human groups.

Many organizations use a *logical framework* as an aid in planning. There are different types of logic in use, but they tend to have a common organizational pattern. *Log frames* are a simplified listing of

Activity	Indicator	Verification Process	Assumptions
Policy Goal			
Strategic Goal			
Program Goal			
Project Output			
Project Input			

Figure 5.3
Sample Logical Framework for Describing a Project

key elements in the means/ends hierarchy as already discussed, usually depicted as a column on the left side of the chart (Figure 5.3). The items might be named, as in the sample shown in Figure 5.3. Then, from left to right, across the top, there will be names of features about the relationships among the items in the left side column.

In addition to being an aid to planning, once a project has been described in a logical framework, the document becomes a condensed summary of much longer documents which also describe the project. The framework is a useful "quick view" of the project for various administrative purposes. And when an external review or evaluation of the project is to be conducted, the logical framework sheet is a very useful tool to persons who are unfamiliar with the project, but are asked to assess it.

For any particular activity in a project, it is possible to explain its rationale with this tool. As an example, in one project, village people collaborated with an outside technician in digging the village well deeper, strengthening its sides, and building a windmill to pump water from it into a common clean trough. In the bottom left corner of the logical framework chart, planners might describe the digging and building activities as *project inputs*. Moving up the chart, the *project output* might be availability of clean drinking water in the village on a year-round basis. The *program goal* might include both improved human health in the village, and time-saving for women who formerly had to walk great distances to find clean water for household use. The *strategic goal* could be to contribute, along with other health-related projects in other villages, to longer average lifespans among rural people. And that, in turn, might be one of several strategies employed by a government to demonstrate a commitment to a national *policy goal* of increased equity between rural people and urban people.

Using the same example, one could complete the other boxes on the logical framework horizontally by describing *indicators* of the project input as the numbers of wells dug, strengthened, and equipped with windmills. The *verification process* might be visits by the project supervisor to each village site to describe and record progress. *Assumptions* might be listed as the willingness of the village people to do the work; the availability of required materials; sufficient wind to power the windmills; and the likelihood that clean water would actually flow throughout the year from the wells. In similar fashion, the boxes for indicators, verification processes, and assumptions could be completed for each of the aspects listed on the left side of the chart.

Our experience in field project operations suggests that in addition to being a useful tool for project and program planners, the logical framework is an aid to project implementation, as it answers the question of all those involved as to why they are engaged in each particular activity.

A similar tool is the *time-phased action plan*. For this, a calendar is constructed including the total anticipated time required to plan and implement a project, often including follow-up evaluations of the project long after it is completed. Then each element of the project is shown on the calendar, from its beginning to its completion. Some elements cannot be started until some earlier element has been completed; other elements can proceed simultaneously. Planners can work from the logical framework, or from an ends/means hierarchy, and construct the time-phased action plan (Table 5.1).

Table 5.1
Simple Time-phased Action Plan

Activity	Year 1	Year 2	Year 3	Year 4	Year 5
Hire Staff	——————				
Training Program	——————		——		
Place in Field		————————————————			
Annual Review	—	—	—	—	—

Another useful tool in planning is the *responsibility chart.* For this, planners and managers can work from one of the aids to planning mentioned in this section, and make a list of each of the tasks to be performed. Then, if it is a new project, the types and number of individuals required are listed adjacent to the name of the task to be done. If the project is to be implemented by an already-existing organization, then the names of actual individuals can be written in on the responsibility chart next to the name of the task to be performed. This is a particularly useful tool not only for planners but for other administrators as well (Table 5.2).

A set of forms like the one in Table 5.2 will also be useful to persons concerned with the impact of the project and its sustainability over time. Since development is designed to make significant changes, and since any change will have an impact on a variety of different aspects of a situation, it is important to have a variety of

Table 5.2
Sample Responsibility Chart
(For Implementing Agency)

Tasks	*Responsible Individual(s)*
1. Personnel Recruitment	Smith and Gonzalas
2. Selection and Employment	Arora
3. Relationships with Local Collaborators	Gonzalas
4. Staff and Collaborators Training	Friedrich
5. Field Placement	Gonzalas and Friedrich
6. Program Monitoring	Smith
7. Annual Review	Arora

systematic ways to estimate the impact of a development project. For example, a project might be designed to increase the incomes of people living in a certain area. If it is successful, it is expected to have a positive economic impact on those people. One dimension of impact analysis would be to measure that positive impact. However, another dimension of impact analysis would be to question the impact on other people outside the intended clientele. Will there also be a positive economic impact on them, or will their economic position deteriorate? Then, beyond economics, there are other potential impacts of a development project. What will be the impact on the environment? What will be the impact on the social structure? on the culture? on relevant government agencies? on the political situation? on the international diplomatic situation? etc.

In addition, there are many types of sustainability questions. How sustainable will the project process itself be? Will it last long enough to complete the project? After that, will the people affected by the project continue its activities, or will they be unable or unwilling to sustain them? And if the project activities are sustainable for a long time, what will be the long-range consequences for all those aspects of the situation mentioned in the preceding paragraph? Which of them will be sustained by the changed situation, and which will be undermined?

Beyond these issues, matters of flexibility and creativity are important to the planning process. All of the planning tools mentioned above are here because they can help planners be more flexible in their work. Practitioners can go beyond merely following old habits, and try new and different *ends* to work toward, and new and different *means* to achieve those *ends*. If that happens they can encourage creative thinking among planners, and stimulate ever better plans. But, because the diagrams are relatively formal, they can also be misused to stifle creativity and urge planners of new projects to "fit the mould" of old projects. This would be a long range strategic error, and it is mentioned here to help practitioners avoid such misuse of these planning tools.

5.7 Evaluation Strategies

It is normal in any organized effort to achieve purposeful planned change and to also attempt to evaluate the extent to which the goals and objectives which have been planned are actually achieved. This is a matter of making a measurement and a judgment. As illustrated in Figure 5.1, planning is preparation for implementation, which may then be evaluated in preparation for revision of the plans.

For example, collaboration between the people of a village and some community forestry workers might result in a plan to protect three different areas around the village to encourage regrowth of both fodder for livestock and fuelwood for home consumption. In the plan, the three areas are marked with stakes, so they can easily be seen. Then families in the village are designated to watch each area every day. If no goats or cattle are to be allowed in the areas, members of the designated families may be required to keep constant watch and report any animal which strays into the area. After the first three weeks people may be allowed to enter area A to cut and remove fodder for two days. In the fourth week area B may be used for a similar process, and in the next week only area C might be open for such cutting. Later on, each area might continue to be open for cutting only two days every third week.

Such a project may be *monitored* by a village committee to determine whether or not the selected families are actually patrolling the marked areas and allowing cutting only on the specified days. In addition to *monitoring* that input (watching the three areas) they may decide to *evaluate* the project. To do that, after several months of project implementation, they may actually weigh the quantity of fodder cut in one of the three areas in a week. That same week, they may weigh the total quantity of fodder which can be cut from a similar size land area not included among the three project plots.

If, for example, production of available fodder is significantly increased by this managed rotation plan, the villagers may evaluate the project as being useful. The evaluation might demonstrate that the total quantity of fodder cut from one area in its assigned two-day period is ten times what could be cut from a similar area not being managed by the project. Village people might then change the plan to increase the total amount of their grazing lands to be managed in the project.

If, on the other hand, the *evaluation* shows that there is only a slight increase in fodder production, they might decide to abandon the project. However, in this example there is a second goal, related to fuelwood production. That might have also been evaluated after six months. If the group had agreed on what would be counted as fuelwood and on how they would measure production (as in count-ing the number of bundles cut, or weighing the actual quantity cut and carried away), then a similar evaluation could be made.

The extent to which achievement of the goals of a development program can be measured tends to be directly related to the extent to which the goals are clearly understood by those responsible for carrying out the program and evaluating it (**5p**).

In this case, like others, there are various levels of precision with which the measurement might be made. Those which give more accurate information tend to cost more. To make a valid and reliable assessment of the fuelwood removed from area A after six months, the villagers might all go to that area on one day, with a weighing device, cut it all, and total the weight of fuelwood. To make the comparison with a similar size area not being managed, since some cutting there might have happened each day, it would be necessary to weigh the quantity cut and removed from the other plot each day for the whole six months. That would be a costly effort.

Actually, *precision in measurement of the impact of development programs tends to be directly related to the cost of that measurement* (**5q**). This has been illustrated in two aspects of project evaluation: the monitoring of inputs and the evaluation of outputs. And in this simple collaborative project involving village people and a commu-nity forestry project, the major input was people's time and energy in watching the three protected areas. Many projects have other tangible and measurable inputs. For example, if this had been a tree-planting project, there might have been inputs of tree seedlings and labor for the transplanting. These inputs could be monitored both in terms of the extent to which the seedlings actually were available and in terms of the timeliness of the seedlings being available. The inputs might have been useful only at the beginning of the rainy season in that village, not at the beginning of the dry season.

As Ponna Wignaraja has pointed out, evaluation is another area where collaboration between "insiders" and "outsiders" strengthens the process.

Outside evaluators themselves have to be participant evaluators. By having identity with the total process and in interaction with the participants they ask new questions. They could also have a facilitating role to play while evaluating ... using only quantifiable indicators and trying to evaluate the inter-related and inter-disciplinary process with questionable statistics is too simplistic (Wignaraja 1990: 139).

Similarly, having both men and women on an evaluation team may result in a more balanced assessment of the effects of a project on all members of the community.

But both the measurement of inputs and outputs are connected directly to the planning of the projects. They might be called direct results of the project. In addition, there are often *consequences* of a development project which are not in the plan at all, but do affect the people involved—either positively or negatively.

In this illustration of community forestry, a positive consequence might be better coordination among villagers in other activities. If they discover in the fodder and fuelwood project that they can work together for the benefit of the whole community, they might decide to use such group action for other types of projects. Thus an *output* of the project might be more fodder for their goats and cattle. A *positive consequence* of the project might be empowerment of the community for group action on other matters where individual families have shared needs—perhaps for a village drinking water supply, village road improvement, or building a school.

Both positive and negative consequences tend to occur during and after development projects, and those consequences may or may not be related to the achievement of project goals (**5r**).

On the negative side, for example, too often successful irrigation projects in arid areas have resulted in water-borne diseases becoming a problem in areas where they were never found before. Thus an excellent new irrigation system brings water so farmers can plant crops in the dry season, but it also brings malaria and doubts about the benefit of the development project.

The nutritionist Kathryn G. Dewey has made an excellent case for examining changes in people's nutritional status as a check on the consequences of development projects. In Mexico, in a study of a successful project growing vegetables for export, she found that:

The Plan Chontalpa has thus resulted in a transformation from a population of mostly self-provisioning peasant families to a population that is almost completely dependent on wage labor. Although this change is not *necessarily* undesirable, in Tabasco the situation has led to an undermining of the ability of families to feed themselves adequately (Dewey 1985: 175).

Her conclusions reflect a common experience when families on small mixed farming systems feed themselves, and then are converted to large scale, commercial, market-oriented production of a crop for sale to the outside world. They have more cash money then they ever had before, but they tend to eat less, as the cost of purchasing their food from a market at some distance is greater than the cash they are earning (and they often use some of that cash for non-food purchases).

Dewey concludes:

> The results of the case study in Tabasco are illustrative of the kinds of changes in nutrition that often accompany development. Although it cannot be denied that the basic cause of hunger and malnutrition in the world is poverty, and that efforts to reduce poverty through development is the only long-term solution, it is critical that development projects be designed so as not to worsen health and nutritional status, which, of course, depends on *how* development is defined and carried out. Social impact analysis, both prior to the initiation of development projects and after they have been implemented, is an essential element in the process of ensuring that such projects are more successful in the future than they have been in the past (Dewey 1985: 176).

Since both monitoring progress and evaluation of results are important for development projects, sometimes a unit with a name like "monitoring and evaluation" is included in the organizational structure of the project, or the larger program. There is an advantage for the personnel who are actually implementing a project to also monitor it. They are involved on a daily basis, and can observe their own project inputs and continuously make adjustments in the plan as necessary. However, for the evaluation, there may be an advantage in involving "outside" personnel. They tend not to have the same "vested interest" in demonstrating success, and may be somewhat more "objective" in their analysis. They also have an opportunity to look beyond the immediate project operations to both positive and negative consequences in the larger project setting.

As suggested by Dewey (1985: 176) there is also a time dimension in the evaluation process. This may begin with *pre-project impact assessment*, which might be months or even years prior to the beginning of project operations. Then there can be *project monitoring during various stages of project implementation*. This is often followed by *post-project impact evaluation*. Then, if questions are to be answered about the sustainability of whatever was put in place by the project, and the sustainability of the larger ecosystem within which the project operates, there may be *post-project sustainability assessment*.

Sustainability of a development project or program can be measured only after time has elapsed (**5s**). This is important, because sometimes there are *second generation* effects of a project which are not visible for some years, or even some decades. For example, when people in an area start pumping water from an underground aquifer, the question of the depth of the wells may not be considered at the beginning of the project. But after some time it may become apparent that the water table has been pulled down by the pumping. Wells at 20 feet in depth may still be working fine, but those only 15 feet down may not be delivering water. That raises the question of possible limitations on the allowable depth for pumping water in the area, and all types of social, economic, and political issues may become part of the solution.

In addition, there is a matter of precision in measurement. If the evaluation is designed to deal with *cause and effect*, to demonstrate that the positive changes were *caused* by the project and would probably not have happened without the project, then it is necessary to gather information from both the area where the project took place and similar areas where the project did not take place. In its simplest form, this is illustrated by Table 5.3.

However, if more precision is needed, and especially if different communication strategies with a project are to be evaluated in

Table 5.3
Simple Control Group Evaluation

	Before	*After*
Project Area		
Non-project Area		

Time 1	Exposed	Exposed	Not Exposed	Not Exposed
Time 2	Made Change	Did Not Make Change	Made Change	Did Not Make Change

Figure 5.4
Eight Box Evaluation Design

comparison with each other, it is necessary to gather data before and after the project among those exposed to its activities, and those not exposed. Figure 5.4 illustrates that type of evaluation design.

The type of design shown in Figure 5.4 can be used within a project to evaluate the impact of particular activities (such as a meeting, a newsletter, and a demonstration) as well as to compare one whole project with another. As with any research, the greater the precision desired from the analysis, the greater the cost is likely to be.

An extreme example comes in the grading of eggs for fresh market consumption. Consumers prefer fresh eggs and resist purchasing eggs which may have already spoiled. Therefore, in countries where consumers are protected by law, there are sometimes regulations specifying egg quality. The specifications in one country state that if an egg is broken open over a clean white marble slab, the yellow yoke in the center will normally stand higher than the white which spreads out around it. Then the regulations specify that if the egg is to be graded "A" it must have a yoke which is at least a certain number of centimeters above the marble slab. In addition, the diameter of the white part on the slab may be no more than a specified number of centimeters. If the diameter of the white is too long, and if the height of the yoke is not high enough, then the egg must be graded "B" rather than "A". If the white goes out even further from the center, and/or the yoke is even less high, it must be graded as "C".

One major problem with this method of evaluation of fresh eggs is that it is necessary to break the eggshell in order to do the evaluation. If you are in the business of selling eggs in their shells, the product has been destroyed in the process. The precision is high with this technique, but the cost is also high—too high!

However, there are other ways to do the evaluation. It has been observed that eggs have an "air-sac" at one end, and the older the egg (which correlates inversely with the quality of the egg) the larger the air-sac. If one holds the egg up in front of a candle (or any other light source) it is possible to see how large the air-sac is without breaking the egg. Therefore, for years, eggs have been evaluated for quality by "candling" them, rather than by breaking them over a marble slab. The precision is less with the candling procedure, but the cost is much much less. And in recent years, in highly mechanized societies, even the cost of the time taken for candling is too high. Since the quality of the egg varies inversely with the length of time between when eggs are laid and the consumer using them, eggs are typically evaluated (and thus graded) merely by date. The container in which the eggs are shipped to market is stamped with the date on which the egg was produced. It is graded "A" if sold within a specified number of days. If it is not sold by that date, it is merely shifted to another box, and graded "B". And if even more time lapses prior to sale, it may further be downgraded to "C".

In this example, three different ways of evaluating the quality of fresh eggs have been described. The first was most accurate, but most costly. With each alternative the accuracy, or precision, went down, but the cost also went down. Similar is the case with other kinds of evaluation, including evaluation of the effectiveness of development projects.

In general, *the impact of development programs may be assessed prior to implementation (planning stage); during implementation (monitoring); or after implementation (evaluation). At each stage, impacts upon the ecosystem may be physical, biological, cultural, social, economic, administrative, political, and diplomatic. The total environmental impact is the sum of all of the positive and negative impacts in all these dimensions* (5t).

While most examples in this chapter have been of development *projects*, rather than *programs*, the planning of a *program* may be considered to be the sum total of the planning of the individual *projects* which make up that *program*. And the evaluation of a *program* may be considered to be the sum total of the evaluations of the *projects* within that *program*.

5.8 Implications for Professional Practitioners

Planning is often thought of as the most stimulating and creative aspect of international development. It is not necessary that all aspects require creative work, and excellent execution can be exciting and rewarding. But for practitioners, planning represents an opportunity to do much more than is typical in current practice.

Practitioners should know what the current literature says about the planning process itself, as well as be familiar with recent examples of the greatest successes and great failures. By knowing the current state of the art and the history of both successes and failures in many different parts of the world, the professional can bring all these to bear on the current planning project, whatever it may be. Similarly, practitioners who have their "hands on" the planning of contemporary projects have an obligation to write about their experiences. If they document what they are learning along the way, others may learn from their experience, and the whole field of international development will be enhanced.

If a project goal is the *empowerment* of local people, then local people must *control* the agenda. That requires practitioners to be willing to release their personal "ownership" of projects so that their local partners can know that as the intended beneficiaries of the project they have the greatest stake in that project. If collaboration is the mode, professional "outside" practitioners cannot *control* planning and evaluation. In collaborative work, outsiders must share fully with insiders. For some practitioners, sharing control is the most difficult aspect of collaboration. And there is often a "donor" agency or an outside "implementing" agency which believes that it should control the whole process. Here the diplomatic skills of the practitioner may be required and professionalism may be in conflict with bureaucratic expectations. But the professional opportunity for genuine collaboration is in the balance, and it is a challenge worthy of the best practitioners.

And if practitioners are to achieve a collaborative mode in programs or projects, the planning process is a critical exercise in collaboration. Collaborating planners cannot plan *for* each other; they can only plan *with* each other. Some donor agencies and some implementing agencies resist this type of planning, because it usually costs more. If collaborators in two countries, for example, are to plan with each other, personal face-to-face work at the site on which the activity is to be implemented is normally necessary. While they can do some work by e-mail and facsimile and telephone, unless the collaborators have been working together for many years, these types of communication are not adequate. Effective collaborative planning typically involves travel and living costs for all who are involved. However, the high transaction costs of genuine collaboration are an investment in project and program success which tends to result in more cost-effective development in the long run.

Collaboration in evaluation is also associated with positive achievements. When those who are intended to benefit from a project or program share the tasks of evaluating it with any others who may have been involved in its implementation, they can jointly judge the extent to which project goals have been achieved. In many types of projects, this joint judgment is more valuable than either the judgments of the implementers or the beneficiaries alone. And for assessing both positive and negative consequences, evaluation is more likely to reveal consequences when it is carried on collaboratively.

Thus practitioners can achieve excellence in both planning and evaluation by entering into full and complete partnerships with any clientele or user group for whom development programs may be intended.

CHAPTER 6

Learning and Communication Strategies for Development

Making sense of this experience was itself an evolving process, punctuated by insights and occasional misplaced hopes. Understanding this reality, with its many surprises, required some simplification and some reduction of the immense complexity into intelligible concepts and patterns. This reassessment led to a growing appreciation of the ever diversifying, contingent nature of physical and social phenomena. Explanations framed in terms of necessary and sufficient causation no longer seemed either necessary or sufficient.

Norman Uphoff 1992: 278

Since development has been defined as *change which is perceived as positive by those who have changed*, then for individual human beings and for human groups, the essential process in development is *learning*. And the primary means by which human beings learn is *communication*. This chapter addresses critical aspects of the learning process and the communication process. These processes may be considered as the "building blocks" of international development programs. In this chapter readers are invited to look within the whole programs and projects discussed in the last chapter, and focus on these *building blocks*.

6.1 Learning and Knowledge Systems

When a human being has learned something, s/he has made a change in some aspect of her/his behavior. If there has been no perceivable change in the individual's behavior, then there is no evidence that any learning has taken place. Human behavior can be classified into *thinking* behavior, *feeling* behavior, and *acting* behavior. Thus, if I have learned something, I have made a change in either what I think, or what I feel, or how I act. In order to design effective development projects and programs, it is useful to be able to recognize different types of learning.

Thinking behavior relates to what a person knows, understands, and is able to use (intellectual skill). This skill may enable the person with knowledge to teach it to others. There are different levels of depth in thinking. For example, when a child learns that the wet material her/his mother uses to wash her/his hands and face is called "water", that child now has a name, or a word, for that substance. Having learned the word, s/he knows what that sound denotes, or means. That may be considered a behavior change in *knowledge*.

A greater depth of knowledge is usually required to change one's understanding. Later in life, the child may learn that water, when heated to a certain temperature, will boil, and become a gaseous substance. Further, the child may learn that when the temperature of water is reduced to a certain point, it will freeze, and become ice. Such learning contributes to a deeper understanding of water. Going further, in chemistry class in school, the child may learn that molecules of water are made of two types of atoms, hydrogen atoms and oxygen atoms. This represents an even deeper *understanding* of water.

And perhaps at a later stage, when the same child is older, and is working for an NGO concerned with clean drinking water, s/he may learn the *intellectual skills* required to teach others how to filter drinking water to remove unwanted substances, or how to boil water to destroy certain micro-organisms in the water which may cause "water-borne" diseases. In this oversimplified illustration, the child has gone from merely *knowing* that there is such a thing as water to *understanding* many things about water, to having some *intellectual skill* in teaching others about water.

Just as thinking can be analyzed in terms of knowing, understanding, and intellectual skill, so both feeling and action behaviors may be analyzed and divided into different categories. All of these can be useful in the design of the learning strategies to be used in development work, both domestically and internationally. A simplified category system for use in designing learning strategies is illustrated in Table 6.1. Many other types or categories could be added to such an analysis. First used by educators in the process of curriculum-building, it is also useful to planners who design development activities, or as they analyze and evaluate development work (Ralph Tyler 1950).

Table 6.1
Types of Human Learning Behavior

Thinking Behavior	*Feeling Behavior*	*Acting Behavior*
Knowing	Interest	Ability
Understanding	Appreciation	Skill
Intellectual Skill	Attitude	Habit
	Values	
	Loyalty	

For example, if an agricultural program is being planned to encourage those who own one or two dairy cows to increase milk production, planners might ask themselves, "Why are these farming people not already producing more milk from their cattle?" As regards *feelings*, the farming families may not be interested in those cows for milk production. They may have *interest* only in the bull calves which might be produced to become draft animals; or they might be more interested in the manure which the cattle are producing. They might not *appreciate* the income they could receive from additional milk production. Or, they might simply not *value* that cash as something they need. If these attitudes are not changed, it is unlikely that the cattle owners will do much about milk production. Therefore, strategically, activities designed to change interests or appreciation may be required.

On the other hand, the problem may relate to *action*. If, for example, farmers do not have containers in which to carry milk to the nearest collecting point, perhaps several kilometers away, they may not be *able* to carry milk there. That physical *ability* is parallel, on the human behavior side, to being *able* to encourage the cow to let her milk down. Farming people have learned, in many cases, how to work with the calf on one side, and the human milker on the other, and then soothe and encourage the cow even without her calf, in order to milk out her udder twice daily. That kind of ability can be learned by people, and is learned by those who become effective cow milkers.

But whether it is milking a cow, riding a bicycle, or playing tennis, merely being able to perform an action is not the end. With practice and coaching, a person can move, on the action side, from being *able* to do something to having *skill* in doing it well. And beyond even the *skill*, people also learn to form the *habit* of taking certain kinds of actions regularly. Many of the daily routines of life have their origin in such learning. A child may first learn to be *able* to brush her teeth; then she learns *skill* in brushing so as to keep them clean and promote dental health, and then, later perhaps, learns the life-long *habit* of doing that twice a day.

Almost all aspects of human behavior are learned. Even our cultural diversity is learned, each person learning the patterns of normal behavior within her/his own group. And each of us, for the rest of our lives, are relatively culture-bound by the patterns we learned as children. The spirit of this was caught by Richard Rogers and Oscar Hammerstein II (1949) in their musical play, *South Pacific*, in the following words:

You've got to be carefully taught
Before it's too late,
Before you are six, or seven, or eight,
To hate all the people your relatives hate,
You've got to be carefully taught.

However, people do not stop learning as they get older; they continue to learn as long as they live. Thus, is it possible for us to unlearn things we have learned before, if we find it appropriate to change what we have learned? As a learning animal, the human being learns throughout life, and changes throughout life. That is why learning is critical to all aspects of social development, including international development.

In development work, it is important to assess the extent to which people who are the clientele, or audience, or target group for a development project have, in fact, learned something of which the project was designed to help them learn. This assessment can be made in terms of changes made. *Learning can be perceived only when the learner makes some kind of a change in behavior. Behavior change can be in* THINKING, *in* FEELING, *or in* ACTION (**6a**). In the planning of development activities, and the evaluation of the activities, it is often necessary for those implementing the activities to make assessments of the extent to which who has learned what.

Too often, in the international development experience, a project has had goals related to a change in *attitudes* of local people, but implemented only activities designed to encourage changes in *knowledge*. Similarly, many projects have goals in terms of changes in *actions*, but carry out activities which relate only to *thinking*. Here is an example from our field notes about a maize production project:

> The project staff had constructed field demonstrations, on farmers' fields, for three years. They demonstrated that in plots where purchased mineral fertilizer was applied, the yields were much higher. But farmers in that region did not start using purchased mineral fertilizer. Informal discussions with several farmers indicated that they usually did not have the cash money required to purchase fertilizer. And the few who said they had money, and wanted to buy fertilizer, told us that there was no fertilizer available in the local market at planting time. Most farmers indicated that *they already knew* that if you put mineral fertilizer on the field, you would get more maize.

In this example, the project assumed that a change in *thinking* was needed. Actually, the problem was not that farmers lacked *knowledge* of the effects of fertilizer. The problem was one of lack of cash to purchase fertilizer, and lack of physical availability of the fertilizer in that village. The problems in farmers' *ability to act* could not be solved by merely trying to help them learn to *know* something—especially something they already *knew*.

In a project in another country, farmers had already used too much purchased mineral fertilizer; the soils had become too acidic, and yields were going down. Farmers tried to solve the problem of decreasing yields by purchasing even more nitrate fertilizer. At the same time, a local factory was set up to crush limestone and make agricultural powdered lime. The idea was to encourage farmers to put the lime on their fields, reduce soil acidity, and increase yields. Here is another excerpt from our field notes:

> Extension officers complained that farmers were refusing to buy the lime, even at a very low price. They continued to buy the more expensive nitrate fertilizer. The extension program was

designed to increase farmers' knowledge of soil acidity, and help them understand that they had a need for lime for more acid soils; they did not have a need for "fertilizer" for more nitrates in the soil. Farmers continued to refuse to use the lime. When we interviewed several farmers, they told us that the price of the new lime was only about one-third of the nitrate fertilizer. Therefore, the lime could not be as good. Their crop was too important to them, and they wanted "only good fertilizer, not cheap fertilizer".

Again, farmers had an attitude toward the "cheap" lime which did not change. The extension program focused on farmers' *knowledge*. It neglected their *feelings* about "cheap substitutes", and it failed to make the desired impact.

The point of all this is that, for development programs designed to enhance people's learning, it is critical to separate thinking, feeling, and action types of learning. *The more careful and insightful the analysis of what the clientele think, and feel, and do, before the project, the greater the chance that the learning activities are likely to produce the desired impacts* (**6b**).

6.1.1 Banking Systems versus Problem Posing Systems

While the analysis of the types of learning required is a critical starting point, there are many other strategic choices in the learning process as it is applied to development, particularly international development. One of these is the choice between what Paulo Freire (1970) called "banking" systems of education compared with "problem posing" systems of education. In the "banking" system, typical of formal education in many parts of the world, the teacher treats the learner as a type of "bank". Lessons are "deposited" in the student the way money is deposited in a bank. Then, when it is time for the examination, the teacher would like to retrieve from the student exactly what has been deposited. Thus students memorize the textbooks and lectures, and try to give back to the teacher exactly what was deposited. This system does not encourage creative thinking on the part of the student; neither does it help the student learn to solve problems. But it does help the student learn some kinds of things, and it is relatively easy for the teacher to evaluate the extent to which the student has learned. It is more effective for the *knowing* kinds of learning, than for *understanding* or developing *intellectual skill*, and it is even less useful in the attempt to help learners change *feelings*. It does, however, have special value in development of certain types of skills.

In the "problem posing" system, by contrast, the teacher does not ask the student to memorize lists of facts, or reading materials. Instead, the teacher asks questions and poses problems. The student must then search for the needed knowledge, and discover ways to use that knowledge in dealing with the problem. This system encourages creative thinking among students, and helps them learn the skills of problem-solving which may be applied to a broad range of issues.

An example from our field notes illustrates the contrast:

The School of Agriculture was in an old palace in the middle of the capital city. It had once had a courtyard full of beautiful formal gardens, but all were now grown up with weeds. I was led up two flights of uneven wooden steps, and down a long hall to a classroom. The teacher was standing at the chalk board in the front of the room. There was a list of twenty varieties of tomato plants handwritten on the chalk board. As I entered in the back of the room with my host (the school head) the discussion featured the English language spelling of the word tomato, and the issue was did it have an "e" at the end, or could it be written without the "e" (English was not the mother tongue of either the students or the teacher). Then it became apparent that they had just had a test, in which each student had been asked to write, in English, the names of as many tomato varieties as he could remember. All names had been taken from a foreign seed catalog.

It occurred to me at the time that probably none of these varieties were available from the seed sellers in that country, but it did make a rather easy examination for the teacher to grade. As he explained to the students, if they were able to name all twenty varieties on their examination paper, they received 100 marks. If they named only 19 varieties, they received 95 marks; 18 varieties gave them 90 marks; and so on down the list. It was an excellent example of a banking type of approach to teaching.

Then I was invited by the College Head to ask any questions I might have, so I asked the instructor which of the twenty varieties he thought would grow best in that city. He looked at me with a mixture of annoyance and confusion, so I asked a second question. "If one of the students were going to plant a tomato seed in a garden, how deep in the soil should the seed be planted?" I was informed that this was not covered in the curriculum. My last question was on the best time of year to plant tomatoes in that location, and again I was told that the class did not cover that. I left with the feeling that neither the teacher nor the students were at all concerned about actually growing the tomato plant, as this was an example of agriculture being taught as literature, not as a practical subject.

Later that same school of agriculture was moved out of the capital city to a remote rural location. The rationale was that if students were going to learn anything about practical agriculture they must be surrounded by farms where farming people were actually growing plants like tomatoes. The new location promoted relevance, but there, too, it was necessary to change from a banking style to a problem posing style before students and teachers, together, got their feet in the mud and their hands on the plants, and began to learn something about tilling the soil and tending the livestock.

6.1.2 Literary Systems versus Practical Systems

Among development-related topics, it is not only in agriculture that the banking system, with its literary approach, is to be found. Vocational and technical education have been introduced through international development cooperation into the formal education systems of many countries. *Practical learning systems* concentrate on the actual work, with the trainee helping the master, who already knows how to do the work, and who continuously demonstrates skills and procedures to the learner. *Literary learning systems* start with students learning to read and write, and then attempt to build from that to learning other things which may be useful in life.

A dramatic experience we had in a southern state of India while working with a World Bank team illustrates the difference between these two approaches. Here is an excerpt from our field notes:

In the morning our team visited a vocational–technical school, run by the government Ministry of Education in the city of Coimbatore.

It was part of the post-secondary education system— all students had to have secondary school leaving certificates to be admitted. It was a two-year program, with examinations and all of the other trappings of formal education. The headmaster took us on a tour of their facilities, showing us where they teach home science, agriculture, automotive maintenance, and secretarial/clerical skills. As we walked, I asked the headmaster about his problems, and he assured us he had no serious problems.

After the tour we met in his office for tea and light refreshments, and he presented us with a list of needs, mostly equipment for the teaching classrooms and laboratories. By then, everyone was more at ease, and I again pressed the headmaster about problems. This time he responded by saying that they had only two. First, it was difficult to find teachers, as government required that his teachers have both a secondary school leaving certificate and an intermediate certificate (two years beyond secondary). The problem was that people with that much formal education usually did not know much about the hands-on skills which this school was supposed to be teaching. Second was the problem of placement of their graduates. He pointed out to us that even in the automotive maintenance program, potential employers were cautious about their graduates, for fear they might want to sit behind a desk with a tie on and manage things, rather than to get underneath automobiles and get grease all over themselves. As we left, the headmaster reminded us of the school's needs, and the opportunity for international development assistance.

That afternoon our team traveled several miles out of the city to a rural location where we visited another vocational–technical school. This was not a government school, but sponsored by a local NGO with religious (Hindu) affiliations. Here again, the headmaster took us on a tour of the school facilities, where the same four technical subjects were being taught. Different from the government school, any student could be admitted, even without any prior school certifications, as long as she or he was willing to work. All students had to work in the shops or fields of their curriculum. But they did not have a fixed time for the program. Each student could proceed at his/her own pace, and would receive a certificate when they had passed the final examination.

On our tour, the headmaster showed us the room where students took their final examination in the automotive maintenance program. It had a large door on one side, through which a motor vehicle could be driven. Then there were three large tables, one at which the front end of the vehicle could be parked, and the other two on each side of the vehicle. In fact, the door was open, and a large, old lorry (motor truck) was parked just outside. The headmaster pointed out to us that the examination in automotive maintenance was a two-part exam. For part one, the student had to start the vehicle, drive it into the room, disconnect the engine, lift it out (using a crane attached to the roof of the building), and put it on the tables. There all parts were to be disconnected from each other, so that no two pieces were touching each other. When this was completed, the student called the examiner. If the examiner certified that no two pieces were in contact; no nut was still fastened to any bolt, then the student had passed part one of the exam. For part two of this examination, the student had to reconnect all the pieces in their proper places, and reinstall the engine in the vehicle. Then he had to start the engine, and back the vehicle out of the examination room. If the student succeeded in this, the examination had been passed. Employers were waiting to hire the graduates from this school.

As in the morning visit, the headmaster provided us with tea and light refreshments, and then walked with us back out to where our vehicles were parked. His final words were, "Don't spoil us with any of your easy money."

The World Bank team was highly impressed with the second school, and its headmaster. Our final report did not recommend "spoiling" either school with our "easy money". But we did all learn something about teaching and learning styles. And we saw the value of the practical approach compared with the literary approach—right in front of our eyes, and all in one day! As usual, most learning strategies are somewhere between these two extremes.

In international development, *learning and teaching styles which are "practical and applied" are likely to be more effective than learning and teaching styles which are "pure and literary"* (**6c**).

6.1.3 Indigenous Knowledge Systems

In international development cooperation, learning strategies are affected by the differences among the knowledge systems of different places. Since each country, region, district, and, to some extent, village, has its own ways of thinking about the world, and therefore its own knowledge systems, interactions among the people of different places provide rich opportunities for enhancement of the human condition. However, the natural reluctance of individuals to be willing to admit that there are knowledge systems other than their own, and then to be willing to learn from the others, is a problem.

In their book on the subject of indigenous knowledge systems, Brokensha, Warren, and Werner introduce the idea this way:

> Throughout this volume, the emphasis is on the necessity for development planners to take into account the accumulated knowledge and traditional skills and technology of the people among whom they work...we are determined to demonstrate the richness, variety, and value of indigenous knowledge.... To incorporate in development planning indigenous knowledge is a courtesy to the people concerned; is an essential first step to successful development; emphasizes human needs and resources, rather than the material ones alone; makes possible the adaption of technology to local needs; is the most efficient way of using western "Research and Development" in developing countries; preserves valuable local knowledge; encourages community self-diagnosis and heightens awareness; leads to a healthy local pride; can use local skills in monitoring and early warning systems; involves the users in feedback systems, for example, on crop varieties.... These positive reasons— together with the negative reasons, such as the likelihood of failure without using indigenous knowledge—constitute a strong case for incorporating this knowledge in development programs (Brokensha et al. 1980: 1–8).

The experience of project planners and international experts with projects which were not successful supports the case for awareness and appreciation of indigenous knowledge systems. In agriculture, for example, outsiders have often developed projects intended to give or sell "superior" seed to local farmers prior to discovering that local people typically save the seed harvested from one crop to use in planting the next crop. Since there may be local reward systems associated with the choice of the "right" seed to save, and punishments for not protecting it adequately until the next planting time, the simple idea of using seed provided by a stranger may be very threatening.

With similar neglect of the indigenous knowledge system, one poultry nutrition specialist invested heavily in research of local products to manufacture feed for poultry. Eventually he developed what he believed was an excellent poultry ration made entirely of locally available materials. When it was time to actually produce and distribute this new poultry feed, however, the specialist discovered that most poultry flocks in that area consisted of only one or two hens, and these birds normally scratch around the family household for their feed. Nobody fed them; they fed themselves! Therefore, people in that area were not interested in purchasing any feed for their chickens, no matter how local the ingredients and how low the cost.

Incidents of this type might not happen were it not for the natural politeness and generosity of many rural groups. It is common to say "yes" to any suggestion made by an outsider, no matter how inappropriate it may be. After all, the outsider would soon leave, and would not know that his recommendations were not actually followed. Byrd Baylor gives an example from Arizona:

The three Indians at the table...have been interviewed by similar young Anglos on similar topics. They have each learned long ago to try to give answers which will most please the questioner.... If a yes or no answer is required, they try to say yes. In most of their dealings with white people Indians find it is easier and more polite to say yes than no (Baylor 1972: 10).

This same attitude was reported by the Nepalese anthropologist Dor Bahadur Bista as follows: "As part of a high caste educated behaviour people learn not to use the negative expression 'no' to anything. It is considered good manners to say 'yes' all the time in response to anything, even when they have absolutely no intention of fulfilling the commitment" (Bista 1991: 136).

Our field notes suggest that the indigenous knowledge of women is often different from men's knowledge.

In the hill areas of Orissa it was the tribal women who explained to the agricultural scientists that they brought certain spider type insects on small branches from the forest, and "planted" them in their fields to attack other pests which would harm their crops. And when the tribal women of the Chotanagpur plateau in south Bihar met with members of the forestry faculty at Ranchi Agricultural University for a day's seminar these women described in great detail the many uses of various forest products. At the end of the day the Dean told the group he "had learned from them all the things he had been taught at school, and more". The traditional cultivators, often women, have a unique store of knowledge that is only beginning to be tapped by the end of the 20th century.

Experience suggests that for international development programs *innovations introduced into any system through interaction with a second system are likely to be rejected by the first system when first introduced* (**6d**). This is explained by the forces of continuity and change shown in Figure 2.2 in Chapter 2. While a particular innovation may be technologically appropriate, there will usually be economic, social, cultural, political, and other reasons why the group will initially reject it. Thus investigation of the indigenous knowledge system prior to the introduction of any new technical innovation can help avoid obstacles to the development process.

Before constructing a new building for a health post in a rural area, and then staffing it with "barefoot" doctors trained in an urban medical school, analysis of the indigenous knowledge system might reveal that there are several families of midwives already in the area. If they are ignored, they may become a force to deny success of the new health post. On the other hand, if they are discovered by the project planners, there may not be a need for a new health post. Or, perhaps they can become collaborators with the outside planners, and design an improved healthcare delivery system for the community which takes advantage of BOTH the indigenous knowledge system (supplied by the midwives) AND the outsider's resources, perhaps with additional training, medications, equipment, and facilities.

In the process of planning many different types of projects, international development planners are encouraged to *explore and discover* the local situation. The more of the indigenous knowledge system that they can discover, the greater is the likelihood that whatever they design will be implementable. And after project implementation, this strategy will increase the probability that the activity may continue after the development project ceases to be supported by outsiders. *A collaborative strategy for both planning and implementing development efforts, involving both outsiders and insiders, will support selection of appropriate knowledge and technologies from both the international and the indigenous systems* (**6e**).

There are many examples of this need when male project planners are involved in the design of activities for women. In many villages, women are often not able to leave their households and the near environment owing to responsibilities of child care and feeding the family. Their absence is resented by other family members. Sometimes religious and cultural norms forbid such absence. When local women are collaborators in planning the location, frequency, and timing of such learning activities as literacy classes, or child nutrition clinics, they may be able to ensure that the project will be implementable. They would know what times of day or night are feasible. They would know how far people would be able to walk in the time available, to a place where others can also be present. And they would know how long they can be absent from the household at different times of the day and seasons of the year. Collaboration with local women in the planning process is often critical in the design of learning activities intended for them.

6.1.4 Learning and Education

Some international development programs involve support for a formal education system. Many do not. All, however, use some kind of learning strategy for the people who are the designated beneficiaries of the program. The word "learning" is used here to refer to both education and research. People learn without a teacher in *research*; a teacher facilitates learning in *education*. Research is that learning in which the learner does not have access to a teacher, a book, or a computer program which can enhance the learning. In research, the learner has a question, or a proposition, or some "unknown" which s/he would like to answer, test, or explore. For that purpose, s/he enters the world, and learns from it.

For example, in agriculture, a farmer may save some seed from the most productive plants and some from plants which produced a better-tasting grain last year. S/he might then plant some of each the following year to see (test the hypothesis) whether there will be any difference in the plants produced by those two types of seed the following year. With a new crop for the area, s/he might also plant some seeds near the surface, and others a little deeper, to see which is best in his/her own garden. This kind of research has been going on among farmers for thousands of years. It is not what today's scholars would call "formal research", but it is more than casual observation. We call it non-formal research.

International development involves both education and research, both formal and non-formal. When the learning has the form of graded levels, entry requirements, and certifications of achievement, it is called formal education, or formal research. Both of these are usually programmed in organized systems which prescribe the steps to be followed, and reward achievement. Much of the learning in international development, however, is non-formal. It has been planned through programs, projects, or other collaborative arrangements, and therefore is not merely casual learning. But it tends to be learner-centered, and focused on the usefulness of the learning to the learner, rather than any process of moving through pre-defined steps.

Non-formal education is a major strategic tool used in international development, sometimes in projects with the word "education" in their name, but more often in projects with names like community forestry, or production credit for rural women, or seed multiplication, or small farmers development. In the latter type of activities, and many others, the goals and objectives do not mention education or research, but project success may depend in part on what the clientele of the project have learned.

Education can be an iterative process between learners and teachers, as illustrated in Figure 6.1. In this diagram, time is flowing along from time 1 to time 2 to time 3. The teacher in time 1 sends some message to the learner in time 1. The learner in time 1 sends a message back to the teacher. By then it is time 2. The flow of this process is back and forth between the learner and the teacher. Such a process is known as an *iterative* process.

In non-formal education, *the more iterations between learners and teachers, the greater the chance that a particular interaction will be perceived by both learners and teachers as valuable to them* (**6f**). This is also true in formal education. When an outsider (teacher) who knows about clay cook stoves which are fuel efficient tries to help village potters (learners) learn how to make that type of stove,

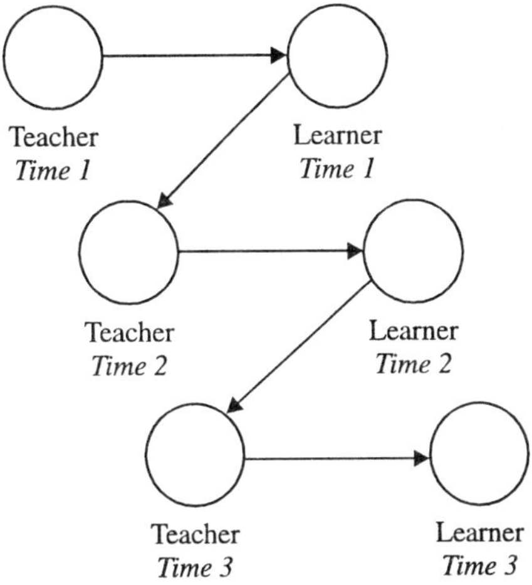

Figure 6.1
Iterations Between a Teacher and a Learner

as an effective teacher s/he will watch the learners as well as the clay. When learners have a question, the teacher stops, and tries to learn from the student what that question might be. Then the teacher responds to the learner, trying to discover whether s/he (the teacher) has understood the question as it was intended, and whether the response was understood by the learner. This process may be seen as a change in roles between the learner and the teacher. The teacher becomes the learner, and the learner becomes the teacher. *Teachers and learners exchange roles from time to time. The greater the frequency of role exchange, the greater the tendency for learning to proceed* (**6g**).

Practical learning is possible if teachers can shake their assumption that if the learner is illiterate, s/he is ignorant. This requires a level of self-confidence on the teacher's part which is sometimes lacking. But many years ago we had the opportunity to observe really effective learning with rural Nigerian women who had never had any formal education.

Maria, the home economics teacher at the new university, went to a local school in the bush to teach a nutrition class to adult women. The class, once each week, was very early in the morning.

The local women, many with babies tied to their backs, walked from their homes or fields to the school. Maria had gone to the local market and purchased foods which most of the women were growing at home. Then she spent an hour with the women describing the food value as well as ways of preparation which preserved the food value and didn't add to the heavy workload these women already had.

While Maria often stressed the need to use clean water, this resource was a real problem in that area, and there were many water-related illnesses. But the water looked clean, so it was a real challenge to convince the women that there was anything unhealthy about that water which would cause sickness. In desperation, Maria chartered the campus bus for one morning and made arrangements in advance to give the women a bus ride through the bush to the campus. Each woman was instructed to bring a small jar with the water she normally used.

On the campus the microbiologist on the faculty welcomed the women to his laboratory where each woman prepared a slide with her own water sample, and then looked through the microscope to see all the things which were in that water. Suddenly they understood that there might, indeed, be a connection between the water and various illnesses in their family. And the reasons for trying to purify the water were clear to them, even if the ways of achieving that were very difficult and not always possible.

Maria's willingness to go to the local school every week helped her learn from the local women, just as they were learning from her. The added benefit was that Maria could better prepare her university students who were going to be working in villages in Nigeria.

6.1.5 Accountability Strategies in Learning

The probability of learning taking place in international development activities is directly related to the extent to which what teachers are trying to teach is relevant to what learners want to learn. This need for relevance is appropriate in all kinds of programs which employ non-formal education approaches. If the education is very formal, learners may participate because of the formalities, and may or may not have any interest in what is being taught.

One of the best ways to increase the effectiveness of non-formal learning activities so typical of development projects is to arrange the project so that teachers are *accountable* to learners. When a project is organized in a collaborative mode, for example, and teachers and learners participate in deciding who needs to learn what from whom, *accountability* is shared. When learners own and operate the system, so that they select and reward teachers, teachers will be *accountable* to learners. *The effectiveness of teachers in most development programs is directly related to the extent to which they are* ACCOUNTABLE *to learners* (**6h**).

This discussion has been about *program* accountability. Much more attention is typically given to *financial* accountability. Financial matters are important, and cannot be neglected in international development activities. However, it is relatively easy to build financial checkpoints into a program, to ensure that money made available for certain purposes is used for those purposes and not for something else. It may require much effort, and constant observation, and thus has its costs. But money is comparatively tangible and easy to measure. Program accountability is much more elusive. People operating a program can claim that they are including the content which the clientele would find practical and useful. However, when the clientele actually control project personnel, then they at least have a voice in program accountability.

A different perspective suggests that there may be quality factors in any program, which can only be protected if program-control is in the hands of more experienced professionals in the central government, or central management if it is a non-governmental program. Proponents of this view will claim that educational excellence can only be achieved when highly trained professionals implement the program. Others will claim that the definition of excellence which is appropriate for development projects uses the criterion of relevance. If it is not relevant, they say, it cannot be excellent. Both views are valuable, and this may be a situation where the *both/and* approach suggested by Norman Uphoff (1992) is more useful than an *either/or* approach.

Like other debates in education, a larger perspective suggests that there is value in both approaches, and both may be used in the design of development strategies. Richard Bawden puts it more eloquently:

The same may be posited for propositional, practical, and experiential learning systems. Instead of the endless and fruitless arguments of dichotomy that persist in the name of curricula reform such as the relative balance between theory and practice in agricultural education, it is much more profitable to systemically explore the nature of their inter-relationship and exploit the "glorious unity of opposites"—creatively born of the inherent tension of difference (Bawden 1990: 312).

6.1.6 Collaboration Strategies in Learning

The perspectives presented above suggest a collaborative mode for planning, implementing, and evaluating the learning aspects of development activities. If people planning and implementing any development project value their clientele—value them as human beings in spite of such differences as culture, language, formal education, experience, economic status, etc.—then a true collaborative mode is feasible. If such collaboration can be achieved it enables both learners and teachers to transcend many of the common problems in learning.

In development projects and in other types of non-formal education it is not unusual for teachers to have a different agenda from that of learners. By agenda, we refer to the general view of why individuals are involved in the process at all. If the agenda of the teachers assumes that the learners are interested in vegetable gardening, for example, and the learners are only interested in flower gardening, they will have problems. If collaboration between learners and teachers was not part of the planning process, it could be the second or third session before the teachers discover that their agenda is different from that of the learners (or, the other way around). If a group of learners and one or more teachers had sat together to decide what should be taught, why it should be taught, and how it should be taught, this problem could have been avoided.

In a village water system project, for example, when outsiders and insiders worked together in planning, the outsiders who had been thinking only of drinking water discovered that the insiders actually wanted to use the water to irrigate small kitchen gardens, as well as for household purposes. This enabled them jointly to plan a different type of water system, designed specifically to meet the needs and interests of the particular village. After that, since the teachers and the learners shared the same agenda, the learning/teaching exercises went quite smoothly.

Another difficulty in learning in some development programs relates to teacher-control versus learner-control. When learners control the program, it is likely to be relevant to their needs and interests. When teachers control the program, it is likely to include content and methods with which the teacher is familiar and skilled. But for effective development programs, BOTH learner interest AND teacher skills and enthusiasm are required. Again, a collaborative mode of program-control should insure a convergence of interest between learners and teachers, and thus further the development process.

Training programs for rural women benefit from teachers who have actually spent enough time in the village to understand the many demands on women's time. In one rural area in India, non-formal literacy classes were planned for evenings when the women's work was completed. The literacy teacher had spent enough time in the village area to know the kind of work the women were doing in any particular season. Together they developed a "curriculum" which built on the words the women used each day to describe seed selection, methods of planting, weeding, and harvesting. The class room, dimly lit with lanterns, was always crowded with women and their slates as they learned to read, write, and handle numbers. And, although they had been awake since early morning and were tired, and perhaps hungry if they hadn't taken time for supper, no one was sleeping. Learning was fun, with lots of laughter as the teacher related the lessons to students' daily activities.

More generally, *the success of any interaction between two individuals or groups is directly related to the extent to which the benefits of the interaction are immediate and obvious to the participants* (**6i**). This has been well known to field personnel of agricultural extension organizations. It is difficult to interest clients in activities like planting fruit trees, when they might need to wait five or six years after planting the tree before they see the fruits. By contrast, distributing drinking water supplies during a drought brings immediate positive response. There are many projects in which positive results are immediate and obvious. For example, when a new, narrower hoe is made available to gardeners so they can cultivate rows of vegetables which are much closer together, the response is likely to be rapid. When those operating a forest nursery are shown how low cost plastic sacks can substitute for heavier and more expensive clay pots, the value may be quickly perceived. While actual programs have both long-term and short-term response segments, field personnel have found it useful to begin with some quick response items. It builds confidence among clientele when they can see immediate positive results. It also enhances willingness to enter into collaboration on further projects.

6.2 Communication

Human beings everywhere learn by communicating with each other. Communication is an essential characteristic of our very humanness, since we learn words through communication with each other. Having attached meanings to words as significant symbols, we use words to think thoughts, and also to exchange thoughts and ideas with each other. Thus communication is the basic process by means of which learning takes place—the root of change—and hence the root of social, cultural, and psychological development.

Communication strategies are a part of every development program and project, whether identified as such or ignored by planners and implementers. Just as we said that *learning* is necessary for any development activity to succeed, here we suggest that *communication* is necessary for any *learning* to take place.

The essential phenomenon of communication can be said to be the making *common* of a thought, an idea, or any bit of meaning between two or more people. It would be more obvious if the word were spelled as *common*-ication. If you know the meaning of a word, or have a thought, you may be able to share it with another through communication. However, although all human groups communicate, different groups have different words, different scripts for written communication, and different ways for exchanging messages with each other.

For international development, given that in any particular place there will be indigenous (local) communication systems and perhaps exogenous (external) communication systems, there will be both appropriate communication strategies and inappropriate communication strategies. In order to describe, analyze, and compare communication systems, it is useful to identify common factors in these systems.

Developing good listening skills may be the most important of all communication strategies for human beings. And when people attempt to communicate with each other across the boundaries of different nations, different cultures, different languages, different professions, and different organizations, the need for effective listening skills increases. Further, when the goal of interpersonal interaction is *collaboration*, as we have been advocating in this book, the ability, skill, and willingness of each individual to listen to others is absolutely critical. Professional listening for practitioners in international development involves the need to know both languages and other dimensions of the various cultures involved.

Listening skills can be learned. It is possible to study the strategies and skills of listening, and for individuals to make significant improvements in their personal ability, skill, and habit of listening to others. Strategically, one can learn to concentrate on what others are saying to them, to "pay attention" to others, and to try to learn what ideas or feelings others are trying to convey. Professional psychotherapists develop great skill in this regard. They learn to *empathize* with the feelings of the other person as s/he speaks. They learn to give "listening responses" to others, in which they merely repeat what the others have said to assure them that they are listening and do understand what is being said. And as with other skills, practice can improve listening skills.

This excerpt from our field notes is illustrative:

It was actually a surprise to begin to see the enhancement of the quality of communication in ordinary day-to-day conversation with Nepalese colleagues which followed my feeble attempts to read the Swasthani Katha. While the two of us had invested a month in the study of Nepali language five years earlier, and then used the language with occasional help from language teachers in several rural communities for two years, that was different. Even when I resumed my attempts to improve language skills several years later in Kathmandu, concentrating on speaking, listening, and reading, I didn't appreciate the value of culture and history. But, because I didn't have sufficient skill to read the local newspapers, I turned to children's books, and then to children's versions of Hindu Scripture. What a revelation! After a few weeks, I found a new ability to put things in context, to understand better what was being said to me, and to appreciate nuances which had previously been missed. I will always be an outsider; not really one of them. But I think I am slowly becoming more able, after working in and out of this country for more than a decade now, to communicate a little more effectively.

Those who have personal field experience in international development may appreciate the difficulties and the importance of communication in their work.

6.2.1 Communication Systems

The simplest type of analysis of a communication system identifies a *sender*, a *receiver*, a *channel* which links them to each other, and a *message* which the sender would like to share with the receiver.

The *sender* can share an idea with the *receiver* by using a *channel* to carry that idea (the *message*) to someone (the *receiver*). If the channel is face-to-face communication, the sender might merely smile. If the receiver's understanding of that gesture is the same as the sender's, and if the receiver can see the sender, communication will have taken place. If the two speak the same language, and have a word which means the same thing to both, the sender can speak that word. If the receiver hears that word being spoken, and knows what that sound means, again communication will have taken place.

While any human communication is a complex, and often difficult, process, for those who work in international development cooperation, where it is necessary to communicate across the barriers of culture, including language, the process is even more difficult and complex. Within a particular society, for example, when two or more people are engaged in face-to-face communication, simple gestures convey meaning and are part of the way a message is processed. A certain motion of the head may indicate approval or disapproval. But when different social systems are represented, the gesture which means "yes, I agree with you" to one individual, might mean "no, I do not agree" to another individual. In Europe and the Americas, when people meet each other, or are first introduced to each other, it is expected that they will take each other's hand briefly and shake it. In some African countries, very elaborate handshakes are customary. In South Asia and Southeast Asia, where people traditionally do not touch each other in public, they show respect for each other by each one holding her/his own two hands together. This is usually done with the palms and fingers flat, and perhaps a slight bow of the head.

These types of gestures communicate ideas and feelings. When they are misunderstood, they can interfere with all other aspects of the communication involved. Thus, strategies for communication in international development need to take into account a great range of social and cultural, as well as linguistic differences.

Figure 6.2 illustrates a strategic communication model which is designed for planners of purposeful communication. Here the assumption is that planners can describe an audience and the audience's situation with regard to some thinking, feeling, or action. Through program planning, a *message* has been agreed upon which is appropriate for that *audience*. Strategic choices include which *channel* or *channels* will be used to deliver the *message* to the *audience*, and how that *message* will be *treated* for each particular channel. The arrow illustrates the direction in which the program hopes the audience will "move".

In this model, the strategic components are the audience, the message, the channel, and the treatment (G.H. Axinn 1969: 260–63).

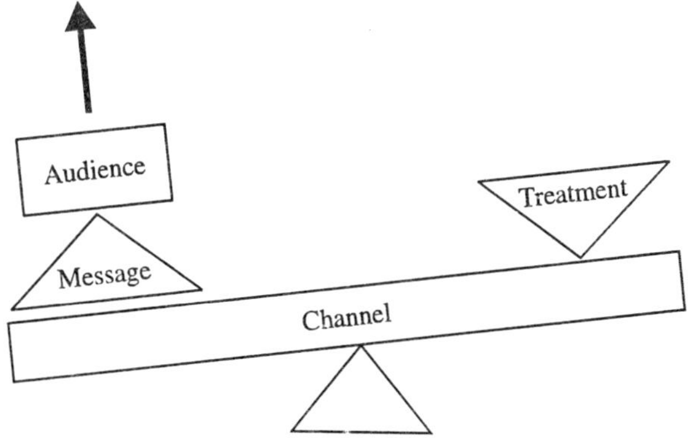

Figure 6.2
Strategic Communication Model

6.2.2 The Audience

The *audience* refers to any individual or group with whom a sender of messages wishes to communicate. In most development projects, the senders are people from an organization attempting to implement the project, and the audience consists of the intended beneficiaries of that project. However, in a collaborative mode, the senders and receivers of messages plan together, and this greatly facilitates communication.

The more a potential sender of messages knows and understands about a particular audience, the greater the chance that communication will be effective (**6j**). For example, if individuals in the audience speak two different languages, it is important for a communicator to know that, and perhaps send messages in those two different languages. If 98 percent of the people cannot read the written language, an informed communicator would not send them printed messages.

6.2.3 The Message

The word *message* is used here to refer to the *intent* of the sender with regard to the receiver. For strategic planning purposes, the project goals or objectives can be stated as the changes planners *intend* should occur within the audience. For example, in a project designed to help farmers control insects which limit rice production, one message might be to encourage the farmers to study the stems of rice plants frequently, looking for indications that the paddy stem-borer has infested the plants. This message is stated in terms of a change to be made by farmers. The assumption here is that farmers in that area are not already making such frequent inspections. If the program planning were done collaboratively, then farmers and project personnel might have jointly concluded that this message needs to be communicated.

Once the *message* has been identified, then further strategic questions about the most appropriate *channels* by means of which to send this *message*, and how the *message* should be *treated* on those channels, can be decided. A precise definition of the message, specifying just which farmers are now making frequent inspections;

which farmers are not now making frequent inspections; and what the differences are between the two groups will be valuable in making further strategic decisions.

To continue with this example, it may be that some farmers in the area already know how to inspect the stem of the rice plant, notice small holes near the base of it, and diagnose the problem as being caused by the paddy stem-borer. Others may not have sufficient knowledge to understand where the holes are likely to be and how to find them. When planners have identified these two groups, it may be that they will divide the message into two subparts. For those who do not have the required knowledge, it may be that the message is to increase their knowledge and ability regarding this particular diagnostic technique. For the other group, more analysis may lead to (*a*) recruiting some of them as the senders of messages (teachers) to the other group, and (*b*) developing specific messages for them designed to increase the skill and habit of frequent inspections of plants in the field.

Since specification of the message is so critical for other aspects of the communication strategy, some development project designers have made tools like check sheets to help them find the message. In the check sheet they attempt to describe in detail (sometimes using categories like *thinking, feeling,* and *action*) what the behavior patterns of the intended audience are at present and what changed behavior patterns are called for by this project in the future. This specific clarification of the message is a critical step in developing all other aspects of the communication strategy.

6.2.4 Communication Channels

Channels for communication vary greatly from one human group to another. A channel has been defined as any tool or instrument which can be used by a sender to transmit her/his message to a particular audience. It includes such things as a face-to-face visit between two individuals, a meeting of a group, a tour of a group to visit selected places, a newspaper, a printed folder, a book, a telephone, a computer network, individual computerized electronic mail, facsimile, radio, television—and many, many other "instruments".

For example, when a village leader in West Africa wants people in the surrounding area to know that a ministry of health official is coming to the village to discuss family planning, he may use the "talking" drum to alert his audience to the message. The drum is the channel. When agricultural assistants in Pakistan wanted farmers to see the difference between Mexi–Pak wheat and other varieties, they established demonstrations by the side of the road. The demonstrations were the channel.

The field staff of a development agency, such as a government agricultural extension unit, a watershed management project of an NGO, a small farmers development project of local banks, or a rural women's pond aquaculture group, typically have access to a large number of channels for communication with their clientele. The staff or volunteers in such an organization may get into the habit of using one or two channels, and then use those channels for all messages. Sometimes it is a personal visit to the homes of the individuals. This is usually an excellent channel, but it takes a considerable amount of time compared to arranging a meeting which most of the individuals attend. If the audience is literate, printed material could be sent to them by a messenger or by post. If they are not literate, drawings on cards posted in public places might be an appropriate channel.

The success of a first line development project worker may be directly related to the extent of use of multiple communication channels (**6k**). For each particular message to each particular audience, some channels will be more effective and more efficient than others.

This is not to say that more channels used by a given sender to reach a particular audience are always better than fewer channels. But there are some generalizations about channels which can be useful in designing a strategy of communication. The two which we now list have been particularly useful to us over the years. *The more communication channels in parallel between a sender and her/his audience, the greater the chance that any particular message sent by the sender will be received by the audience* (**6l**). Conversely, *the more communication channels in series between a communicator and his/her audience, the less the chance that any particular message sent will be received accurately (with high fidelity) by the audience* (**6m**).

Communication channels may be said to be in *parallel* when several of them link the same sender with the same receiver (Figure 6.3). Communication channels may be said to be in *series* when

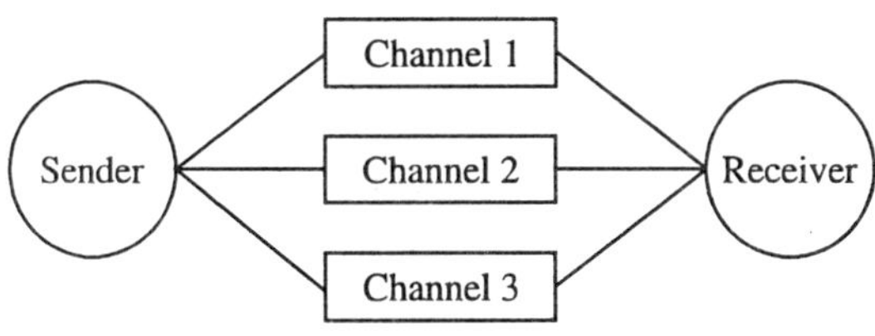

Figure 6.3
Channels in Parallel

a sender uses one channel directly, while a different channel is used by the receiver (Figure 6.4). In such cases, a third person must receive the message on one channel and send it on the other channel.

For example, the three channels in parallel in Figure 6.3 might be a printed notice sent via post, a personal telephone call to each person, and a meeting of thirty people. The notice may tell receivers that they are invited to join a new village organization and that it will meet at a certain date, time, and place. The second channel used by that same sender might be a personal telephone call to each invited person, answering questions they might have about the new organization, and reminding them of the time, date, and place of the meeting. And the third channel might be the meeting room itself, where the sender meets all the receivers who attend. An example of two channels in series, as shown in Figure 6.4, might be the sending of a letter to a third person, who, in turn, makes a telephone call to the receiver.

An advantage of more channels in parallel is that if a receiver does not pay attention or attend to one, s/he might attend to another channel. Also, repeating the message may increase the chance of it being received and understood. A disadvantage of more channels in parallel is that there is some cost (in time, money, or other ways) involved in each use of each channel.

A disadvantage of more channels in series is that the third person is not likely to send exactly the same message s/he received. Each

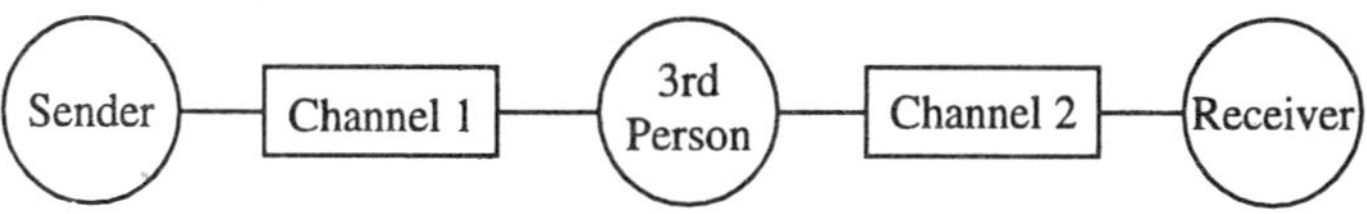

Figure 6.4
Channels in Series

time an intermediate person receives a message, interprets what the sender is trying to communicate, and sends it on to another person, there is a tendency for some of the original message to be modified.

In addition to the multiple use of channels, each individual channel has its own strengths and weaknesses. Radio, for example, has the advantage of immediacy—listeners would hear the message in almost the same moment that the sender speaks. A disadvantage is that after the moment of transmission, unless the receiver is using a tape recorder, there may be no record of what was said to aid memory. For a receiver without electricity the radio may be useless; unless it is a battery-operated radio. Then the only problem may be acquiring a fresh supply of batteries. As with every other channel, there are costs to the sender and costs to the receiver.

From our field notes:

Once when we were stopped in the mountains in Nepal we heard lovely music bouncing off the hills and reaching us on the road deep in the valley. Our eyes searched the hills and finally we saw two men—just small spots, they were so far away—climbing high above us, playing their radio as they climbed. One of our group reflected on the effort required to come all the way down those hills to the bazaar to get new batteries for that radio which might last little longer than the time it would take for them to climb back up the hills to their home.

The radio has some advantage when there are a large number of people in the audience. A newspaper article might also reach a large number of receivers, but it takes more time to do so. The newspaper has the advantage of lasting longer, as readers can save an item, show it to others, or even pass the newspaper from one receiver to another. Of course, the newspaper depends on the receiver's ability to read the language. Radio does not require literacy, but it does require broadcasting in the same language which a receiver understands. Radio can reach very remote areas. In development communication, some projects which use radio may repeat the same broadcast in several different local languages.

Electronic mail (e-mail) is a highly effective and efficient channel with many uses. But it requires both the sender and the receiver to have access to computers which are connected to telephones or satellite systems which, in turn, have access to the internet or another computer network. E-mail has advantages over facsimile and telephone for long-distance communication. These three electronic media (fax, telephone and e-mail) have today reduced the volume of telex and telegrams. Communication is much more immediate and reliable. This strengthens collaborative efforts.

Although some channels are promoted as being better than others, our experience is that this varies with the particular audience, the particular message, and the particular sender. Under some circumstances, one channel will have advantages over another, but under different circumstances it may be the other way around. However, each channel does have its own special characteristics.

Before the development of electronic channels for communication, many traditional societies used drama as an effective channel for communicating messages. Even today, at the turn of the century, there are times and places where drama is the most effective and accepted way to get new ideas, especially relatively complex ideas, introduced in a community. In some places, a drama group moves from community to community, perhaps sponsored by the commercial product it is introducing to a new area. Or, there may be particular times of the year when drama is featured in a village, giving many people in the community ways of sharing feelings or thoughts with the group.

Here is an excerpt from our field notes when we were living in a remote village in the terai of Nepal:

During the Desain holiday we were invited to join the villagers in an evening of drama. They told us "twenty-eight items" would be presented. The program included satire, comedy, music, poetry, and little plays which many villagers took turns presenting during the evening. Most of the "items" reflected on events in the community which all the audience had experienced.

Immediacy is a characteristic of communication channels which is important to development project planners. Channels like radio and television can deliver a message to an audience instantaneously. If there is a heavy storm coming and farming people are to be advised to bring their newly harvested grain under sheds or into other places where it will be protected from the rain, that message may be heard by listeners within minutes. The telephone also features this type of immediacy. By contrast, a newspaper may be read after a few days, and a book may take several years before its audience is exposed to its message. On the other hand, the latter two channels, although they lack immediacy, have greater *capacity* for quantity of information and detail.

All of these factors are important in the strategic planning of communication. Further, on the economic side, each channel will have certain costs and certain potential benefits. Keeping the costs low and the benefits high is usually part of the economic strategy. A useful generalization suggests taking advantage of whatever communication channels are already in use among the audience rather than introducing new ones. *The cost of sending a message may decrease to the extent that existing communication channels within any particular social system are utilized* (**6n**).

6.2.5 Treatment Strategies

The *treatment* is the design given to a *message* as it is sent via a particular *channel*. If the *message* is the *intent* of the communication, the *treatment* is the *content*. Given a particular message intended for a particular audience on a particular channel, there are an infinite variety of treatments which could be employed. For example, if the message, "use one bag of superphosphate fertilizer per hectare at the time you plant your new wheat", is to be sent to literate farmers in the fortnightly newspaper of the ministry of agriculture, there are a great number of ways in which this message could be treated. For example, the whole story could be told in words. Or pictures could be used. If the message is to be printed in text, it could include a direct quotation from the minister of agriculture, urging everyone to use superphosphate. Or, it could be a success story quoting one farmer who used superphosphate on his/her new wheat last year, and the story could tell of his/her success and the profits made. Or, it could be a large photograph of a demonstration, with an article by an agricultural assistant in which s/he tells how much greater the yields were on a plot where superphosphate was used, than on another where superphosphate was not used. All these are different *treatments* of the same *message* to be sent via the same *channel*.

Another example might be a signboard on a new rural health post conveying the message that healthcare is available at that particular place. The channel is the signboard. But the variations in treatment are, again, unlimited. What color should the background of the sign be? It could be white, or red, or black, or green, or yellow, or some other color. That might depend on materials and paint available, but from a design perspective, these are all different treatments. If the board is to be all in one color, what color should the letters be? Going further, what size should the letters be? Should the name be in larger letters, and additional information (like the days in which the place will be open and the hours of each day) in smaller letters? Again, the particular choice of treatment depends only on the creative ability of whoever is designing the treatment.

The language used is a critical part of the treatment. Often outsiders or technical experts have limited skill in the local language and this creates problems for them. From our field notes:

When I was traveling with agricultural scientists in a remote hill area in Eastern India, the plant breeder in the group told me there was only one "progressive" farmer in the area. When we stopped to visit that farmer we discovered that he spoke the language of the state, as did the plant breeder. The other farmers, women and men, spoke their own tribal language. They may have been just as "progressive" but not in the language the plant breeder understood.

It is important for outsiders who are participating in collaborative activities to develop as much skill in the local language as possible. Often this means listening carefully to the way words are used in the local setting and hearing particular phrases which have local meaning that is important. Professionals should also recognize that illiterate people are not ignorant. There are many creative ways to communicate with people who are not literate but who are very wise. This is particularly important in developing programs for rural women who may not have had the time or the opportunity to gain literacy skills but have real need for technical information.

There are many excellent examples of effective communication with and among non-literate people. Many projects have developed sets of large cards with illustrations on them which tell a story. The best of these have no written words at all on them, but they do allow a facilitator or development field worker to communicate more effectively by showing the pictures and explaining in the local language. Non-literate women who have farming production responsibilities in many parts of the world can receive technical training through use of creative treatments. Here is an example:

When a fertilizer program in eastern India was developing materials to teach non-literate farmers the best ways and times to apply mineral fertilizer, a series of large, laminated flash-cards were produced. These illustrated the steps in the process by showing only the farmer's hands and the plants. The hands had bangles (bracelets) on the wrists, which women in that region usually wear. Without any written or spoken word, it was obvious that this was a lesson for women, who normally have the responsibility for fertilizer application in that place.

Others have worked out "safe" ways of helping non-literate people communicate, such as giving them written "prescriptions" for insecticides or fertilizers which look like a medical doctor's prescriptions, but which help them buy the right thing at a market. And still others have used the spoken word in songs and drama. Non-literate rural people have often invented their own ways of communicating effectively without the written word.

On the other hand, there are also some "horror stories" when outsiders failed to appreciate the value of the local language. Here is one from our field notes:

When Don first came to our village, we urged his project manager to give him time to learn the local language *before* starting his research work. But the manager said that his work was technical, as a plant breeder, and that therefore it would be a waste of their project funds to allow him to take time for that, and they also refused to pay for tutors. But Don was an experienced and dedicated plant breeder, and he worked with local counterparts in arranging many field trials of different maize varieties on local farmers' fields.

As a serious professional, he visited his plots on the farms often, and developed a warm personal relationship with the farmers. They helped him put numbered signs on each plot, although all the numbers were in English. And as it came nearer to harvest time, some farmers even followed him in his tours of the plots. They knew he was a good man trying to help them. When harvest time came, he went out to the farms with a scale to weigh the grain and numbered sacks in which to retrieve the grain, harvested and weighed separately from each plot.

Unfortunately, when Don arrived at the site, he was greeted by a group of happy farmers who had saved him a lot of work. They had harvested all of the grain and put it in one large sack! Because it was impossible for him to know how much of what quality had been produced on each plot, he had lost the value of his whole year of work. But he knew the farmers had been trying to help. So he hid his tears and thanked them. That night we cried together, for his lack of the local language had prevented him from communicating the purpose of his experiments to them. If they had only known, both the outside researcher and the insider farmers would have learned so much more.

The demonstration of different wheat varieties, as mentioned, with the demonstration as the channel, is also subject to many different treatments. For example, if the agricultural assistant had planted the wheat on the south side of the road, in certain seasons viewers would have difficulty seeing it, as the sun would be shining into their eyes. By using the same channel (demonstration) on the north side of the road, the treatment would have been more effective, as the sun would be behind the viewers. Language is a factor here too if the demonstration has signboards. Are they in the local language? Or in the language the ministry officials or donors can read?

One critical question in the design of a treatment is who should the receivers perceive as the sender of the message? For example, if a professional within the staff of the education ministry writes a letter to all headmasters of schools, s/he might sign the letter herself/himself. Or, s/he might arrange for the director of his/her division to sign. Or, the secretary of the ministry might sign. Or, they might prepare the letter for the minister to sign. Neither the audience, nor the message, nor the channel is different among these choices, but they are four different treatments.

In most human communication, there is a great advantage in face-to-face personal contact. *The success of development projects in any particular locality tends to be directly related to the extent of personal contact between the people of that locality and the staff of the development project* (**60**). To the extent that such personal contact can be designed into the treatment strategy, the effectiveness of communication is likely to be improved.

6.2.6 Comparison of Communication Factors

The word *effectiveness* is used several times in this chapter. An effort to send a message to an audience will be considered to be effective if the audience makes the change in behavior the message was designed to achieve. The extent of that change is called the *impact* of that communication. The *impact* is the extent to which the audience has made the change in behavior intended in the message.

For example, if the message is to plant some new variety of oil palm seedlings which an NGO has made available, and the audience consists of 100 farmers, then the impact can be measured in terms of the percentage of farmers who, in fact, planted some of the new type of palm seedlings. To be sure that this change on the part of the farmers was affected by the message, it is necessary to compare that group with a control group (perhaps another 100 farmers in a different district) which was not exposed to that communication. The measuring of impact is a complex process, but it can be done.

Since measuring the impact of a particular effort at communication is a way of evaluating that effort, it may be resisted by many development practitioners. If no one measures the effectiveness, the project cannot be said to have failed. Actually, it is difficult to present evidence of success of efforts without measuring effectiveness. From a communication standpoint, without measures of effectiveness it is difficult to know which channels are best over time for reaching any specific audience.

Especially if different messages are being sent to different audiences as part of a development project it is important to know that someone actually received the particular message. Part of measuring effectiveness is knowing if the message resulted in the change of behavior being recommended.

Beyond knowing that some people in the audience made the change, the effectiveness will depend on how many, or what proportion. Therefore, effectiveness can be said to be indicated by the *impact per person* multiplied by the *number of people* with whom that impact was achieved.

This can be stated as:

Effectiveness = impact per person × number of people.

Thus if ten farmers out of the 100 farmers in district A (where the channel had been a meeting) planted the new oil palm trees, and thirty farmers out of the 100 farmers in district B (where the channel had been a demonstration followed by a meeting) planted the new trees, it may be said that the effectiveness of the program was greater in district B.

However, there is another dimension to comparing communication factors, and that is the *efficiency* of the particular effort at communication. Efficiency can be said to be the effectiveness divided by the cost. For development projects that cost typically involves the time of the personnel involved in sending the message plus whatever cash costs there might be. This can be stated as:

$$\text{Efficiency} = \frac{\text{Effectiveness}}{\text{Time} + \text{Money}}$$

In a development program, the strategy of communication is typically an effort to design it in such a way that the impact per person is achieved with as many people as possible (effectiveness) and at as low a cost as possible. Often development practitioners will invest even more of their time and money in a particular effort at communication, because the greater effectiveness that strategy might achieve will make the effort more efficient than it would have been if they invested less time and money. For example, sometimes a local development worker will decide to take the time to visit the home of each of the members of a production credit society, rather than wait to see them all together at a meeting. Perhaps the worker is new in the area, and believes s/he can learn more about each one by going to their homes. The worker's decision was to invest more in the communication in order to achieve greater impact on each person. The same professional field worker might choose to use the meeting instead of the home visit for another message at a later time, and both times s/he would have made the most efficient choice.

The choice of communication strategies can be one of the most stimulating aspects of planning and implementing development activities, since the opportunities for individual and group creativity are so great. It is also an aspect in which personal experience can be invested wisely. What a development practitioner learns in one project can be utilized in the next and future projects.

From the perspective of the professional practitioner, this chapter has only very lightly touched upon the literature on the communication process in international development. Follow-up could be very fruitful by reading such authors as: Crowley and Mitchell (1994); Lerner and Schramm (1967); Lull (1995); Mattelart (1994); O'Sullivan et al. (1994); Rao (1966); Rogers and Svenning (1968); and Röling (1994).

6.3 Implications for Professional Practitioners

A further complication in the complexity of interaction between insiders and outsiders in international development activities is what Robert Chambers has called the "two cultures of outsiders". He explains:

> Outsiders polarize into two cultures: a negative academic culture, mainly of social scientists, engaged in unhurried analysis and criticism; and a more positive culture of practitioners, engaged in time-bounded action. Each culture takes a poor view of the other and the gap between them is often wide.... Academics are trained to criticize and are rewarded for it. Social scientists in particular are taught to argue and to find fault.... When it comes to rural development, they look for faults. Their peers, too, award them higher marks for a study which points to the bad effects of a project than one which highlights benefits.... The typical practitioner, in contrast, is more exposed, and tied to the deadlines of budgets and seasons, to targets, and to political demands.... So while academics seek problems and criticize, practitioners seek opportunities and act. Academics look for what has gone wrong, practitioners for what might go right (Chambers 1983: 28–33).

Clearly, there is a need for professional personnel in development work to have one foot in each camp. Learning strategies can be enhanced when both planners and implementers avoid the "negativeness" of the academic and the "positiveness" of the practitioner. In that sense, the professional practitioner can become more than merely a practitioner. S/he can know what the literature says, and all the potential for difficulties and failures along the way, but can, at the same time, "look for what might go right", and appreciate the successes along the way.

The practitioner will also appreciate the role of learning in development strategies, and be able to assess the state of thinking, feeling, and actions at the beginning of a project, so as to identify what needs to be preserved in a situation, as well as what needs to be changed. Beyond that, practitioners can be familiar with the differences between banking-type approaches and problem posing approaches; between practical and literary approaches, and will appreciate the values in indigenous knowledge systems. The practitioner may have experience with various types of informal, non-formal, and formal learning and teaching strategies, and be able to relate current problems to the world experience in these matters. And a practitioner should understand accountability strategies and collaboration strategies not only from what the books say, but from what field experience has taught.

Just as some grasp of the human being as a learning animal is helpful in both the planning and the implementation of development activities, some understanding of strategic alternatives in human communication is also helpful. The men and women who are serious practitioners in international development do not achieve professional stature without considering these "building blocks" in the process.

The most effective practitioners have learned the skills to be able to use all means of communication available in their setting. This means writing, speaking on the radio, doing effective demonstrations, using technical equipment such as an overhead projector or slide projector where these (and electricity) are available. Effective communication can also be by drawing pictures in the sand if that's what's available. Also, practitioners in international development have greater need of excellent listening skills than do professionals in many other fields. Probably no other single ability is as significant as the ability to listen carefully, to understand what someone else is trying to communicate, and to empathize with others who are different.

The practitioner of international development does not need to be a "communication professional" or a "professional educator". However s/he does need to appreciate the role of communication in any development program, and the strategic choices which are part of the design of development activities. To be concerned with such matters as effectiveness and efficiency of whole development projects *includes* the need to be concerned with the effectiveness and efficiency of the learning and communication strategies within that development project.

PART 3

Implementation and Administration

CHAPTER 7

The Administration of International Development Collaboration

Bringing together contrasting expertise involves learning some part of one another's disciplinary language, a willingness to make underlying assumptions transparent, a sensitivity to the historical and political dimensions of the debate, a more reflective handling of the data, and, above all, a respect for one another's humanity.

Jiggins 1994: xvi

7.1 Basic Concepts of Administration

In international development cooperation, as in other planned and organized human endeavor, the desire to change the world and make it better is a necessary condition; but it is not sufficient. The ideas which have been planned must be implemented to have any impact. Beyond the planning, implementation requires *administration*.

Administration is found in all organized human effort. It is necessary in traditional hierarchical, top-down activities; and it is also necessary in highly participatory, collaborative joint efforts among equals. Administration is more than a science, and it is more than an art. Administration is a combination of art and science. Chapter 7 attempts to describe this combination, as it is being played out at the turn of the century, in international development cooperation.

The implementation of any type of program or project requires administration. But international development is a special type of activity and requires a special type of administration. Development transcends the traditional disciplines. As described in Chapter 2, it includes *technology*, but it includes *more than technology*. It includes *economics*, but it includes *more than economics*. The same was said for biological, physical, cultural, social, political, diplomatic, and *even* administrative dimensions. They are ALL found in development activities. From the perspective of a professional practitioner, international development is a highly complex phenomenon.

Administration is also highly complex. Like *development*, it transcends the traditional disciplines. In universities, administration is taught in colleges of business administration. But administration is also taught in departments of political science and sociology, although differently in each. Educational administration is taught in colleges of education; industrial engineering taught in colleges of engineering also includes administration. There are many more special types of administration. Besides the sciences of sociology, psychology, and anthropology, the arts of interpersonal relations and such human characteristics as trust, caring, consideration, friendship, love, commitment, dedication, and service are all important in administration.

William H. Newman has described the complex, continuous cycle of administrative duties, which include *planning*, *organizing*, *assembling resources*, *directing*, *controlling*, and *again planning*, *and so on* (Newman 1951: 16).

In 1966 Ferrel Heady did a helpful review of the politics of development in discussing administration in developing nations. Although this was written in the era of international assistance, it remains relevant as we prepare to shift into a collaborative mode in the 21st century. Bureaucracies don't change that easily! The historical background of traditional elites, colonial administrative heritage and the rise of nationalist elites affects administration differently in each country. However, Heady points out:

The colonial administrative heritage includes one incidental feature that has lasting effects. The colonial version of British, French or any other system of administration was suited to the requirements of colonial government rather than government at home. It was more elitist, more authoritarian, more aloof, more paternalistic. Remnants of these bureaucratic traits have inevitably

carried over to the successor bureaucracies in the new states...
(Heady 1966: 70).

Heady suggests that bureaucratic activity is often directed by a
"carryover of deep seated values from a more traditional past...
those attached to status based on assumption rather than achievement" (Heady 1966: 71). He also mentions that public service can
be a substitute for social security.

About the administrative process, Floyd Reeves says "*it may be
described and analyzed in terms of four aspects: Planning, Organizing, Staffing, and Directing. These are interrelated, and take place
simultaneously*" (**7a**) (Reeves 1956).

In this chapter, there is a discussion of several critical concepts
which are significant for all aspects of administration. After a review
of *institution-building*, there are brief discussions of *accountability*,
responsibility, and *authority*. Then we return to the central theme
of this book, *collaboration*, and discuss it from the perspective of
administration. This is followed by a series of practical strategic
alternatives in *organizing*.

7.1.1 Institution-building Concepts

*Sound administration depends upon a statement, or at least a clear
recognition, of overall goals to be achieved. For any organization, this
may be called its "doctrine"* (**7b**). This is the perspective of a group
of scholars and practitioners of international development, among them
Milton J. Esman and William J. Siffin, who focus on *institution-building*
as a major strategy used by government and non-government agencies
in international development.

The term "institution" is somewhat more abstract and elusive than
its cousin "organization". Institution, as used in institution-building
terminology, refers to "the normative qualities of an organization,
as distinguished from technical characteristics", and indicates "that
the *institution* established by institution-building is not just an
organization, but a set of continuing patterns of action that encom-
pass both the organization and its transactional relations with its
environment" (Esman and Siffin 1975: 17).

Esman and Siffin and their colleagues have identified five features of any organization which are important in institution-building:

1. *Leadership:* the group of persons actively engaged in the formulation of the doctrine and program of the institution, and who direct its operations and relationships with the environment.
2. *Doctrine:* the specification of values, objectives, and operational methods underlying social action.
3. *Program:* those actions which are related to performance of functions and services constituting the output of the organization.
4. *Resources:* the financial, physical, human, technological, and informational inputs of the institution.
5. *Internal structure:* the structure and process established for operation of the institution, and for its maintenance (Esman and Siffin 1975: 17).

The institution-building group has also analyzed the relations between an organization and its setting, and identified four classes of "linkages" between an institution and its environment, as follows:

1. *Enabling:* relations with entities that control the allocation of authority and resources needed by the institution.
2. *Functional:* relations with organizations performing functions and services which are complementary in a production sense, which supply the inputs and use the outputs of the institution.
3. *Normative:* relations with organizations which incorporate norms and values relevant to the doctrine and the program of the institution.
4. *Diffuse:* relations with elements in the society which cannot clearly be identified by membership in formal organizations (Esman and Siffin 1975: 18).

7.1.2 Accountability

One of the critical concerns in the international development field at the close of the 20th century is *accountability*, as discussed in Chapter 3 of this book. It is a crucial aspect of administration. In sum, it can be put as follows: *The success of a development program*

in any particular locality is directly related to the extent of
ACCOUNTABILITY *by the staff of the development organization to
the people of that locality* (**7c**).

ACCOUNTABLE, as used in this book, is defined in the *Oxford
Paperback Dictionary* (1983: 5) as *"obliged to give a reckoning or
explanation for one's actions"*.

In an organization, there are different alternatives for the direction
of accountability. Some development organizations owe their
accountability only to higher-level members of a bureaucracy. These
organizations take very different actions than a development organization which is accountable to its clientele. The direction of
accountability in many organizations is spelled out in their *doctrine*.
In others, it is a reflection of the *organizational structure*. In all, it
is reflected in their *linkages*.

For example, there are many cases where a group of village people
in a particular place form an organization to provide themselves
with water for irrigation and household use. They may pool their
labor and other resources to build themselves a dam (or barrage or
weir) across a nearby stream. From that they may dig canals to each
family's land, or perhaps even connect plastic pipe from the reservoir behind the dam to each household. Such groups often establish
rules for use of the water, for maintenance of the dam and canals,
and perhaps give work assignments to all members. Some of these
types of organizations have been in operation for many decades.
Some have annual meetings in which members are held *accountable*
for their share of the work and their share of the water. In this type
of organization, the clientele are the same people as the owners and
operators of the organization. The norm for them is that the whole
organization, and any "staff" it may employ to carry out its functions, is directly accountable to the clientele.

Shivakoti, in his study of "user-controlled" irrigation systems in
Nepal in comparison with "non-user-controlled" irrigation systems
in that country, found that farmers in user-controlled systems approached neighbors and relatives to resolve water system problems,
while among non-user-controlled systems, a majority of farmers
approached the village council functionaries to resolve problems
(Shivakoti 1991: 109).

The same situation has been found with local irrigation systems
in many parts of the world. If, for instance, the members hire one
of their young people to turn on the water flow in various canals

on a weekly schedule so that each family gets its share of the water, the members will hold that person accountable to them. If s/he fails to do the work properly, they may punish that person, or even replace that person with someone else. On the other hand, if the job is done very well, the water users may reward that person with a bonus of some kind. The accountability is clear and enforced. (See examples in Abel 1975; Coward 1980; Martin 1986; Martin and Yoder 1987; Yoder 1986.)

Contrast this with the situation where an outside agency, perhaps a government ministry of water supply, or even an NGO from the capital city, decides to "help" the people of that village by installing a water system "for them". In this situation, it is typical for the outside organization to arrange for outside engineers to design the water system, and either contract with outsiders to build it or use village people for labor on the project. When it is completed, the outside group will usually manage it according to its own rules and regulations. And normally, they will employ someone from outside the village to be the one who turns on and turns off the water, arranges for cleaning the canals, etc. In this type of situation, the employee is usually *accountable* only to higher levels of management within the organization, not to the people of the village.

The experience of the Gal Oya irrigation scheme in Sri Lanka was one which, over the years, shifted accountability for the program from the government irrigation department to the farm families who took responsibility for the maintenance of the canals and made distribution decisions to better serve the "tail-enders" in the system (Uphoff 1992).

The global experience with irrigation systems and drinking water systems demonstrates the consequences of the direction of *accountability*. In systems run by outsiders, with little or no accountability to the local people, it is typical for villagers to complain that they do not get water on their fields when they need it; they do not like the way distribution is made among them; and the proportion of the "command area" of the system which is actually receiving water during dry seasons tends to be low. Conversely, in systems where local staff is accountable to the villagers, the water users tend to be pleased with the way in which the system is being managed. More important, perhaps, a higher proportion of the "command area" of the system tends to actually have water during dry seasons.

Agricultural research and agricultural extension provide many examples of the importance of client-accountability. In Thailand, by the late 1970s, a large and nation-wide agricultural research system was developed by the central government. There were local research stations scattered throughout the country. Professional agriculturists from other parts of the world assumed that such a system would be responsive to the needs and interests of local farming people in each agricultural zone. But when we were sent there to analyze the situation, we discovered that it was quite different. Here is an excerpt from our field notes:

Visits with the heads of several local agricultural research farms revealed that decision-making was not local. When these persons were asked about the results of last year's research, they responded that they didn't know. It was the normal practice for such local managers to receive instructions from central government officers in Bangkok each year. They were sent seed packets, for example, along with specific instructions for the design of field plots, planting dates, fertilizer and plant protection instructions, and dates on which data on the crop were to be gathered and reported. These data were then sent to Bangkok, where they were summarized and analyzed. The next season, different packets of appropriate inputs were sent from Bangkok, along with appropriate instructions. Each year the local manager merely followed instructions from higher officials in Bangkok, to whom he was accountable, and tried to do all assigned tasks in a timely and effective manner. Local farmers rarely visited the research farms, for their staff had very little knowledge of local agriculture, and not much to offer to local farming people.

This may be contrasted with the rubber growers' organization in Malaysia. There, at about the same time, an agricultural research unit was owned and operated by the rubber tree growers. Staff at those research farms were in daily contact with local growers; did practical, applied research on the problems currently faced by the rubber producers; and were well-known to the growers.

In the Thailand example, individual professionals doing agricultural research had no accountability to local clients. As a consequence, the research results they produced were of little value to local people. (Analysis of personnel management in that system in the early 1970s, not surprisingly, demonstrated that the size of salaries received by the professional research staff varied inversely with the distance to Bangkok. The highest salaries were received by those posted in the capital city; the lowest salaries were received by those in the most remote places. And, incidentally, the government of Thailand later changed the system to make it more responsive to local agriculture.) In the Malaysia rubber case, since the rubber producers owned the research system, individual professional agricultural researchers were fully accountable to the growers. The research results they produced were used regularly by their clientele.

Similarly, in one West African country, the government was interested in expanding oil palm production among small farmers. From our field notes:

Agricultural extension officers were sent to several villages where land was not owned individually, but assigned each year by a Council of Elders to each family according to the size of that family. The typical pattern was for husbands to reallocate that land among several wives, based on the number of children each had. Since the major crops were yams and cassava for family food, husbands typically managed those crops, and their wives interplanted peppers, tomatoes, and other vegetables among the root crops. And bananas, citrus fruits and coconuts grew along with the other crops. With this intensive multi-level agriculture, there was little interest among individual farmers in allocating land to the government's oil palm seedlings. Even when extension officers provided the tree seedlings at no cost, most farming families did not plant them.

Since the extension officers were not at all accountable to the farming families, they did not discuss needs and interests with them. The accountability was to the central government; the oil palm program was in response to central government needs; and the extension personnel failed to "convince" most farm families to plant any of them in their "gardens".

In Honduras, outside extensionists had a similar experience when they tried to introduce the velvet bean in communities where the hills were not very steep, and where farming people saw no advantage in the beans as a soil building crop. In other locations, the velvet bean had been a great success. Those were places where the steep hillside pattern of slashing and burning a field, then planting for a few years, then moving on to a new location, could be dramatically changed with this new crop. This leguminous crop was planted into other field crops, strengthened the soil after the other crop was harvested, and allowed families to stay in one place, and continue to farm the same fields for many years. But what was appropriate in the steep hills, was not suitable for the more gently sloping hills. Agriculture extension systems which are *accountable* to local farmers are less likely to make this type of error.

In all of these examples, where local personnel are *accountable* to their local clientele, the clientele tend to receive services appropriate to their needs and interests. Where staff are not accountable to local people, the services they provide may or may not be appropriate to their needs and interests.

7.1.3 Responsibility, Authority, and Accountability

Practitioners of administration have used the ideas of *responsibility* and *authority* for many years. The concern with *accountability*, as used in the last section, is more recent.

In a formal organization, *responsibilities* may be specified for each individual within the organization. These are the specific tasks or functions which that individual is expected to perform. In very formal organizations, there are written job descriptions, which distinguish one position from another, and tell each individual what s/he is "supposed" to do. These are listed as the individual's *responsibilities*. For example, in an urban retail food supply firm, some people will be responsible for receiving shipments of food from suppliers, and placing that food in appropriate displays. Other people may be responsible for running a cash register (counting the items a customer is purchasing, assessing the cost of each, summarizing that cost, collecting the money from the customer, and giving the customer a receipt). Still others may be responsible for helping the customer carry what has been purchased from the firm to the customer's home, or to his/her vehicle. Yet another person may be a manager in the firm, responsible for supervising the work of others. Each responsibility is described in its own way, and personnel may be trained for each specific responsibility.

In much less formal organizations, individuals still have specified *responsibilities*. If there are draft animals in a typical farming family in South Asia, it may be the responsibility of the man of the farm to manage those animals and work with them in the fields (ploughing the soil, or pulling a cart, etc.). In that same family, it is likely to be the women who have the responsibility for feeding the animals, milking cattle, and otherwise looking after the livestock. Similarly, children may have responsibility for taking small ruminants to local pasture areas and looking after them, for cutting and carrying grasses and leaves for the animals, and other tasks.

In both cases, and in many types of organizations which fall between the highly formalized example and the very informal example, there are *responsibilities*. Individuals know their own *responsibilities* and the organization can only function when individuals perform their assigned responsibilities. This phenomenon is found in all manner of human groups, from symphony orchestras to restaurants to soccer/football teams. Everyone playing in or watching the soccer game understands that only one is "assigned" the responsibility of being the goal tender. Other players have other responsibilities. When each person understands his/her special functions, and what they are responsible for doing, the whole team can function.

Authority is a different aspect of the individual's role and function in a human group. Unlike responsibility, *authority* is given to individuals by a higher level in the larger social/political system. Authority in some traditional societies is ascribed to the village chief by virtue of his having been the first-born son of the former village chief. Other human groups have different rules, and choose a leader by an election in which certain people are authorized to vote, and the individual who wins the election receives his/her authority by virtue of having won that election. An individual who has authority in an organization may share some of that authority with others, but does not lose his/her authority for the larger organization. The president (or chief operating official or chief executive officer) of a large corporation may assign another individual authority over the marketing division of that organization, and give a third person authority over the production division of the firm. But the chief executive officer still retains authority over the entire organization. The head of a national government agency may share authority for the northern districts with a junior officer, the southern districts with another, the eastern districts with a third, and the western districts with a fourth. But the agency head still retains authority for the whole agency.

Traditional authority patterns, usually always male, help explain why sometimes programs designed for women do not get beyond the planning stage. If the authorities demonstrate by example and practice that they are really convinced of the value of a women's program, those responsible for implementing the program (male or female) are more likely to be successful.

One type of organizational authority is vested in an individual by appointment to a particular assignment. Another type of authority is earned by an individual through his or her demonstrated competence. This is called "earned authority". An example is the authority of ideas which a practitioner achieves by virtue of an excellent record of performance. Another example is the village leader who has the respect of the community because of his/her demonstration of being able to do good things, or perhaps because of a willingness to put in long hours of hard work on behalf of neighbors.

These key phenomena in the administrative process, *responsibility*, *authority*, and *accountability*, are discussed below. They are manifest differently in different cultures, different social systems, and different types of organizational structures. The concepts are introduced here as tools for use in the discussion which follows.

7.1.4 Collaboration in Administration

A critical contemporary issue in the international development arena, as we have seen, is *collaboration*. From an administrative perspective, it is possible to plan, organize, staff, and direct a human group in which all members are collaborators with each other. It is also possible to manage a group where collaboration is not the mode; where those in authority expect all others to follow orders, do as they are told, and do not see themselves as collaborators. And there are all types of intermediate forms of administration between these two contrasting approaches.

Different types of functions may require different types of collaboration. Military organizations are known for their need to maintain a top-down discipline. If the general orders his troops to enter the battlefield, it is not the type of situation where he is likely to wait for discussions with all members of the group, give each an opportunity to express his/her views, and then try to achieve some kind of consensus prior to actually taking the action. He might have a heavily collaborative relationship with a few other officers in his immediate staff; but when the moment of final decision comes, it is expected that all will look to the general, who has the *authority* to make the decision, and is *responsible* and *accountable* for it.

A small medical research team might find that the team is more productive when it takes a highly collaborative approach. Although there will normally be leadership among the members, the leader's role could be to ensure that each member makes inputs regarding what should be done, why it should be done, how to do it, etc. Then the leader might encourage each member to clarify his/her position with all other members, and then jointly make the decision when consensus has been achieved among all members.

Many African villages have traditionally followed a pattern of collaborative decision-making similar to this medical research team. When an important matter is to be decided by the village chiefs and elders, they conduct an open discussion of the alternatives at the weekly village market. With a four-day week in villages in West Africa where we worked in the 1960s, this meeting took place every fourth day. The ground rules were simple: First the chiefs and elders put the issue to the people. Then everyone present was allowed to ask any question or speak as long and as frequently as s/he wished. Sometimes the meetings went late into the night. Decision was by consensus vote. That is, if even one person did not agree with the "majority" decision, the meeting continued. Important decisions often took several weeks of discussion. Finally, when everyone agreed and consensus was reached, one part of the decision-making process was completed. Then, a select group of villagers took the next step, by going to a special house dedicated to the spirits of village members who had died. After consultation with the spirits of the dead, the group reported on whether or not the decision of the living could be implemented. After that came the third and final stage of the decision-making process. For that, another designated group went to a second sacred house to consult with the spirits of unborn generations to come. If they also came out agreeing that the decision of the living and the former members of the village should be implemented, then the decision was implemented. This type of collaborative decision-making has much to offer those concerned with sustainability.

These illustrations demonstrate some of the differences between a "straight-line" or top-down administrative style and a collaborative administrative style. The contrasts are not always so sharp. For example, members of a group of jazz musicians may each be given freedom to play variations on the theme during a performance. However, they typically have a leader who gives signals as to when they will begin to play, when they will end, and perhaps some other aspects of the performance about which each had some inputs. A spectator might consider that a more collaborative approach than a symphony orchestra concert, where the conductor holds a baton, signals not only the beginning and the end, but also the tempo and emphases along the way.

The experience in the 20th century with international development activities suggests that *the more the collaboration among the various "players", the greater the chance that the activities will achieve success which will be sustainable over time. "Players" refers to the residents of the local place where the development activity is to be implemented, the personnel of local agencies and organizations which are involved, and the personnel of national and international agencies participating in financing, authorizing, and implementing the activity* (**7d**).

One of the issues is, development from inside or development from outside? Certainly, the perspectives are different, and when insiders and outsiders do not collaborate, there tends to be problems. The Small Farmers Development Projects (SFDPs) in many Asian countries, illustrate the difference in perspectives. The programs are organized to provide production credit to families who operate very small, mixed-farming systems and usually consume most of what they produce. They usually do not conduct sufficient cash sales of farm products for banks to consider them creditworthy. The projects start by organizing small groups of farmers (around eight to twelve individuals), so that the group can borrow money. The group becomes the collateral. The members monitor and discipline each other—if one is slow making repayments of a loan, the others apply social pressure and force him/her to take responsibility; if one has a catastrophic loss (like the death of a goat which was purchased with credit), then the others provide funds from their own pockets to cover the loss, protecting the group's creditworthiness and ensuring continuity of the group. Saved in this way by neighbors, the person with the loss is likely to regain her/his financial position, and eventually pay back funds provided by the neighbors (Clark 1975).

The SFDP groups, which were originally organized to obtain bank loans, have frequently expanded to address other issues, such as family size, which impinge on the ability to repay loans (W.G. Axinn 1992).

Banks which participate in programs like these may set aside certain funds for "high risk" creditors, and then employ field officers who help organize the groups, train farmers in the procedures, and act as intermediaries between the local bank branch and the SFDP groups. But when is such a program successful? Insiders and outsiders may have different criteria. Both may see SFDP groups as successful when they have a high rate of repayment of their loans. Beyond that, however, differences arise.

One such group in Nepal was so "successful" after a few years of operation that its members accumulated considerable cash savings. Since they had learned to cooperate in the SFDP, they started their own internal credit system, and did not require further loans from the bank. From the perspective of the local SFDP organizer they were a failure, because their lack of active involvement with him resulted in him seeing them as a "dropout" group. Instead of counting nine active working SFDP groups in his area, he could count only eight. On the other hand, from the perspective of many "insiders" in that SFDP group, they were more successful than those groups which were still borrowing from the bank. From one perspective, the group which no longer requested credit was a failure; from the other perspective, the same group, no longer needing outside credit was a great success. It had been empowered by the process, and could now take on many other group activities because of their beginnings in SFDP!

There are international development programs which demonstrate that collaboration in development projects, involving a great variety of insiders and outsiders, can be very successful. There are also many failures in international development, where insiders and outsiders do not collaborate. From an administrative perspective, the following issues are involved:

- Who should define the needs?
- Who should be the field personnel of an international development project? Should they be insiders from the particular district, or

the country, or should they be outsiders, who might come from a different part of the world with some special knowledge which is needed?

- If there are to be "experts" for the project, who should select them?
- If there are to be training programs for people involved in implementing the project, where should the training be, and who should conduct it?

7.2 Internal Organizing Strategies

Another major aspect of administration is *organizing*. International development activities are normally carried out by organizations. To be defined as an organization, a group must have a purpose and a structure. *An organization is a group of persons, together with their positions and jobs, and the interrelations of such positions and jobs with a unified purpose* (**7e**).

Organizations may be formal or informal. A group of people who gather at the village market one day each year to clean it and make minor repairs to market stalls is likely to be quite informal. Leaders will issue instructions to followers, but they will probably work out informal ways of getting cooperation and coordination as they go along. If they meet again the following year for a similar purpose, they may work out very different "organizational" arrangements. A large government bureaucracy, by contrast, is likely to be a very formal organization. In it, there will be higher-level positions which have authority over lower-level positions; and perhaps even written job descriptions for each person, describing the level of that position in the hierarchy, to whom it reports above, those below who report to it, and details of functions to be performed.

Size is a major factor in organizations. The larger the group of people involved, the more formal it is likely to be. Without certain standard and expected patterns, a large group would have great difficulty deciding what to do, and who will do what. While large formal organizations tend to have a tradition of top-down control, some have worked out ways in which members at all levels can participate in decision-making. The smaller an organization is, the easier it is to maintain interpersonal relationships and less formality is required.

Since so much of international development activity is carried on by large, far-flung organizations, often in partnership with other organizations of a variety of sizes, the structural or organizational dimensions of administration are particularly important in international development. There is considerable literature on the subject, and it is growing.

Coralie Bryant and Louise G. White are among the more insightful scholar/practitioners addressing organizational matters:

> Developing institutional capacity is both the most essential task in a development strategy and the most difficult. It is not enough to rely on the good intentions of staff, or a good project design. Institutions have to be developed so that local organizations can establish procedures and practices that encourage local participation. Unless institutions are developed, projects and their results will not be sustained over time. In the late 1960s the field of development administration placed a similar emphasis on building strong institutions. However, these did not necessarily encourage participation, and by stressing strong central organizations, they often impeded it. Participation by a wide variety of stakeholders requires institutions to expand, encourage, and manage that participation. Recent experience tells us that instead of emphasizing institutional lines of authority, it is crucial to develop processes for decision making and implementation, processes that include different interests and allow for interaction and learning (Bryant and White 1984: 15).

The continuous nature of the planning process in international development work was discussed in Chapter 5. We must stress here that *organizing* is also a continuous process. Administration cannot merely develop an organizational structure for a development agency and then assume that it will continue to stay the same as the years go by. Human organizations are living, growing, learning, and changing entities. And those in development work must be especially sensitive to this evolving process.

Elinor Ostrom has concentrated on organizations which manage irrigation systems and has learned much that is widely applicable in international development. She writes, "Crafting institutions is a continuing process because of the complexity of devising institutions which match the unique combinations of variables present in any one system *and* adapt to changes in many of these variables over time. The system is never really stable" (Ostrom 1992: 63).

While Ostrom has written about organizations concerned with irrigation, professionals in the administration of international development find similar situations when they work on programs for healthcare delivery, education at all levels, agriculture (including supply, marketing, credit, extension, research, and production), finance (including everything from women's savings organizations to cooperatives to banks), transportation systems, forestry, taxation, law and order, and other aspects of change in the human condition. In a changing environment, human organizations are also continuously changing.

Most large organizations, and those engaged in international development cooperation, tend to be structured by disciplines. Examples of these include organizations like the UNDP, World Bank, USAID, and FAO. Typically, all economists are in one unit, agronomists are in another, and veterinarians are in a third. Large international development organizations may have twenty or more such specialized units. However, in the latter years of the 20th century, it is being increasingly recognized that the problems of development are interdisciplinary. Most organizations now involve a large number of different disciplines, all required for the design and implementation of one development program, or perhaps even for one project.

For example, a watershed management project might have need for engineers to build a dam, for other engineers to design hydroelectric generating facilities as part of the dam, for irrigation specialists and agriculturists to arrange for irrigation systems downstream of the dam, and for soil and water conservationists to arrange for protection of the environment upstream of the dam. But that is just the beginning. There may also be need for political scientists, sociologists, and anthropologists to work with the people who may be displaced upstream of the dam in the area which will become a large reservoir. Economists may be required to estimate costs and benefits of electricity transmission facilities from the power generated at the dam; agricultural economists to study alternative crops to be produced in the newly irrigated land, as well as marketing arrangements for new farm products to be produced on the irrigated land, and the supply of seed, pesticides, and fertilizers. Further upstream, there may be need for foresters and animal husbandry specialists to participate in an analysis of the mixed-farming systems with a view to reducing siltation, as well as for flood control specialists to arrange a system for early warning and protection in the event of excessive rainfall, not to mention administrative, accounting, and clerical support staff.

An appropriate organizational structure for a project such as watershed management can expedite cooperation, coordination, and communication among a mixed group of individuals from a variety of disciplines. In addition to the lack of cross-disciplinary cooperation, an inappropriate organizational arrangement often leads to competition among specialized groups, and sometimes even outright conflict. Arranging the organizational pattern for maximum effectiveness is a serious challenge to administration.

In a project like the watershed management example just presented, and in many other international development cooperation projects, there is also the issue of indigenous organizations versus exogenous organizations. Outsiders usually bring their own organizational patterns with them. Insiders usually already have local organizations with different ways of working. These may compete with each other, and attempt to defeat each other's programs, or, with special attention, can become collaborators and partners. For long-run effectiveness, and for the sustainability of activities initiated during such a project, special attention to these organizational characteristics is necessary.

Without appropriate attention to these dimensions of organization, projects have serious difficulties. In irrigation schemes, if local people are prepared for *ownership* of the project from the earliest planning stages, they are much more likely to be willing to cooperate in the maintenance of canals and the allocation of water later on when these matters become problems. In one case in India, there had been no such involvement in the early planning. Here is an excerpt from our field notes made during a visit to that project:

A group assembled in the village to discuss the allocation of water to farmers' fields with local government officers who had been put in charge. We were less than a mile below the dam, and the irrigation canals had just been completed. The government workers proposed that villagers form their own organization, and take responsibility for fair sharing of water among themselves. One of the village elders rose, and pointed to the high dam which could barely be seen in the distance. Then he said, "We know that there will be conflict among us in sharing this new irrigation water. But, see that dam over there. You did not ask us whether or not to build it, or where to build it, or anything else. You made all the decisions yourselves. Now we think you should continue to make the decisions, and you can try to cope with the conflicts among us." Then he sat down.

Overlooking the indigenous organizations, which had been there in the villages for a long time, was a strategic mistake. It is possible to establish linkages among organizations of insiders and organizations of outsiders, and for the projects to succeed, it is necessary.

7.2.1 Formal Organizations and Informal Organizations

Formal organizations can be described with simple diagrams. These are called organization charts, or organograms. The simplest type may have only a few boxes, with lines connecting them to illustrate responsibilities. For larger organizations, there may be dozens or even hundreds of boxes, with many types of lines connecting them.

Figure 7.1 illustrates an organization of four people. One is the designated head of the organization, or chief. The other three are all subordinate to the chief, but equal to each other, as they are on the same "level" of the organization. A more complex organization (Figure 7.2) may have more levels than this, for example where the chief has four department heads reporting to him/her, and each department has two or more sections within it.

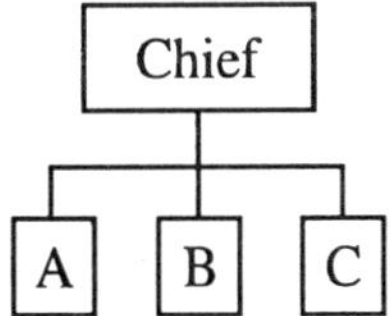

Figure 7.1
Simple Organization Chart

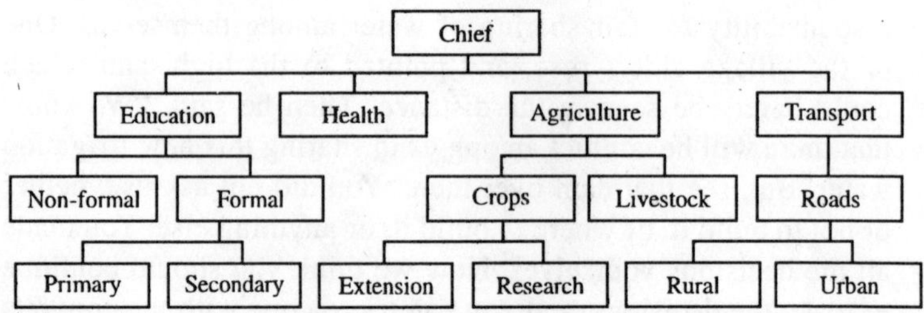

Figure 7.2
Complex Organization Chart

In Figure 7.1 the "span of control" for the chief is three persons, that is, the number of people who report to him. In Figure 7.2 the span of control of the chief is four persons. Since each of those four persons has several more people reporting to them, the chief actually has authority over a much larger group, but from an organizational perspective, the span of control of the chief is still four persons.

One of the issues in organizational design is, how large should the span of control be? Some types of work and some cultures suggest a rather level organization, in which all members report directly to the leader. This is effective in smaller organizations, and does promote participation and collaboration. In other situations, particularly with larger organizations, it is more effective to reduce the span of control. *The higher in a hierarchy a particular position may be, the smaller the span of control should be for that position. However, the more similar the functions of people reporting to one person, the larger the span of control may be* (**7f**).

When it comes to the question of how many units or departments there should be in an organization, that will depend on how its personnel are specialized or differentiated. *Factors of specialization, or differentiation, suggest departmentalization in accordance with such factors as: (a) function, (b) location, (c) kinds of work, (d) time of work, (e) public interests (pressure groups), and (f) personal trust* (**7g**). In international development organizations, *location* is a critical factor. A global agency of the UN, for example, might have one large headquarters office in one city in one country. But it might also have a regional office on each continent, and a representation in each country where it is conducting operations. Similarly, an NGO operating in one district in a country might have a central office in one town, and then several branch offices in different villages in the district. They might also need a small liaison office in the national capital.

Even if an organization operates in only one *location*, it might be carrying out several different *functions*. A small firm manufacturing water pumps might have one unit which purchases supplies and inputs, another which fabricates the parts of the pump, a third which assembles the pump, a fourth which stores and transports the products, a fifth which is responsible for sale of the pumps, and a sixth which provides administrative support services to the other five. An organization chart might show a chief with some aides at the highest level and six assistant chiefs, one for each of the other divisions, at the next level. Under each assistant chief there would be lower levels.

For larger organizations, administrators need special assistants for certain functions. These are usually called *staff* functions, to separate them from the main *line* functions in the organization. The *line* functions get their name from the vertical lines on the chart and indicate the flow of administrative control from the top to the bottom of the organization. The heads of these units are often called *line officers*. These are the persons who need help from people on a level with them (not in the *line*), who are called *staff officers* (Figure 7.3).

There are LINE *functions and* STAFF *functions in organizations. Staff functions, such as planning, budgeting, and personnel management (staffing), should be done at every level, since fundamental decisions require information from every level* (**7h**).

In Figure 7.3 the person in charge of personnel and the person in charge of finance are both *staff* officers. The persons in charge of agriculture, education, and health are *line* officers.

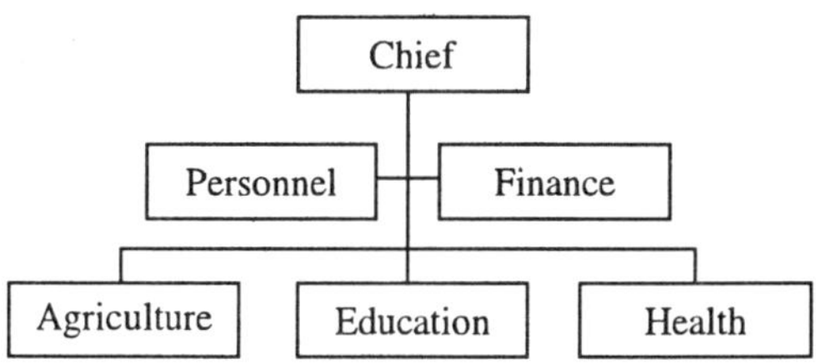

Figure 7.3
An Organization Chart Showing Line and Staff Functions

In a formal organization, it is important for each individual to know to whom s/he is accountable. To whom does s/he report? Or, who has the right to tell whom what to do? And, similarly, each person should know who are those below on the organization chart who report to them. The administrative ideal has been that each person should report to only one other officer, not two or more. In fact, there is literature warning against the dangers of "dual supervision", or situations where two different senior officers give different instructions to someone in the organization. The general proposition can be stated as, *the extent to which unity of command is achieved is a measure of the effectiveness of administration. It is never totally achieved* (**7i**).

In the real world, everyone has a variety of demands upon her/his time, attention, and activity. Therefore, while there are many advantages of "unity of command", it has been observed many years ago that there are actually a milieu of forces acting upon people, in the workplace, at home, and elsewhere (G.H. Axinn 1957). In times of crises, however, the effectiveness of an organization in coping with immediate problems is directly related to the extent to which everyone in it is willing to ignore all other conflicting demands on them, and devote full energy and attention to what is being requested of them by the leadership of the organization.

However, no matter how firm the formal lines are in an organization, there tend to always be informal lines of communication, and often cooperation. People in different branches of an organization may know each other because of family relationships, personal friendships, "old school" ties, ethnic similarities, and for many other reasons. Thus they share thoughts and ideas about the workplace even when they are meeting in other locations for other purposes, or when they are having their lunch hour or coffee break together. Insightful leadership, which can encourage collaboration beyond the formal organization chart, can do much to enhance the effectiveness and efficiency of an organization. *Informal organization is the most important aspect of organization. For success, the order of importance tends to be people, process, and then structure* (**7j**).

Nevertheless, *the effectiveness of organization and administration may be related directly to the extent to which delegated responsibility and authority are commensurate* (**7k**). As supervisors are heard to say, "Don't hold me responsible for the work of others over whom I have no authority."

To get the best of both worlds in organization, *the effectiveness of administration is often directly related to the extent to which informal organizations within the structure are in accord with the purpose of formal organization* (71). For example, if the top leadership does an excellent job of communicating the *doctrine* of the organization at all levels, then members of various informal groupings within will also be able to discuss it and explain it to each other. If there is consensus, then informal groupings will support the programs of the organization. If there is doubt and misunderstanding within the organization, then informal groupings may act as subversive elements, trying to defeat the overall purpose of the organization.

7.2.2 Geographic Organizing Strategies

One organizing strategy which has been effective for some agencies is to set up special work teams, utilizing members from several different units of the organization, but putting them together on a temporary basis to accomplish a specified task. These may last for a period of weeks, months, or even years. An example from agricultural research is the effort of some organizations in farming systems research. In order to comprehend the whole farm as a system of interrelated components, and to attempt to understand the relationships among those components, agricultural research units globally have had a serious problem. They are usually staffed with highly specialized technical personnel. Some are agronomists, who know about field crops. Others are horticulturists, who know about fruits and vegetables. Others are animal scientists, who know about cattle, sheep, goats, and poultry. Still others may know about soil and water conservation. Some human ecologists know about farming families, and their internal production and consumption needs. Some social scientists know about local farming people's organizations, and local cultural and ethnic differences. And other scientists, at the same agricultural research organization location, may know about farm management economics, or marketing of farm products.

The problem is that each of these dimensions of farming life is related to all the others. Identifying problems "within" any one of these areas, and even working out solutions to those problems, may not be helpful to the farming family. It is not unusual, for example, for an agronomist to be told by a worried farmer that his/her cow is down with a warm wet nose and unable to stand up. If the agronomist says, "I'm sorry, but you need a veterinarian for that problem", the farmer will find the scientist useless.

The organizational problem is how to arrange the organization's structure so that people from various specialized fields will be willing and able to exchange information with each other. Better still, they might develop respect and appreciation for each other, learn more about the linkages among the separate components about which they were trained, and become more useful to the small mixed farming systems in which most rural people live and work. At the end of the 20th century, this problem had not yet been solved. However, some national and a few international agricultural research organizations have found it feasible to put together temporary teams of scientists from a variety of disciplines. This group may be physically housed in one cluster of laboratories and offices, spend much of their time together, visit farms together, and learn to appreciate each other as persons. These relatively informal, temporary teams have been able to overcome the barriers which normally develop between departments or other units of a large bureaucracy (G.H. Axinn 1991b; N.W. Axinn 1990a; Merrill-Sands et al. 1989).

Team-building among members of an organization is normally difficult. It is necessary for the ideal collaborative mode of operation referred to several times in this book. International development organizations have a long experience of assigning an "outsider" to work as the counterpart of an "insider" in project or program design and implementation. The pair of individuals is known as *counterparts*. As with other human relationships, this has sometimes been a success, sometimes a failure, and sometimes an utter catastrophe. For individuals who have been engaged in interpersonal competition and conflict, whether they are local persons or international personnel, team-building is a significant cross-cultural challenge. It requires a high tolerance for insult. Because of so many cultural and professional differences, even well-meaning individuals attempting to work together often inadvertently insult each other. The situation requires *diplomacy* and *patience* on the part of all those involved.

However, the evolution of a genuine collaborative mode can transcend the *counterpart* problems if the individuals involved are sufficiently committed to it and professionally prepared for it. This happens when those involved realize at the beginning that sharing goals and working together among people whose whole backgrounds are different requires an investment of time and energy.

One of the strategic choices involved in large organizations spread over a wide area has to do with the mode of organizational structure in the physically decentralized locations. For example, if a development agency has three main program areas (health, education, and agriculture, as an illustration), there are two different basic strategies for structural arrangement. The most common has been to organize by program areas. At headquarters, in addition to basic administrative services, there would be three main divisions: one each for health, education, and agriculture. If such an organization were operating in a country with four geographic areas (for this illustration, call them north, south, east, and west), in each geographic area there would be one branch for health, one for education, and one for agriculture. In each of the four areas, the head of each program area would report directly to his/her chief in that same program branch at headquarters. If a very large geographic area is being covered, the organization might have a third level of structure, at the subarea (or county, or district) level. Again, each subarea office might have a person designated in charge of health, another in charge of education, and a third in charge of agriculture. The lines of authority would all be going up and down their organizational chart, from field personnel at the bottom, straight up to people in the same program area at each level. This type of structure can be called a function-based organization (Figure 7.4).

An alternative structure is to organize by geographic *area*. With this mode, using the same illustration, there would still be central offices at the highest level, other offices at area level, and offices at the subarea level. But in this type of structure, one individual would be designated in charge of all programs at his/her level. Thus, there would be an officer in each of the four area offices who would formally be assigned to all of the duties and responsibilities which the head of the whole organization has at headquarters, but s/he would have them only for his/her own geographic area. There would be one person (and, thus one office) in the north area responsible for *all* programs in that area, another in the east with similar responsibilities, and the same for the west and the south. Again, at

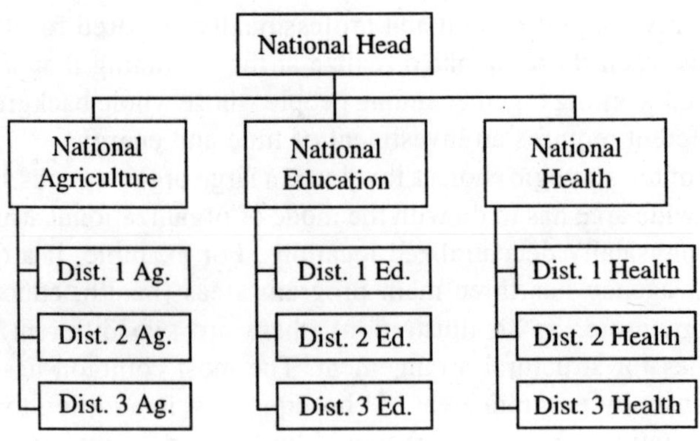

Figure 7.4
Function-based Organization Chart

the subarea level, the organization would have one person responsible for *all* three programs in each subarea. The organizational chart, for this structure by area, would have fewer vertical lines on it, but many more horizontal lines. Communication and coordination would be basically among the individuals concerned with health, education, and agriculture at each level, horizontally, rather than up and down, vertically, between persons at each level concerned only with one of the three program areas (Figure 7.5).

There are advantages and disadvantages of each of these two basic alternatives. Most very large organizations have some kind of a combination of the two. They might be basically structured by area, but maintain informal vertical communication lines between individuals in the same field, or discipline, at all levels of the organization. Or they might have a basic structure by program area, and try to encourage some horizontal communication among personnel from different program areas in each geographical location.

An advantage of the functional organization pattern is that professionals in each of the separate program areas tend to be more up-to-date in their own disciplines. They seek rewards, recognition, and promotion within their own specializations. That works well in some situations, but it is a serious disadvantage when there are problems or opportunities at a given level which cross over from one field to another. In such situations, there tends to be pressure from "higher up" to stay with each individual's professional field

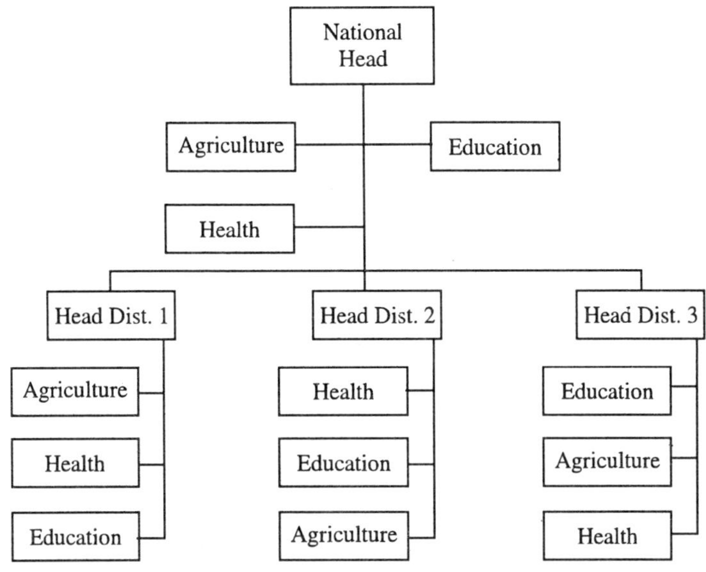

Figure 7.5
Area-based Organization Chart

and not "waste time" helping the others. If, for example, local political leadership in the north area becomes concerned with the nutritional aspects of health, and wants an integrated program in which education personnel help build training programs for both health workers and agriculture workers about human nutrition, there may be conflicts. The organization is simply not structured for interdisciplinary activity.

The area type of organization has an advantage for integration of such programs along geographic lines. The disadvantage may be a lack of incentive for personnel to keep up with their own specializations. And rivalries may develop among personnel assigned to different geographic areas. However, in development work of various types, the increasing need is to take all relevant components of the whole system into consideration, so there is a trend in the direction of more organization by area and less by function. In reality, both are required, and large formal organizations need to maintain communication, co-operation, and coordination among both functional specialties and different geographic areas.

7.2.3 Field Level Operations

Another organizing strategy is related to control of the field level operations of a development project or program. Figure 3.1 in Chapter 3, which illustrates the difference between acquisition systems and stimulation systems, is relevant. *One way to facilitate accountability of an organization to its clientele is to build two-way communication channels between the clientele and the staff and leadership into the organizational structure* (**7m**). There is no better way to achieve this than to work through an organization where the staff and leadership are the clientele, or are persons hired by the clientele. That is an acquisition system.

This strategy is related to the strategy of *decentralization* which has become increasingly popular, especially in Asian nations like Indonesia and the Philippines, at the end of the 20th century. Many national government planning units have come to the conclusion that one central government organization, headquartered in the capital city, cannot manage the great variety of different activities required of it, especially if one of its functions is to enhance development. Variations in everything from climate to topography to ethnic differences to distance from markets are so different and vary locally from place to place that relevance demands decentralization. Concurrently, many are discovering that the sheer difficulties of travel and transportation as well as communication are making it difficult to hold their large organizations together.

One potential solution is to divide up the area into many smaller divisions, or local units, and then have local units organized to serve their special needs while representing national policies of central government levels. Toward this end, many large organizations, NGOs as well as governments, have decentralized. But decentralization takes many forms. In some, for example, physical offices and personnel are decentralized, but control of programs and personnel, and financial matters is retained in the center. In others, local units may generate their own financial resources locally, and control their own personnel and programs. And there are many variations between these two quite opposite approaches to decentralization. The second approach is sometimes called *devolution* instead of *decentralization*, as more of the control is *devolved* to the local units (Uphoff 1986).

From the perspective of development, two great advantages of the decentralized organizational structure are the ability of local operations to be under the control of *client-accountable* local organizations, and the ability to enhance *collaboration* among local people, and between local people and outside organizations.

7.3 Implications for Professional Practitioners

From the perspective of practitioners in international development, the *collaborative mode* has emerged toward the end of the 20th century as an ideal condition for state-of-the-art international development cooperation. Because of the great diversity of the needs and interests of the agencies, organizations, and individuals involved, *collaboration* has evolved as a means to the end of successful implementation. The challenge to administration is how to plan, organize, staff, and direct development activities so as to ensure maximum collaboration among those who have a vested interest, the so-called stakeholders in the activity.

Ideally, the professional practitioner in international development should be able to use the *institution-building* concepts to clarify and better understand the *leadership, doctrine, program, resources,* and *internal structure* of the agencies in which s/he is working. Such a professional should be able to identify and analyze significant linkages of such agencies to enable and facilitate development activities.

The practitioner might also recognize how *accountability* is manifest in the particular culture/social system where s/he is working, as well as identify ways of broadening accountability patterns to enhance collaboration. Similarly, the ability to comprehend and manage arrangements for responsibility and authority in international development practice is a mark of the professional practitioner.

Concern with organizational aspects of administration is a part of professionalism for the practitioner. Manipulation of organizational structure is one of the opportunities for learning and adjustment within an agency. Sometimes, when serious personnel problems plague an organization (like having the wrong person in a key job) the problem can be ameliorated by a change in structure. Sometimes, when the personnel of a whole agency are demoralized and productivity has become low, it is possible to rejuvenate everyone through structural reorganization. Since this is both an art and a science, it has to be done with care and concern for the individuals involved, as well as attention to the larger political, economic, technical, and other pressures impinging on the organization.

Practitioners of international development have responsibilities to both their clientele and to donors or sponsors who provide their resources. As professionals, they have an obligation to know the organizational alternatives, to be familiar with global experience in various fields, and to be able to make forecasts of the advantages and disadvantages of different choices. While they may not be able to forecast the future with accuracy, they should understand history well enough to be able to anticipate potential consequences.

CHAPTER 8

The Organizations and their Personnel

Although the concept of development has been and remains imprecise, it connotes steady progress toward improvement in the human condition; reduction and eventual elimination of poverty, ignorance, and disease; and expansion of well-being and opportunity for all. It entails rapid change, but change alone is insufficient; it must be directed to specific ends. Development involves societal transformation—political, social, cultural, as well as economic; it implies modernization—secularization, industrialization, and urbanization—but not necessarily Westernization. It is multi-dimensional, with scholars and practitioners disagreeing, however, on relative emphasis, priority, and timing.

Milton J. Esman 1991: 5

This chapter addresses two of the major dimensions of administration of international rural development: the organizations which implement development programs and projects, and the staff, or personnel, which make the organizations work. The implementation of development policies and strategies depends on the organizational arrangements of the human effort, and how well the personnel within these organizations are managed.

The first part of this chapter describes the main types and characteristics of the organizations involved in international development at the close of the 20th century, and the second part analyzes special considerations in personnel management for these kinds of organizations.

8.1 The Organizations which Implement
International Development

There are thousands of agencies and organizations involved in international development collaboration. A few are very large and operate globally. Most are very small, and work within one nation state. Some are rich and powerful; others are poor and weak. Some are very effective; many are not. In this section we describe the great range and variety of types of organizations which plan, finance, and implement international development. And readers are encouraged to reflect on the choices which various human groups may have—to enhance their own development independently without outside help, influence, and pressure, or to let outsiders in. And if outsiders are allowed in, which outsiders? for how long? and to do what?

The global system of these agencies and organizations may be viewed as a systemic whole. And this holistic view testifies that there are all kinds of interactions between and among these units. A holistic approach demands recognition that the organizations themselves are composed of a variety of different individuals, with different specializations, different values, different cultural backgrounds, and different perspectives on the process of development. But there is need for analysis. Michael Carley and Ian Christie point to this need as follows:

> Within the traditional bureaucracy there is often little motivation to learn from past experience and even less to admit, analyze and learn from past mistakes. Raking over past failures is generally considered poor form, and seldom brings any career benefit. But accepting the need for such learning is essential for the type of adaptive environmental management argued here, for it provides the rationale for active monitoring to generate feedback for making the necessary incremental adjustments to policy and implementation (Carley and Christie 1992: 161).

The international organizations of "outsiders" are typically related to domestic, or local, organizations of "insiders". That relationship may be a linkage between only two organizations, or may involve networks of large numbers of organizations. And the relationships among these organizations involve cooperation and collaboration, but communication is rarely efficient and effective, and there is often conflict and competition among them. These organizations include government organizations, non-government organizations (NGOs), religious organizations, private foundations, educational institutions, international development banks, and others.

Since this great variety of organizations operates at many different levels, the discussion in this chapter is arranged according to the *base*, or *control*, of the particular organizations. There are sections on *locally-*, *nationally-*, and *internationally-based* organizations, and on *interorganizational collaboration*. Our warning to our readers and to ourselves is that everything in this field is changing and evolving. Some organizations, which had different policies and strategies five years ago, are much more similar to each other now; and others which were trying to so the same thing in similar ways ten years ago are very different from each other today. And both situations will be different tomorrow.

8.1.1 Locally-based Organizations

Most communities have groups within them which are concerned with improvement of the situation within that community. On the government side, public schools, hospitals, postal services, transportation systems, and planning cells are examples of these. NGOs may be involved in the same functions. Some are related to religious organizations. Others may be purely economic, such as a local women's savings circle, a local farmers' irrigation association, or a bull ring (which owns, feeds, and cares for one bull which services the cows of all members).

These locally-based organizations may be self-supporting, or they may be funded by outside groups. In India, local upper caste/class people, motivated by the Gandhian philosophy, often organize marginal tribal or lower-caste people (Harijans) into groups which attempt to combine some religious base with self-improvement through economic programs. These are quite successful if they have adequate technical expertise to combine with religious motivation. Other local groups are self-generating, often in response to environmental resource threats, such as the Chipko movement by women in north India to combat deforestation efforts.

One of the issues on the local level is the extent to which "outsiders" (from national and international levels) should be asked for help, or allowed to interfere. On the government side, national governments tend to control their own units, even those which operate locally. Governments may decentralize and allow more or less local control of local units. But even NGOs may offer "help" from outside, and some of them may dominate large numbers of local units. In contrast, there are situations in which local people, because of political, military, or other forces, are unable to facilitate *development* work without some outsiders present to *buffer* and *protect* them. Thus the issue of how much control of program and staff should be local and how much should be national or international is a very live issue in international development.

In Africa, village level self-help and age group societies have been a tradition for centuries. In Zimbabwe the NGO Africa 2000 Network (UNDP program) gives support to groups of village women who come to them with their own statement of problems and needs, rather than one developed outside the community.

A recent review of local programs in Africa where villagers took collective action to change their conditions noted "there has been a proliferation of smaller, more diverse organizations which are closer to the grassroots. These new organizations are making civil society and democracy more vibrant and resilient wherever they appear" (*New Internationalist* 1995: 30).

Local banks and more wealthy people in small communities all over the world contribute to local organizations promoting local development. If the programs they support are not successful, they usually disintegrate quietly. If they are successful, they may not receive notice outside their own community, since "development professionals" are not earning a living reporting on them.

Successful outcomes nurture self-confidence and encourage networking and exchanges among such groups. These may become regional or state-wide organizations which can then impact on national resources and programs.

8.1.2 Nationally-based Organizations

Almost every sovereign nation state has branches of government at the national level which deal with development. These include ministries of education, health, agriculture, forests, water resources, transportation, and many other types of ministries or departments. There are also central government staff units which support development activities, such as national planning commissions and ministries of finance. These may also have regional offices, and often local offices, so while they are grouped here among nationally-based organizations and their base is national, they may also operate at local and international levels.

Many of these organizations will enter into contracts or make agreements with internationally-based organizations for the implementation of development activities. They will also negotiate loans or grants from international organizations for domestic development work. Thus, while they are nationally-based, they are often part of global networks of development activity, as well as involved in local operations.

Separate from these national government organizations, there are usually national NGOs, as well as universities, research institutes, religious organizations, banks, and philanthropic foundations within each country that are active in development. And it is typical for these non-government agencies to participate in networks of local organizations and also to have links with international organizations. Comprehensive directories and listings of many types of NGOs are available; their numbers are very large. As an example, the Philippines, alone, is reported to have over 17,000 NGOs.

Reflecting on the NGO side of the picture, Reinhold E. Thiel has noted:

It is a myth that these groups are egalitarian grassroots organizations. Those that actually function, at the village as well as at the regional or national level, do so thanks to the selfless involvement of individual persons, who are able to motivate others, come up with ideas, coordinate efforts, and bring about decisions.... The real chance for NGO leaders lies in the fact that they do not have to prevail against a rigid, bureaucratic apparatus, which tries to stop novel ideas just because they are new. On the other hand, this constellation also harbours the danger that imperiousness and autocratic structures will expand within the NGO sector just as at the state level (Thiel 1994: 3).

Lori Ann Thrupp and her colleagues have pointed to the importance of participatory methods, and the range of approaches being used at the grass-roots level in order to involve local citizens and groups in projects:

> These kinds of challenges are slowly being addressed in Latin America, partly as a result of innovative collaboration among NGOs, people's federations, and a variety of international and government agencies. Good examples include the Grupo de Estudios Ambientales (Environmental Studies Group) with the Tropical Forest Action Program in Mexico, the Organization of Tropical Studies with municipal governments in Costa Rica, COMUNIDEC and the Ministry of Agriculture in Ecuador, and the International Potato Center (CIP) and local NGOs in Peru. Yet much more work is needed to realize the strong potential from innovative convergences of approaches, institutions, and policies (Thrupp et al. 1994: 82).

Among non-government organizations, but sometimes not included in lists of NGOs, are many types of local and national religion-based organizations which are involved in development activities. Missionary groups from urban areas link with rural temples, churches, and mosques to facilitate rural development. Some have linkages with international or global religious organizations. Some have other agendas beyond development. But all are part of the system of organizations involved in international development.

On the government side, within agriculture as an example, most countries have national agricultural research systems which are a part of the national ministry of agriculture. These units typically have divisions operating within states or districts of the country. In addition, they are linked through various types of agreements and contracts with international agricultural research centers, as well as with units in the global UN system. All of these are actors in the international development arena. And similar situations are found in such fields as health, education, transportation, and commerce.

In addition to nationally-based development organizations whose purpose is to conduct development activities domestically, many countries have nationally-based organizations whose purpose is to further development activities in other countries. While these also may have such other objectives as the conduct of international diplomacy, support of military power among friendly nations, and the promotion of trade, they typically have names which emphasize international development. Examples are: Australian International Development Assistance Bureau (AIDAB); Canadian International Development Agency (CIDA); British Overseas Development Administration (ODA); Japanese International Development Agency (JICA); Swedish International Development Agency (SIDA); Swiss Development Cooperation (SDC); German Agency for Technical Cooperation (GTZ); and US Agency for International Development (USAID).

In the international development field, these are often referred to as "bilateral agencies", since they tend to work through bilateral arrangements between themselves and governments or other organizations in other countries. While it is beyond our scope here to describe these individual organizations, they all publish annual reports, brochures, personnel directories, and other materials which do describe them in depth.

8.1.3 Internationally-based Organizations

In addition to the organizations discussed in the last two sections of this chapter, there are many organizations which transcend the boundaries of any particular nation state. These include the UN, and its large system of specialized agencies; global and regional development banks; multinational private corporations; global and regional NGOs; and global religious organizations.

8.1.3.1 The United Nations System

The United Nations system has been growing and evolving over the last half of the 20th century. While its political, diplomatic, and peace-keeping activities have received much publicity, it is the work of the specialized agencies which has been most significant to international development. Among the organizations involved in this effort are: the United Nations Development Programme (UNDP), the Food and Agriculture Organization of the UN (FAO), the United Nations Educational, Scientific, and Cultural Organization (UNESCO), the United Nations Children's Fund (UNICEF), the World Health Organization (WHO), the United Nations Development Fund for Women (UNIFEM), the International Labor Organization (ILO), the United Nations Population Fund (UNFPA), the

World Food Program (WFP), and many others. These are mentioned in examples in other parts of this book. Much has been published by them and about them, especially during 1995, the 50th anniversary of the UN (UNA–USA 1995).

In terms of international development collaboration, these agencies have set global standards, and have been willing and able to transcend international boundaries, even in the most difficult of political and military conflicts, when bilateral agencies could not. They have encouraged research and information exchange on all kinds of serious human and environmental problems; and have participated in many types of collaborative partnerships with bilateral government agencies, banks, NGOs, and educational institutions. In addition, the UN has organized major global conferences on such critical topics as the environment, gender, population, and other social issues like poverty. These have brought together both governments and NGOs, and have had an impact on policies and strategies within countries and globally.

Nevertheless, the UN system is an intergovernmental arrangement and under constant pressure from its member states, each of which has its own political and diplomatic agenda. One strength of the specialized agencies is that they have governing bodies made up of representatives of each member government. And, when important decisions are to be made, like selection of a director-general, approval of a biennial budget, or approval of program documents, each member-country gets one vote. (That is quite different from the international development banks, mentioned below, where each country's voting power is directly related to the amount of money it puts in, so the rich countries dominate.) Like all the other organizations mentioned here, the UN is less than perfect. Here is a sample of the criticism during 1995:

> To sum up, there is much that is problematic about the present-day context in the UN for development. Development continues to be downgraded (indeed almost marginalized) as a priority as compared with peacekeeping, by the Secretary-General.... The excellent standard setting achieved by the UN interlinking human rights, development and democracy is being nullified with UN development agencies and others, at best, blithely ignoring such standards or, at worst, flouting them with impunity. Corruption scandals linked to large megaprojects in development are tending to destroy the very credibility of development. Calls for good

governance, transparency and democratisation of development processes must not go unheeded (Dias 1995: 16).

Realistically, the UN system is no more immune than bilateral, NGO, or other systems, from the factors of human greed and corruption mentioned in Chapter 3. But like the other agencies, its staff also contains large numbers of professional, hardworking women and men trying to do the right thing for humanity. These are among the professional practitioners for whom this book has been written.

8.1.3.2 Non-Governmental Organizations (NGOs)

Like the UN system, NGOs also include a great variety of globally-operating organizations. Many have been mentioned elsewhere in this book. Examples also include the World Council of Churches, International Institute for Rural Reconstruction (IIRR), International Voluntary Services (IVS), Volunteers in Technical Assistance (VITA), Christian Rural Overseas Project (CROP), Save the Children, World Vision, Catholic Relief Services, Christian Children's Fund, CARE, The Freedom from Hunger Campaign, Food for the Hungry, Foster Parents' Plan, World Neighbors, OxFam (UK), and OxFam (USA). They are all different from each other; they have similarities; and like the other international development organizations, they are continuously changing their names, size, alliances, and modes of operation.

There is increasing interest in NGOs by both government and multilateral international development organizations, since they see NGOs as partners which can give them access to local people. Martina Vahlhans summarized the situation:

NGOs have in fact specific characteristics which governments have not which make them more suited to the achievement of success in poverty alleviation. Their relationship to their beneficiaries is based on voluntarism which is the main factor allowing NGOs to achieve meaningful participation. Furthermore NGOs recruit and motivate highly qualified motivated staff on the basis of shared values and a belief in the social mission of the NGO.... Moreover, NGOs are free to organize according to the perceived organizational needs in relation to their activities. This enables NGOs to be more flexible and respond better to the specific needs than (highly bureaucratic) government organizations. NGOs thus have—in theory—potential comparative advantages over government organizations (Vahlhans 1994: 20).

Certainly, "the scale, scope, and influence of NGOs concerned with development has grown enormously in recent years" (Pretty and Chambers 1993: 25; Farrington et al. 1993).

8.1.3.3 The International Development Banks

Similarly, the international development banks operate globally or regionally. They are not part of the official UN system, but they are typically supported by many member governments, and dominated by the wealthiest investors. They include the World Bank group with the International Bank for Reconstruction and Development (IBRD), International Development Association (IDA), International Monetary Fund (IMF), Asian Development Bank (AsDB), African Development Bank (ADB), Inter-American Development Bank (IDB), International Fund for Agricultural Development (IFAD), and others. They invest heavily as "donors" in international development, and often intervene in the operations of governments and multilateral agencies.

Like other categories of international development organizations, the banks are not perfect and are much criticized. But they do play a significant role. Gita Sen points to many weaknesses in the current "consensus" among international development agencies and their sponsors. The weaknesses include:

Growth may not pick up for many countries.... Growth may occur but employment generation may be weak.... Both growth and employment may rise, but the jobs created may provide neither economic security nor human dignity.... Growth may occur at the expense of significant and irreversible environmental damage.... The processes of economic structuring that are argued by the Bretton Woods institutions [the World Bank group] and others to be essential to generate faster growth have very high social and human costs, including greater insecurity of livelihoods for many, sharp increases in the work burdens of women and reduced access to services such as education and health. The pent-up frustrations created by the poor employment prospects of young people, the worsening distribution of consumption and income, and the aspirations generated by an increasingly multinational media are vented through the rise of fundamentalism, fascism and ethnic conflicts (Sen 1995a: 12).

From a different perspective, Susan George and Fabrizio Sabelli have critiqued the World Bank, and what they term its "Secular Empire". Here is an excerpt from their enlightening analysis:

The Bank's project can also be analysed, however, as a religious utopia. Structural adjustment does not *set out* to make countries fail. But nor can these countries be allowed to succeed with the "wrong" policies as the case of Zimbabwe shows. The Bank must, again and again, affirm the rightness of its teachings, in the teeth of all the evidence.

The Bank did not invent neo-classical economics, liberalism, free market orthodoxy, or whatever one cares to call this doctrine. It did not even invent the notion that the doctrine works in all places and at all times, regardless of the historical and social context and the relationships and inequalities between nations. The formalist school of economic anthropology has claimed the same thing for half a century.

The Bank was, however, the first (along with the IMF) to put this doctrine into practice and to convince most of its contemporaries that the greatest good for the greatest number will necessarily emerge from its adoption, voluntary if possible; if not, then under duress (George and Sabelli 1994: 72).

8.1.3.4 The Foundations

While all of these categories of international development organizations are fluid and changing in their relationships with one another and within themselves, the private foundations are perhaps even less likely to fit any category. They are sometimes registered in only one nation, but often have operations in many. Some act like bilaterals; others are very much like multilaterals. Most are primarily donors of money, but they also become involved in actual execution of projects and programs and have their own strategies. All are "trying to make the world better", but each has its own approach. They include such organizations as The Ford Foundation (USA), Aga Khan Foundation (Pakistan), Gettillo Vargas Foundation (Brazil), Fredrich Ebert Foundation (Germany), Rockefeller Foundation

(USA), W.K. Kellogg Foundation (USA), Carnegie Corporation (USA), Pew Charitable Trusts (USA)—and thousands of others. Directories of these are available in libraries, and they also publish annual reports, brochures, announcements of grant programs, etc.

Because foundations are not usually a part of government, they have a certain freedom to address issues and processes which governments cannot. They are able to test creative new project ideas which government agencies may fear involve too great a risk or are politically unpopular, such as projects on diseases like AIDS, projects on special education for disadvantaged groups, or projects for preservation of ancient art. They also enjoy greater flexibility of movement from place to place and in selecting and releasing personnel than most other types of organizations. Since in many countries their status as a giver of gifts to those in need relieves them of the need to pay taxes, they must necessarily move money to maintain their legal standing.

8.1.4 Interorganizational Collaboration

Perhaps the high degree of interorganizational collaboration is the most significant aspect of the organizations involved in global international development at the turn of the century. Government agencies have discovered NGOs and are inventing new ways to collaborate with them. Bilateral agencies are collaborating with each other and with multilaterals in what is called "multi–bi agreements". UN agencies have departments within them which actually belong to development banks. And foundations collaborate with each other, with governments, and with UN agencies in governing international centers.

At the same time, there is plenty of competition within and among these organizations. Banks compete with each other to finance development projects, and UN agencies compete with each other to execute projects. Bilaterals compete with each other to execute projects in individual countries. But all are learning that collaboration is a more effective and efficient mode of operation in the international development arena than competition and conflict. A positive example comes from a 1995 issue of the FAO periodical *Ceres* which points to the collaboration between FAO and NGOs:

A First: NGOs Advise FAO on Forestry.... FAO has an unparalleled opportunity to build bridges with all interest groups which seek to influence the future directions for forestry. Both representatives of the industry and non-governmental organizations were invited for the first time to meet with the FAO staff in Rome prior to the FAO Committee on Forestry (CFO) meetings, to inform the meeting of permanent representatives and ministerial meeting which followed (*Ceres* 1995: 14).

Similar cooperation between the UN and NGOs took place in developing the Platform for Action at the 1995 Beijing Global Conference on Women. The newsletter of the International Women's Rights Action Watch reported thus:

In eighteen months the document changed dramatically, in direct response to demands of governments—who were listening to their citizens. From the very beginning of the preparatory process, NGOs were active in articulating the equality and rights issues, working as responsible participants in the process. They succeeded because they showed that they knew what they were doing. By the time of the Beijing Conference, it was clear that governments had recognized a constituency of women—the official delegations were full of NGO representatives. We worked with IWRAW friends and colleagues in the delegations of Malaysia, the Philippines, Mali, Sri Lanka, South Africa, Colombia, Bangladesh, Australia, Canada... (*Women's Watch* 1996: 1).

USAID has been moving toward greater cooperation with NGOs through the decade of the 1990s. In 1993, 17 percent of its non-military aid was delivered through private groups, and by 1995 this had increased to almost 30 percent. While this is an example of positive collaboration, it also has risks for NGOs which might become dominated by their government partners. Some NGOs resist this, and are careful to control the quantities of funds they will accept, and the types of activities they will conduct on behalf of more wealthy donors.

Another major example of global collaboration among a great variety of different types of organizations is found in agricultural research. Although there have been government and private agricultural research organizations scattered throughout the world for over a century, and there was some exchange of information and biological materials among them, a new type of unit was born in the latter half of this century. It began with the International Wheat and Maize Improvement Center (CIMMYT) in Mexico and the International Rice Research Institute (IRRI) in the Philippines. Both were started by US foundations, with support from the local governments. Scientists from many different countries were assembled to focus on increasing productivity of specific crops.

As the years went by, other international agricultural research centers were established, with increasingly less specific crop-centered mandates. Among them, in addition to the first two, are the International Center for Tropical Agriculture (CIAT) in Colombia, International Institute for Tropical Agriculture (IITA) in Nigeria, International Center for Dry Lands Agriculture (ICRISAT) in India, International Food Policy Research Institute (IFPRI) in the USA, and International Service for National Agricultural Research (ISNAR) in the Netherlands. Although each had a headquarters in one particular country, they engaged in field activities in other countries. Over the years they established relationships with many national agricultural research systems, which had been competitors for personnel and funds. Financial support spread from both bilateral and multilateral development organizations, as well as some of the international development banks. And as the network spread, NGOs of various types and sizes also became partners.

By the 1980s and 1990s, the international agricultural research centers had formally organized the Consultative Group on International Agricultural Research (CGIAR) for the express purpose of strengthening the links among the several different international centers, national agricultural research systems, and their major donors.

Another illustration of such interorganizational collaboration is a national government program in Nepal called Production Credit for Rural Women. While it is officially a section of a government ministry, small groups of women in many villages are organized as local NGOs. Although they have ties to district "delivery systems", which are, in turn, connected to the central government, they are local "acquisition systems". In addition, the program, as mentioned earlier, has been supported by several international bilateral and multilateral development agencies.

8.2 The Personnel of Development Organizations

The life blood of any international development organization is its personnel—the human beings who are the staff of the organization. And for any domestic organization attempting to facilitate development internally, the people within the organization are the most important consideration. Thus staffing, or personnel management, is one of the most significant aspects of administration of international development.

There is a large body of professional literature in the field, and the attempt here is merely to call attention to some of the key aspects of personnel management. In his book on the subject, Randall S. Schuler (1986) identifies seven personnel management functions, as follows:

- Planning for human resource needs
- Staffing the personnel needs
- Establishing effective relationships
- Appraising and motivating employee behavior
- Training and career development
- Improving the work environment
- Managing effective union–management relationships

In the following sections we deal with (*a*) levels and types of personnel; (*b*) recruitment, selection, and placement; (*c*) gender and language considerations; (*d*) training; (*e*) reward systems; (*f*) interpersonal relationships; (*g*) conflict management; (*h*) economic pressures; and (*i*) local culture relationships.

8.2.1 Levels and Types of Personnel

In international development cooperation, there are special problems of staffing which go beyond those typically found in organizations within one nation state. These stem from the interaction between local personnel (professional civil servants, technical specialists, and clientele) and foreign personnel (expatriate technical experts brought from outside, administrators and program officers who manage the outsiders' organizations). Bihari K. Shrestha, at a seminar in Kathmandu in 1983, mentioned some of the problems relating to the role of expatriates, one of which is the high cost of the outsiders compared with Nepalis. He has described the situation as follows:

> According to those figures one man-year (of an expatriate) is roughly budgeted at one million rupees (excluding agency overhead), depending on the grade, of course. On the other hand an average gazetted HMG official costs the government anything between say 20,000 and 30,000 rupees per year which gives a ratio of one expatriate for 30 to 50 of our counterparts. An informed source has it that currently there are a total of 334 expatriates working in Nepal for several bilateral and multilateral projects covering almost all the development sectors in the country (Shrestha 1983: 219).

After listing some of the other problems of the relationship among professional insiders and professional outsiders in development projects, he has concluded:

> In the context of the foregoing experience in Nepal, the following conclusions are inescapable. Firstly, when an expatriate is good and hard working he tends to gradually take over the role that legitimately belongs to his Nepali counterpart who is effectively shielded from action. Rarely does he have the skill to operate in a way that does not forfeit the role of the native official and deprive him of the opportunity to gain greater experience and confidence on the job. Rarely is an expatriate able to put into practice the realization that he is involved only temporarily in what is essentially a long-term government project. Secondly, looking from the recipient's angle, most expatriates are not as dedicated and sincere, nor as skillful and talented as their position demands. This then results in a mutually uneasy relationship in which the government officials are increasingly intolerant and resentful of this very expensive individual. And finally, it is a colossal wastage of resources whose opportunity costs happen to be very high for a resource-scarce country like Nepal (Shrestha 1983: 239).

A great variety of types and levels of personnel are involved in international development operations. These range from local volunteers to employed project personnel at the local rural village, to staff at district headquarters, to officers in both technical and generalist positions in national capital cities. To that may be added the personnel of international agencies, again both technical and general, in local field operations, in host country capital cities, as well as in international headquarters cities. Under these conditions, personnel management may be an overwhelming challenge.

And yet, the individuals actually doing the work are ABSOLUTELY critical to the conduct of international development. Here are a few of the relevant generalizations on this point. *The success of a development program in any particular locality is directly related to the extent of respectful personal contact between the people of that locality and the staff of the development organization* (**8a**).

First-line workers are those who are in face-to-face regular contact with the clientele. In education, these are the local primary or secondary school teachers. In healthcare delivery, these are the "bare-foot" doctors and nurse-midwives who actually assist people who come to the local health post for help. And in agriculture these are village level workers in extension, in farm input supply, in purchase of outputs from farmers, etc. *The success of a development program varies directly with the extent to which its "first line workers" are local persons who are selected by and accountable to the group (clientele) to be served* (**8b**).

8.2.2 Recruitment, Selection, and Placement

The basic tasks of staffing include: finding suitable people, selecting them, and placing them in the right positions. And finding suitable people is a challenge at every level—from the global UN specialized agencies, to national government ministries, to local government branches, to NGOs, and to village level acquisition systems.

At the village level, the development worker must be able to communicate with local people. That includes being able and willing to listen to them, hear what they are saying, and understand what it means to them. It also requires the ability and skill to communicate with outsiders who may have something to offer to the village, or from whom the villagers want certain goods or services. And it also includes being able to translate what the outsiders have to say or offer into messages which will be understood within the village.

Many agencies and organizations have complex and well-organized systems for finding suitable people. Where large numbers are recruited in places where there are many unemployed people, there are great pressures on recruiters to select people from their own families, or at least from their own ethnic, social, and economic groups. When the clientele are mostly from different human groups, this can be counter-productive. To protect against misuse of power by recruiters and those who manage personnel selection, large organizations and govern-ments often develop complex sets of procedures. Sometimes these become so burdensome that the whole process breaks down.

For example, most agricultural extension systems require staff who have a certain amount of formal schooling, as well as some training in agriculture. However, on some occasions this has not been possible. When staff in some locations have had to be doubled in size (as a result of government acceptance of large international loans for this purpose), recruiters and personnel managers have had to ignore the rules, and accept anyone who was unemployed or transferable from other positions. Similarly, since political power is everywhere, sometimes government personnel officers are pressed by local politicians to employ people for political reasons, rather than because of any qualifications or interest in the performance of the job. Since these "abnormalities" are real, professional personnel workers have been able to (*a*) attempt to minimize their occurrence, and (*b*) take various steps in placement to minimize the damage to the program and the organization.

At higher levels of technical training, there are additional prob-lems of recruitment. One can assume that well-qualified highly productive people are already employed doing work they like to do. There are exceptions, of course, but part of the challenge is to entice such people to leave their present "good jobs" and take on chal-lenging development work which needs to be done and where the professional challenge may be even greater. Further, it is easy to specify "well qualified", but not as easy to determine the particular qualifications appropriate for a particular assignment. A technical person, for example, may have excellent "paper credentials", such as advanced degrees in the subject matter, but have relatively little practical experience in actually doing the work. Others may have great practical skill in doing the work, but not sufficient formal training to qualify according to job specifications. Too often the persons doing the recruiting confuse the preparation for competence (as indicated by paper credentials) with actual competence, which comes only from practice in doing the work.

Some suggestions in this regard were made to the World Bank by the environmental economist Herman Daly, after six years of work within the World Bank, and on the occasion of the naming of a new president of that organization:

There are two entry paths to become a bank staff member: as a mid-career recruit, or as a Young Professional, usually straight out of graduate school. Rapid promotion of the latter by powerful bureaucratic patrons in return for filial loyalty soon results in there being two kinds of people in the bank: those who are Somebody within the bank, but nobody outside the bank (Promoted Young Professionals); and those who are Somebody outside the bank, but nobody within the bank (mid-career entrants). Abolish the Young Professionals emphasis, rely more on mid-career recruits who have some independent experience. The bank's unique combination of external arrogance with internal obsequiousness results from the too-rapid promotion of young loyalists to their level of incompetence (Daly 1995: 10).

At their best, recruiters are able to encourage large numbers of qualified people to apply for vacant positions within an organization. Then the next task is to *select*, from among those persons, the individuals to be appointed. In selection, personnel workers can examine application forms, letters from applicants telling why they should be employed, letters from other persons (referees) who recommend the person, interviews with the individuals who are applying, and interviews (sometimes by telephone) with others who have worked with the applicant.

A generalization in this area is: *In selecting new recruits, get opinions of those listed as referees and those not listed as referees; those for whom the person works, and those who work for the person; and then have the person observed by people for whom that person will work, and people who will work for that person* (**8c**).

Personal interviews are also important, especially when they are conducted on a face-to-face basis. However, there are risks in first impressions, just as there are risks in having to make the decision without the opportunity for face-to-face communication. There is an old saying among personnel managers which goes something like this: *The selection interview results in important decisions being made on the basis of insufficient evidence collected under artificial circumstances by incompetent observers.*

One way to improve the quality of the evidence is to add a practical demonstration of competence to the "talk only" interview. For example, in selecting a chef for a restaurant, in addition to the personal interview and study of opinions given by referees, it is sometimes possible to give the chef a menu, send her/him to the kitchen with time to prepare the selected meal, and then have the selection committee interviewers eat what has been prepared. This is normal practice in the selection of typists, for example, where, after the interview, each candidate for the job is given an assignment to keyboard some material. The practical demonstration of hands-on skill adds validity and reliability to the information being gathered. (In one case, for example, when the typist had excellent paper credentials testifying to the number of words per minute and errors of past performance, as well as a personal claim to great skill, it was only when confronted with paper in his hands and a typewriter in front of him that it became obvious that he had never before inserted paper into a typewriter.)

In international development activities sometimes personnel selection involves such practical test possibilities. However, there are other instances where such concrete evidence of ability and skill is not feasible. The opinions of others may be the only available evidence. One learns to be suspicious of current employers who recommend an individual very highly. There is always the possibility that the great recommendation is given because they would very much like the individual to leave their employ and go somewhere else (anywhere else, even to your organization).

Here are some additional relevant generalizations: *If all other things are equal, in personnel selection, choice of a person from within the organization, for whom the new position is a promotion, is better than someone from outside. It builds morale* (**8d**). *In recruiting, there is a tendency to see the strong points of people from a distance, and see the weak points of people up close* (**8e**). *In recruiting, the larger the organization, the smaller the number of key people who must be brought in from outside* (**8f**).

For larger organizations, after new people have been selected, the next important step is *placement* in the appropriate job. This is particularly important in rural development organizations, whether they are NGOs working with volunteers who may be available for one or two years, or government organizations, which may be committed to personnel from the date of their first assignment for many years until retirement. If the organization has many different field locations, it is often feasible to assign a new recruit to a location where a senior, experienced staff member can provide a positive role model. It is also possible to rotate new personnel to a variety of different locations during the first years of service, as this provides a better understanding of what the whole organization is doing.

Sometimes in rural development work there is great advantage in assigning a person to the individual's "home district". It may help very much in the development work if a person posted to a place knows the local language well and appreciates the local customs. On the other hand, if the new worker is too well known (as the son of someone "no better than" themselves, whose boyhood may be remembered for some of its mistakes), he may have difficulty convincing anyone, for example, that his training in healthcare or agriculture helped him learn some things they could use. There are advantages and disadvantages in such location, and each placement has its own unique characteristics.

Careful placement of individuals may include some years in a variety of different locations. Some of the major global international development organizations have a policy of rotating professional staff from field posts (in countries where they are executing projects) to the international headquarters, with some years in each. Other global organizations tend to keep field people in the field, but move them from country to country as the years go by.

Continuity is also a major factor in the success of field staff. It may take more than a year for an individual to comprehend enough of the uniquenesses of a particular location to become an effective collaborator with local people. For a professional from another continent, with a different language and culture, it may take more than five years. Effective personnel management may compare the advantages of continuity with the disadvantages. For each profession, for each particular program or project, and for each organization, there will be differences. In international development, this is one critical aspect of personnel management.

8.2.3 Gender and Language Considerations

Gender is a key factor in all aspects of personnel management. For selection and placement it can have a significant impact on program success. For example, in much of the rural world, most farm work is done by women. In selecting field agriculturists to work with farmers, whether the organization is an NGO, a farmer cooperative, or a government agricultural extension system, if most farmers are women, women field workers have advantages over men. They have access to a higher proportion of the women farmers in more different locations and at more different times of day and night. Where women have been recruited for such assignments, they have tended to be more effective than men. Sometimes, lack of sufficient formal education in agriculture has been used as an excuse for not recruiting women field workers. The experience from around the world is that even with less formal training, women are likely to be more effective than men; and as for women with appropriate formal education, they are both willing and able to go to remote rural places, stay there, and do the work.

In many social systems, the placement of women in appropriate locations is particularly sensitive. While traditions in some cultures encourage women to live only within their parent's or husband's household, professionally trained women development personnel have made significant contributions even when their travel burdens have been greater than those of male colleagues. Better access to women clientele gives women field staff a great advantage over men in many types of development programs and projects. Some development organizations have been willing to rearrange program schedules and provide extra travel allowances in order to utilize this advantage.

In Nepal, for example, when the government's Women Development Section first attempted to recruit women with university degrees as field staff in the Production Credit for Rural Women program, they were told that no such trained women would even take the jobs. In the first year, however, they were able to recruit and place six women in six districts. After five years, the program had thirty-two women professionals serving in thirty-two different districts. In Kerala state of India, in 1988, almost half of the professional field agricultural extension officers were women, some of them with more than a decade of successful field experience with both men and women farmers.

According to Vandana Shiva, writing about India,

The recognition that most women in India are farmers necessitates a reorientation in agricultural research, development and extension. An urgent need exists to match research and production systems to the roles women play, and to create mechanisms that strengthen and enhance their roles so that they can contribute effectively to agriculture and food security in the country (Shiva 1991: 18).

The case has been made by many scholars and practitioners that agencies which plan and implement development activities need to increase the proportion of women in their professional staffs. The rationale is found in excerpts like this from Janice Jiggins:

The involvement of women in technology development has to begin from different premises, on the basis of an understanding of the distinctive ways in which women use and develop agricultural technology. If scientists and field-workers talk only or mainly with male farmers, women's distinctive knowledge of plant characteristics, production sites, processing qualities, and so on will never enter the technology development process of modern agriculture. Conversely, incorporation of women's knowledge increases the relevance and effectiveness of scientists' work (Jiggins 1994: 209).

And in a report for the World Bank, Nancy Axinn identified practical actions in personnel management this way:

Clearly, in the South Asian context, an increased number of well-trained professional women are needed in the agricultural extension system to more adequately involve women farmers in extension programs. There are a number of examples in South Asia to refute the assumption of men in bureaucratic and policy positions that well educated women will not live in remote rural areas and assist women farmers. Admittedly, it cannot be assumed that all women will succeed as agricultural extension field level staff, but of the few who have been employed, some are functioning extremely well. In the more conservative areas of each country, there are issues of accommodation and transportation of women staff which have to be resolved. In most instances, government rules and provisions must become more flexible to permit region-specific resolutions of these problems (N.W. Axinn 1990b: 23).

There seems to be broad agreement that the vast cadre of male extension officers already in place at the village level must be encouraged to more effectively involve the women farmers of their locality in extension programs. Increasing the present extension staff's awareness of women's roles in farming, including women's decision making involvement, is the most important first step (N.W. Axinn 1990b: 29).

Similarly, language is a crucial factor. While more wealthy rural people in most districts may know/speak the national lingua franca, or even an international language, in most rural areas many people, especially women, speak only the local language. Field workers in most types of development programs have a much higher probability of success if they know/speak the local language. Often, those who do not know the language upon arrival in an area are able to learn it. Time invested in training and practice to learn language is usually a highly effective investment. This is as true for international experts moving from country to country as it is for local experts moving from district to district within their home country.

In one instance, local researchers from a university planned to interview rural women in a remote community. In response to a request that someone in the group be able to speak the local tribal language, the scientists said that would not be necessary, as everyone spoke the official state language. However, upon reaching the remote site, it was discovered that only men in a few of the most wealthy families spoke the official state language. Everyone else, including the women to be interviewed, spoke only the local tribal language.

In addition to the operational need to have appropriate language skills, some attempt to learn a national language can be a significant asset to international personnel. The simple *attempt* to learn the local language may be perceived as a sign of respect for the people of that place and their culture. International development practitioners who make that attempt find themselves more genuinely accepted by local personnel. The attempt to learn demonstrates seriousness in the enterprise. Beyond that, internationalists who have gone far enough to gain reading knowledge of written languages have access to a rich literature which informs them of cultural, religious, and historical dimensions of the context for their work. This mark of professionalism is associated with the effectiveness of international development activity.

Like language and gender, many other factors—including culture, transportation, ethnic background—affect *placement* of personnel. Those responsible for the administration of staffing in international development can enhance their effectiveness by being sensitive to all of these dimensions of *placement* and taking them into account for each individual being placed.

For international development activities in which *collaboration* is the mode, and the aspiration for operations is that insiders and outsiders work together as full partners, the issues of personnel recruitment, selection, and placement are even more complex. In many ways, the process is more like matchmaking for arranged marriages than like industrial or commercial staffing. Instead of the organization or one of its officers deciding what kind of person is needed, personnel within an organization are seeking partners with whom they can come to basic agreement upon ends to be achieved, even though each comes to the table with a different background, world-view, and perhaps a different basic value system.

Collaborative international development requires consensus among two or more organizations, so that already employed staff may be allowed and encouraged to work with "outsiders" from a different organization. Thus collaboration is called for at two levels: between the different organizations involved and among the two or more different human beings involved. Recruitment may be a career-long extracurricular activity for professionals who are always interested in other professionals as potential collaborators. And selection and placement become a process of extended negotiations which proceed simultaneously at both the interpersonal level and the inter-organizational level.

8.2.4 Training

Another critical aspect of staffing is *training*. It is directly related to *recruitment* and *selection*, as persons better qualified for a position may require less additional training for it. If persons are selected who do not have the necessary level of competence to perform in a job, then a staffing responsibility is to *train* them to be able to do the work.

The success of any training program may be directly related to the extent to which its participants carry out all of the significant activities about which they are learning "with their own hands" (**8g**).

An issue in training which many international development projects encounter is the location of training. Should an individual health worker in rural Bolivia, for example, be trained right at his/her health post, or be sent to La Paz, the capital city for training? Should a livestock worker in Kenya be trained at a school of agriculture within Kenya, or should s/he be sent to the UK or the USA for training? Since many international development agencies support training both within the countries where their projects are located and also abroad, there is often a choice to make. Overseas training may lead to advanced degrees in internationally known universities, which lends prestige and status to the trainee in later years. But the topics studied may be less relevant to situations in the home country. Local training may or may not be more relevant to the local situation; trainers may or may not be less well qualified; facilities may or may not be as adequate as those found abroad.

As with other factors, the gender aspects of training need careful consideration. The cultural traditions of attitudes toward women in any particular region or country are important at all levels of program responsibility. Women who are being trained to work in their own communities need to have training sessions scheduled around daily responsibilities at home or in the field, rather than when it is convenient for the trainer to be there. This often means mid-day or evening classes.

Training programs for women professional development staff who will work in large areas need to begin with consideration of appropriate transportation, office arrangements, and housing. Sometimes this means planning for two women to live and work together in a central area and travel out to their specific districts. In some parts of the world it means hiring women who have family member's (relatives) homes where they can live, rather than expecting them to live with strangers. Increasingly, once cultural norms are understood, women demonstrate willingness to "progress" to new ways of getting to work, such as by bicycle or motorcycle. But these aspects need to be included in the training program so women can assume their positions with confidence. Some training programs, for example, have included swimming lessons for women who did not know how to swim so they would feel more secure walking through rivers.

One of the most important gender-related components of training is designed for the men who are in supervisory or other administrative positions in the organization. While this factor is usually ignored, the men working with women also need training to appreciate the skills and insights women can bring to their programs. If successfully carried out, this kind of training enables women to achieve program goals much more effectively.

In collaborative international activity management, training becomes a process of facilitating two-way communication. Ideally, all training should involve two-way communication. But for operations in a collaborative mode, each party to the collaboration has a responsibility for learning from the other collaborators, *and* s/he has a teaching responsibility to help the others learn. Each collaborator must learn the relevant aspects of the ends and means of the program as seen by the other collaborators, *and* each one must help the other collaborators learn what they need to know about her/his own activities and the rationale for them.

8.2.5 Reward Systems

There are many different ways in which the administration can reward effective performance among staff, and there are ways the administration can discourage (if not punish) poor performance among staff. In a collaborative mode, often the very sharing of professional goals and expertise is the major reward. International training opportunities can be a significant reward for excellent performance. Large organizations usually have formal procedures for rewarding staff with increases in salaries and wages, with increase in rank or job title, and with special recognition like prizes and medals.

For field operations, the means of transportation can be part of the reward system. Village level workers who walk from the office to meet their clientele may be encouraged when a bicycle is provided to them. Some development organizations maintain bicycle pools for such transportation. Others offer low cost loans to personnel who buy their own bicycles. And for those who are "promoted" to larger responsibility, a motor bike may be substituted for the "push" bicycle. At higher levels, four-wheel motor vehicles may be provided, or funds for use on public transportation (such as buses, trains, or airlines).

Incentives for performance of personnel may be related to the reward system of the organization, the reward systems of the culture, and the reward systems of professional reference groups. These three groups of reward systems may be in competition with each other, or they may be mutually supportive (**8h**).

Among agricultural research officers, at least three types of orientations have been identified. Some are really interested in farming people and how to work with them to make life better for them (*clientele-oriented*). Others are more oriented to *professions* such as agronomy, plant pathology, or farm management (*profession-oriented*). And a third group is highly oriented to the agricultural research system, and strives to someday head it (*organization-oriented*) (Cano 1981). Effective personnel management may monitor individual staff in terms of these three types of orientation. Maintaining a balance among the different orientations is associated with effective performance of the organization.

The best managers and administrators are able to identify the most relevant reward systems for their staff members, and provide rewards which will be incentives not only for better performance of the work, but also for personal and professional growth.

For that, however, it is necessary to discover something about the effectiveness of performance of the individual. If the rewards, like salary increases, are merely given for length of service, management is simple. At the end of each year, each individual receives a predetermined salary increase until s/he reaches retirement age. However, while these systems are easy to operate, they do not provide incentives for performance, and tend to militate against personnel investing extra time, energy, and creativity in doing the job. Systems which reward performance do offer extra incentives for good work, but they are much more difficult to administer.

Many organizations make a list of criteria which are used to assess the performance of individuals. This is never a simple matter, but for some jobs it is a matter of describing a product to be produced and then establishing a range of the number of items to be produced, daily or weekly, which is desirable. Then, a supervisor counts what is produced. Even in this simple type of performance evaluation, there are all sorts of complications, as each worker may have a different type of relationship with the supervisor and all types of human phenomena make the measurement complicated. But in international development operations, the criteria themselves are inexact, slippery, and elusive, and estimating the quality and quantity of an individual's performance is difficult.

In a large development organization, the criteria on the list are continuously changing, since the work itself is continuously changing. Robert Chambers, examining professional personnel in international rural development work has contrasted "normal professionalism" with a "new professionalism", which he describes as follows:

The early project process is dominated by engineers and economists, and preoccupation with infrastructure, budgets, schedules, and quantification. The way professionals and organizations think and operate biases the process against poor people. A new professionalism and a new paradigm start with people rather than things, and adaptive processes rather than blueprints. Practical implications for this approach include the need for calibre, commitment, and continuity in field staff, restraint in funding, use of methods of rapid rural appraisal, and support for "learning projects" without deadlines or targets (Chambers 1993: 76).

When a development organization is operating in a collaborative mode, small teams of collaborators approach performance evaluation in a collaborative manner. The team might meet together to assess the extent to which they have jointly achieved objectives, and their successes and failures, both in making project inputs and achieving project outputs. Then each individual member of the group might be asked to make a self-evaluation of her/his own performance as a group member, as well as a similar evaluation for every other member. Especially in groups which have invested time in getting to know each other professionally and personally, these evaluations are shared among all team members. Then the group decides what to change for the year ahead and what to continue in the current manner.

A different dimension of the reward structure of an organization is the extent to which personnel can make a career for themselves within that organization. Some have a "career ladder" which provides for entry of younger people, who may expect further training and professional advancement within the agency over the years. Others merely select and employ people needed for a particular assignment, give them short-term rewards in order to attract them, and then separate them when they are no longer needed. In international development, some government agencies, universities, and UN agencies make provisions for career development within their systems. Others, particularly some NGOs, private consulting firms, and some foundations maintain only a very small administrative core staff, and all others are offered employment on a short-term basis. For some individuals, it is a reward to have the safety net of an organization which offers job security for one's whole career. For others, this is less important. It is a significant matter when the strategy of rewards is being considered for any international development organization.

8.2.6 Interpersonal Relationships

Beyond the aspects of personnel management described above, there are many types of interpersonal relationships which are characteristic of any international, global, or cross-cultural work, and they are important for international development cooperation. These relationships are important because, as William Foote Whyte put it, both individuals and organizations must continuously learn to change.

> In the past, one of the most common strategies used (in agricultural development) was to present farmers with a package of recommended practices and inputs, which were designed to benefit farmers under a wide variety of local soil and economic conditions. In some cases the agricultural bank would not grant a loan unless the farmer agreed to apply every element of the package. This requirement conflicts with the widely reported results of research and experience around the world: In many cases farmers would benefit more if they applied some elements of the package and omitted others while fitting the new elements into their own farming systems. In other words, the package strategy assumes that the professional experts have all the answers the farmers need and what farmers have learned from experience and their own experiments is of no value (Whyte 1991: 65).

Since the global experience in the 20th century has demonstrated that in international development cooperation both professional experts and local people have something to contribute to the process, as well as something to learn from it, the quality of this work is directly related to the effectiveness of two-way cross-cultural communication. A major task of administration is to enhance the interpersonal relationships involved so that all types of people can learn from each other.

Differences in culture *do* make a difference in day-to-day project and program administration. In some cultures, the workplace is very important, and when a person gets promoted on the job, his/her family will reward him/her at home for it. In other cultures, as John and Ruth Useem have demonstrated for South Asia, actual "significant others" are in the family, not in the workplace. There, when a person arranges a very high-status marriage for a son or daughter, others in the workplace may reward them (Useem and Useem 1955).

From the perspective of international development cooperation, there are always interactions between people from one culture and people from another. In addition to interactions of those from one or more outside countries with insiders from another country, there are often interactions with people from a variety of cultures within each of the countries involved.

As those who become professionals in international development cooperation practice in several different cultures, they become changed themselves. Similarly, those from a particular culture who collaborate with outsiders for a number of years also become changed. All of these individuals no longer "fit" as members of their own culture, and especially their own local subcultural modality. Instead, they become members of a *third culture*. Third culture people have transcended their own cultural roots, but not completely, and have also taken on some of the cultural patterns from other cultures, but not completely. This third culture is a phenomenon about which scholars have made significant contributions (Useem et al. 1963).

Becoming a part of the third culture is both an asset and a liability for practitioners of international development cooperation. It helps them in communication and collaboration with each other. It makes it more difficult for them to *represent* their own group in negotiations with the others, as they are able to understand the situation from the perspective of the others. That is why many nation states will rotate diplomatic personnel from country to country. They fear that

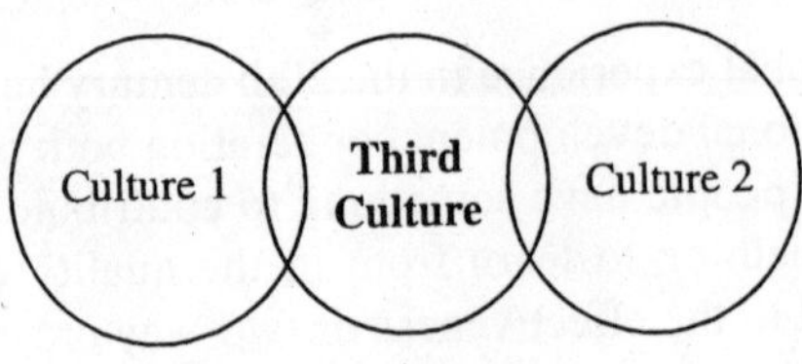

Figure 8.1
The Third Culture

the professional will begin to represent the views of the place to which s/he is assigned, rather than the views of the country which sent her/him. The third culture is depicted in Figure 8.1.

There are other personal and family concerns. Third culture children may have difficulty moving from one school system to another, and some are unable to return to the formal education system of their own country because they lack some of the formally specified "requirements". The depth of the personal problem is illustrated by this event recorded in our field notes.

A colleague at the university (in an African country) invited me to go back to his home village with him for a special ceremony. He had left the village many years before to attend a missionary boarding school, and then had gone to Oxford for two university degrees, but had been back in his homeland for more than a decade. It was the night of the full moon, and we all sat around in a big circle; Ben's father, an elder of the village, sat between Ben and me. Musicians played and drummers drummed. Different groups of men went to the center of the circle, and danced with vigor and enthusiasm. The dancers were grouped by age grade, each group knowing its members very well, and all joining in as appropriate without introductions. At a certain point, Ben's age cohorts moved to the center, and began their dance. The dancers then begged Ben to join them, but he refused. After a few minutes, the dancers came close to where we were seated, and tugged at Ben to join them. Finally, he agreed, and moved to the lively center with them. A short time later, Ben's father, still sitting next to me, shook his head in disappointment. When I asked him what the problem was, he said, "Poor Ben. My poor son. He can wear neither shoes nor sandals. My poor son!"

Ben's father had recognized that his son was part of the third culture. He was no longer "one of us". And the village elder was wise enough to recognize that his son was "really" not one of them either. He had become a highly effective collaborator with foreigners in the international development cooperation activities of his own country. But he had to pay a personal price.

8.2.7 Conflict Management

There are other aspects of interpersonal relationships which add to the challenge of administration. In the leadership of any large organization, and certainly in administering relationships among organizations, there are always conflicts which require management. But when many of the individuals involved are operating outside their own culture, and outside the jurisdiction of their own national governments, there are unique situations in which many minor conflicts must be managed.

Individuals from one system in temporary residence within a second system may develop a "superiority syndrome" (8i). That is because people may remember mostly the good things about "home", and forget the painful and bothersome things there. On the other hand, when venturing into someone else's world, there is a tendency to see things which are less attractive than those remembered at home; to see the painful and bothersome, and minimize the positive. Thus international sojourners often meet in a foreign land and reminisce about the great things back home, and the difficulties at the place where they are trying to work.

When faced with this "superiority syndrome" in some members of a collaborative team attempting international development cooperation, other members who see the world differently will develop stress and in turn, inflict that stress on their "superior" colleagues. When each begins to downgrade the culture of the others, it leads to a downgrading of professional competence and the quality of the disciplines represented, and collaboration degenerates.

The task of personnel management in such situations is to minimize stress by providing positive reinforcement to all concerned. Each situation is different, but all are improved by nurturing a *high tolerance for insult*. Professional practitioners have a special opportunity in these situations, as they can share examples with team members of other situations in which teams like theirs transcended national, cultural, and professional differences in order to get on with the work. If they share with each other in mutually consultative decision-making, and realize others will continuously insult them by virtue of the natural differences, the really professional individual can ignore the insult and get on with the task.

Before leaving the topic of conflict management, there is another aspect of conflict which should be mentioned in a book on international development. In the real world, sometimes nation states, and particularly their governments, become involved in conflicts with each other. Similarly, within any particular nation state, conflicts arise from time to time which can be violent and devastating. Wars, revolutions, and other military encounters arise whether or not the places involved are in the midst of international development programs.

In these situations, collaborative relationships between *insiders* and *outsiders*, when accompanied by friendly interpersonal respect, can be a great advantage to all those involved. *Insiders* can keep *outsiders* informed regarding what is actually happening. And *outsiders* can provide various types of support to *insiders*. The issue for international personnel involved in development work is often whether to withdraw from the scene completely, or attempt to stay with their team and make the best of it. If they leave, there is the hope of being able to return and resume after some months or years, if those then in political power are willing. To stay may mean to attempt to continue in spite of extreme difficulties and personal risk. There are no easy answers to this type of question, and every situation is different. Professional personnel management of international development calls for some thought and preparation for such contingencies.

8.2.8 Economic Pressures

Human greed and corruption were among the issues discussed in Chapter 3. Economic pressures are the most visible manifestation of human greed in the world of international development. Those with the most economic power may be the same people who have the most political and military power, and they may be quite reluctant to share that power with those who have less. This has been a reality of the human condition throughout written history. It is not a new situation. But, the issues relating to human greed constitute an area where well-meaning planners, scholars, and administrators are typically *defeated* politically by powerful commercial, industrial, and agricultural forces.

An example is river water pollution by industries. Planners and government officials may support schemes which can clean the water, or at least make it relatively safe for drinking by people and their livestock. But on every continent—from Malaysia to the US, from Brazil to Kenya, from Poland to Australia—there are examples of national decisions where the economic greed of a few with power has defeated the efforts to protect the natural resource of water for future generations.

In India, when factories dumped toxic waste into rivers in one location, the minister of environment threatened to close the plants. But wealthy industrial investors had more political clout than she did, and were able to defeat her environmentally sound effort. Heavily polluted streams have been a concern of activists and some government officers in South Asia over the years, but the pollution remains. As in other parts of the world, the level of political corruption in South Asia is a continuing concern. It is also a concern in Argentina and Russia and Nigeria and China and Italy and Mexico and the USA.

The economic pressures include a wide range of circumstances. They range from the multimillion dollar international scandals, to the "normal" expectation of small bribes for any service rendered by local petty bureaucrats, to traditional cultural requirements. Thus, if the local colleague of an international development worker is given a home in which to live during service on a development project, relatives may assume that their children will be allowed to live in that (perhaps larger and better equipped) home. From that innocent beginning, it may later be assumed that, if an international scholarship program is involved, of course other relatives will be selected. And beyond that, other economic pressures are likely to be placed on the worker. Managing these can be an overwhelming series of problems, or it can be made part of the expected routine of administration.

Some types of family pressures are not related to misuse of public resources, but do interfere with development activities. For instance, many projects in rural development are in relatively remote locations without access to the amenities found closer to urban centers—like schools, hospitals, shopping centers, and cinemas. For such locations, it is difficult to find personnel who are willing and able to take up residence and perform the work. This includes technicians, international specialists, administrators, and all other types of persons who might be involved.

When an excellent agricultural researcher in Ghana is offered an assignment in the remote Afram Plains, he might agree with enthusiasm. But as travel plans materialize, and as his wife and children make preparations to change their residence to the village, it is not unusual for grandparents to intervene. One might say, "You are not going to take my grandson to that place. There will be no proper school for him, and his later career will be spoiled." Another might observe, "If you force my granddaughter to live in a place like that, she might never reach three years of age. There are no proper hospitals, not even a modern health post! What will you do if she contracts a serious disease? You are definitely not responsible parents!"

Similarly, for a two-career couple, either the wife or the husband might discover that there is a much wider array of job opportunities in a metropolitan area. Why should the family relocate to a remote place? Headquarters personnel in international agencies are notorious for resisting field assignments on the grounds of their children's education. Again, creative program administration will take into account the fact that all staff members are human beings, and attempt to make provisions for health, education, appropriate lodging, transportation, etc. Sometimes a leave of absence is necessary; for some locations these must be more frequent than for other locations. And sometimes, salaries and allowances must be adjusted in order to make remote locations more desirable.

8.2.9 Local Culture Relationships

Those who live in the vicinity of a rural development activity are important potential partners. Whether it is a new irrigation scheme, a health post, a school, or a rural credit program, it will tend to be rejected by local people when it is first introduced. There is always a local power structure; there is always politics; and there are always pressure groups. *The more pressure groups have been involved in the early planning of a project, the easier it will be for implementation administration to gain their support as the project moves along* (**8j**).

But professional personnel management requires acknowledgment that local people are also human. They have needs and interests. They were around before the project began; and they may be expected to be around after the project staff are gone. If their support can be gained, the probability that project objectives will continue to be achieved after the outsiders have gone is much greater. It may be desirable to employ some of their sons and daughters. It may be necessary to adjust working days and hours to local customs. It may be desirable to participate in local reward structures. When special personnel support services (such as a clinic, a primary school, or a store for basic foods) are brought to an area for use by project personnel, it may be appropriate to share them with local residents.

To the extent that the operations utilize a collaborative mode, the more local people see themselves as equal collaborators with the outsiders, the better the chances for project success. Collaboration between project implementation personnel and local residents may be the most significant collaboration in international development cooperation. Outsiders tend to need insiders more than insiders need outsiders. Getting outsiders to appreciate that and make daily efforts to demonstrate genuine collaboration is another critical task for development administration.

8.3 Implications for Professional Practitioners

The large number and diversity of organizations in the international development field, and the complexities of personnel management within them, are important areas about which international development practitioners need some understanding. Directories, annual reports, periodicals, and other publications are available, and through them one can keep informed about the changing collection of organizations which conduct most of the work in this field.

There is a tendency for individuals with experience in one particular type of international development organization to assume that it is the only kind, or that all the others are like it. The professional in this field is aware of the great variety of agencies and organizations involved, of the different strategies they utilize, and of the career opportunities they offer.

Not all professionals can be trained in personnel management, but all need to be sufficiently acquainted with the field to realize it can help. They must be aware that there is a literature about staffing, and that professional help can sometimes be accessed in such matters as recruitment, selection, placement, training, reward systems, performance evaluation, and interpersonal relationships.

The practitioner can be aware of cultural/social biases which may need to be challenged to bring about effective staffing. For example, in diplomatically-sensitive situations in which women personnel are actually better able to implement certain activities than men, but where the surface social pressure says that is impossible, the practitioner may be able to identify the types of individuals who can legitimize such recruitment. The professional practitioner may also be able to support women staff members within local cultural limitations. Careful, sensitive, informed practitioners may be able to achieve what is typically not achieved in such situations.

The practitioner of international development encounters the same range of personnel problems that face any administrator. But the professional practitioner should recognize that there are *ideals* in personnel management, and while the *real* situation seldom matches the *ideal*, there are opportunities to move in that direction. That recognition, in itself, is a step toward more effective performance in international development cooperation.

CHAPTER 9

Directing Development Organizations

We are all part of a world system that perpetuates poverty and deprivation. Those who are poor and deprived do not wish to be poor and deprived. We who are well off and have power say that poverty and deprivation are bad, and should be reduced or eliminated. Yet poverty and deprivation prove robustly sustainable. Why?

Robert Chambers 1995: 14

Every organized group needs direction. In some organizations, there is a formal designation of one individual as director. In other organizations there are different titles for the designated individual, such as chief, president, administrator, coordinator, dean, head, or chairman. The function of *directing*, however, is typically carried out by many individuals in an organization, and they might include the top administrator, several co-workers at the top of the organization, and then the heads of various units within the organization.

9.1 Leadership

When an organization emphasizes internal collaboration, the directing function is usually widely shared, with each collaborator participating in decision-making. However, if the organization is involved in international development cooperation and strives for a collaborative mode, that shared decision-making includes persons in the collaborating partner organizations. The organization gains strength in two ways from this collaboration. Programmatically, the goals for local activities and the means for implementing them are more likely to fit local conditions when local people are genuine collaborators. Administratively, the interpersonal partnerships themselves provide vigor, energy, and enthusiasm for the joint work of the international development cooperation.

Reflecting on his experience in Sri Lanka, in an international development situation where genuine collaboration was involved, with insiders and outsiders learning from each other, Norman Uphoff identified *ideas*, *ideals*, and *friendship* as three sources of social energy. Using the "zero-sum" concept mentioned earlier, he summarizes the relationships as follows:

1. Ideas are positive-sum because *they can be given to others without being lost*. There is some loss of control over them, and there can be a loss of meaning and sharpness in the transmission. But passing an idea through someone else's mind, with its own experiences and insights, is likely to add to the richness of the idea rather than reduce it. And ideas shared with others usually acquire more significance and power. So the sharing of ideas usually has more pluses than minuses.

2. Ideals are positive-sum because *they direct thinking toward common interests* and away from purely selfish notions. They justify actions that serve interests beyond one's own by identifying one's own interests with those of the community. The Golden Rule of "doing unto others as you would have others do unto you" is the most elementary of norms, but it can be elaborated in more elegant philosophical theorizing. Ideals, however insubstantial they may seem, can produce substantial results.

3. Friendship is positive-sum because *it leads people to mutually value each other's welfare*, expanding the satisfaction obtained from finite benefits to either person. At micro and macro levels, it multiplies the effort people will make to achieve common goals or to maintain the status quo in the face of adversity. Selfish motivation can accomplish the same, so it should not be disdained. But to reduce "human nature" to only selfish motivation and to exalt self-centered behavior ignores and even discourages the potentials for productivity and creativity that exist... (Uphoff 1992: 379–80).

These ideas are relevant to the *directing* function because directing an organization is more than the management of it. It also involves leadership, and leadership is qualitatively different from management. Toward the end of the 20th century, organizations of many kinds had perfected management abilities and skills, but tended to be suffering from an extreme shortage of leadership!

Leadership must provide inspiration to the membership of an organization. It must also convince those outside the organization to support it. *A major responsibility of top leadership is to explain and clarify the doctrine of the organization, on a continuous basis, to the staff of the organization, to the clientele, and to those who provide or might provide outside support to the organization* (**9a**). Thus a successful leader must thoroughly understand the doctrine of the organization, and have skill in interpreting it to personnel of the organization at all levels, as well as to those it serves and those who support it.

9.1.1 Leadership Styles

Administrators of organizations exhibit many different types of leadership styles. In international development cooperation, different styles may be appropriate and necessary in different locations, even for one individual administrator. There are no generalizations, or recipes, for effective leadership which will work everywhere. But matters of authority, responsibility, and accountability are important everywhere. Therefore, many propositions are presented in this section, in order to be helpful to practitioners.

There are three ways in which administrators get things done: (a) command, (b) authorize others to act, and (c) stimulate people to act in the direction desired (**9b**). In this regard, the skills of an administrator are similar to an effective teacher or a good communicator. If s/he can stimulate others in the organization to take the actions seen as desirable by the administrator, the organization will be more likely to achieve its programmatic goals.

In many places, a sound leadership style is for the administrator to continuously interact with staff of the organization by expressing satisfaction with their work. Whenever anyone accomplishes something, no matter how large or small, the administrator will express appreciation to the individual, and also make that appreciation known to others in the organization. *Leadership in some cultures may be strengthened by providing positive reinforcement to follow- ers* (**9c**). In other cultures, leadership may be more effective if it never shows appreciation for workers' performance, and may always need to be negatively critical about performance, no matter how excellent it is. Thus, leaders need to know the cultures, and even the subcultural modalities, of their personnel and react to them appropriately. For those in global organizations, where many different cultures are represented in the staff, excellent leaders must transcend these differences and inspire different groups within the organization in ways appropriate for them.

An anthropologist who analyzed public administration in his own country came to this conclusion:

> As the level of responsibility increases within the administration, fewer decisions are actually made. Making decisions can be a very risky business. By making decisions you can make mistakes or sometimes hurt the interests of an individual who, in all likelihood, is a member of a powerful *afno manchhe* (one of us) circle. Doing something means taking responsibility for it, and when something is done badly, then failure is attributed to incompetence. To keep an administrative position for as long as possible, the best strategy is to act as little as possible, so that the danger of dismissal is diminished. A general rule for working in such a bureaucracy is: The lower you are the more active you are, because you have high aspirations and are working hard to realize them. The higher you are, the greater you are at risk and the less you do (Bista 1991: 110).

Some generalizations, as presented in this section, are useful in many international development situations. After all, *administrators everywhere make decisions, delegate, implement programs, and give direction to programs (and sign many documents)* (**9d**). The parenthetical quip at the end of this proposition was added after one two-year assignment as national head of a UN agency in one country. Administrators at higher levels, because they are accountable for everything done by the organization, and all of its members, must put their signatures on many, many documents.

This reflects the reality that higher administrators can delegate *authority* to others, who will then be authorized to carry on certain functions within the organization. However, they cannot DELEGATE

ULTIMATE *responsibility*; that aspect of administration can only be SHARED, NOT DELEGATED. In the simple matter of signing letters, some organizations delegate authority to sign to many individuals. Other organizations merely delegate responsibility for taking actions (like drafting letters) to lower officials in the organization, but insist that the higher administrator is the only one "authorized" to sign the letter. In either case, the highest administrator is responsible for what is done, no matter who does it, and can be held accountable for what is done by others in the organization.

For example, in the simple organization chart illustrated in Figure 7.1 in Chapter 7, if the chief authorizes A to be the treasurer and keep the organization's money, he may share responsibility with A for that money. But if A takes the money and leaves the country, the chief is still responsible for what happened, and can be held accountable by higher authorities. Thus, a major consideration for all administrators is *what and when to delegate. The effectiveness of administration may be related directly to the extent to which duties and authority delegated are in inverse relationship to their importance* (**9e**). Therefore, top administrators must sort out which duties to delegate and which to retain. The more critical a duty is to the survival of the organization, the higher in the structure should be the delegation.

Administrators make mistakes in both directions—sometimes they delegate too much; sometimes they delegate too little. For example, in financial matters, the top financial officer of an irrigation scheme may delegate authority to field officers to purchase necessary small equipment up to a certain amount of money. For larger sums of money, they might need to make a written request in advance to the financial officer. If the pre-delegated amounts of money are too small, then individuals will frequently interrupt the other financial officer with requests for more money. Top officials drown in an excess of small tasks if the delegations are too small. On the other hand, if the delegated amount of money is too large, some field officers might make purchasing errors which result is serious losses to the irrigation scheme.

Whenever you have the right to delegate, you have a right and a responsibility to withdraw the delegation if you cannot correct its misuse. But there is a danger of withdrawing too much (**9f**). As mentioned, knowing what and when to delegate is part of the art of administration. Experienced administrators learn to know their staff, and know the duties and responsibilities involved. Delegation, like other skills, is learned through practice, with trial and error, some risk-taking, and gradual increase in individual skill.

An administrator may be more effective if someone else is assigned to be "acting" when s/he is away for any length of time, or beyond communication. A permanent type of delegation (used as and when needed) tends to be best (**9g**). It is typical in a large formal organization, when top administrators are away from their assigned posts, to have formal letters or announcements sent throughout the organization designating the individual who is "acting for" an absent administrator. For diplomatic assignments, when a representative of an international organization will be away from her/his place of assignment, official notification of such acting assignments may be sent from international headquarters to the protocol officer of the country involved. In these situations, it is often appropriate for informal discussions to take place first with appropriate officers of the host country, consulting with them about the need for the absence, and the competence of the "acting" individual to serve as temporary replacement.

In contrast, in small collegial groups, it is common to merely inform everyone about "acting" assignments by word of mouth. To the extent that the group uses a collaborative mode, all members might be involved in the decision. And in such groups, all members may take turns serving as acting head.

9.1.2 Leadership versus Management

Leadership styles have been discussed in Section 9.1.1. As mentioned, one of the major tasks of the administrator is communication with the members. *The extent to which the goals of any development program will be achieved is directly related to the extent to which they are clearly understood by those responsible for carrying out the program* (**9h**). Just as it is important for leadership to constantly explain the doctrine of an organization to all those involved, program goals must also be communicated. The more collaborative the organizational behavior, the more likely that those involved in carrying out programs will know and understand the goals. That is because they helped select the goals. In any event, since leadership is accountable, it is appropriate to take steps to be sure everyone involved understands what the programs are trying to accomplish.

In international work, since there are great variations in cultural expectations, leadership must be expressed differently from place to place, and from time to time. Nevertheless there are some commonalities. *Characteristics of effective administrators include: flexibility, high intelligence, creativity, ability to work with and judge other people's performance, and unusual energy* (**9i**).

Leaders attempt to achieve organizational objectives through COMMUNICATION, COOPERATION, COORDINATION, and CONTROL. These are different from each other, with communication generally being the easiest to achieve, and control the most difficult. And all of them are more achievable with a COLLABORATIVE mode of organizational style than with the more common TOP-DOWN type of style. *The effectiveness of administration tends to be related directly to the extent to which an administrator is successful in gaining cooperation of informal groups within the organization* (**9j**). Moreover, *morale is a key to effective administration. Wide participation of the group is related to high morale* (**9k**).

Communication, as discussed in Chapter 6, refers to the exchange of ideas among people. Like the other "C" words in the previous paragraph, communication is the essential process by means of which human beings relate to each other, and therefore the essential process of organized human activity, and thus of administration. The other words refer to more than that. *Cooperation* means all parts of an organization functioning in harmony; the act of working together jointly. *Coordination* implies some control to assure cooperation, and perhaps systematic assignment of functions, either among units within an organization or among different organizations. Coordination is frequently resisted among members of different organizations (as, for example, among the specialized agencies of the UN system) because each feels their own territory, or sovereignty, is being intruded upon by the others. But vigorous, creative leadership is often able to achieve coordination.

Control means securing effective action or integrity, or both. *Power* means the right to determine the action of others. However, power based on the "right to power" is not the only kind of power. There is also a power, even an authority, which comes from personal qualities, like superior skill and superior knowledge. For example, knowledge itself bestows upon the holder a type of power which can be used within the organization, or outside of it.

An administrator may have to compromise on minor things in order to get agreement on major things; a gradual meeting of the minds is better than compromise. Compromise, at the right time and level, is the essence of statesmanship (**91**). Unanimity can sometimes be developed through getting the facts and sharing them among all those involved (collaborative mode). Experienced administrators gain these leadership abilities and skills through trial and error, although there are various types of training programs designed to help people understand the important ideas and work toward acquiring these abilities and skills.

9.2 Leadership Tasks

Administrators have many tasks to perform. These usually include some of the functions they performed before they were assigned to administration, some tasks which others in the organization also perform, and other tasks which are uniquely those of administrators. *Time management* is a task which is required of everyone in the field of development, as in other walks of life, and is culturally conditioned.

9.2.1 Time Management

In some cultures, if you ask people if they would like to eat dinner, they look at their watches. You may get responses like, "It isn't even 7 p. m. yet, and I don't usually eat until closer to 8 p. m." In other cultures, people may not even have access to a clock, and will give you answers in terms of how hungry they are. (And in still other cultures, eating is a sacred ritual, and people do not eat with strangers at all; only in the intimacy of their immediate family.) The point is that the concept of *time* has different meanings in different situations.

In administration, however, time is a concern for several reasons. One is that the individuals involved in an organization *always* have other demands on their time, beyond the demands of the organization. But administrators, who are human beings, also have other demands upon their time, and are more or less effective in their performance depending on how they are able to manage their time. Ineffective time use by administrators can reduce the effectiveness of others in the organization. Effective management of the administrator's own time can improve the performance of the entire organization.

Here is a generalization which has been useful to some administrators. *Division of time and attention: determining what to do is policy; execution is doing it. The higher an individual is in the hierarchy, the more of her/his time and attention should be devoted to policy and the less to execution. Conversely, the lower an individual is in the hierarchy, the more of her/his time should be devoted to execution, and the less to policy. (But policy is actually made at every level.)* (**9m**).

Time management often requires difficult decisions. It is not a matter of choosing to invest time in an important task versus an unimportant task. Typically there are many tasks, and all of them are very important. Then the choice relates to what is crucial, and what can wait for a later time. Sometimes it is necessary to be very tough, even crass. This happens in such matters as allocating time to one's family versus the organization. It also happens in time allocation to one's personal health and fitness. When an administrator decides to avoid luncheon meetings, and save the time for physical exercise, criticism will come from others in the organization. If an administrator decides to accept invitations to small dinners, but avoids participation in large dinner meetings, there will be criticism. The task is to know which events are really the highest priority, and then be prepared to withstand the criticism. Actually, a high tolerance for criticism is an important characteristic of top leadership.

9.2.2 Decision-making

Making decisions is a central task of leadership. Important decisions are the most difficult, because they are not simple matters of choosing between the "good" choice and the "bad" choice, or the "right" answer and the "wrong" answer. They are decisions in which there are several alternatives, and none of them are completely desirable. Often, they are a choice between one undesirable alternative and another undesirable alternative, and the issue is which of the two "bad" choices will have the most severe negative consequences afterward. If the "bad" choice must be made in a time of stress, collaborators can be a great asset. Unfortunately, those are the times when committed collaborators tend to be hard to find.

There are no general rules for decision-making, as each serious situation requires identifying the alternatives, weighing the alternatives, attempting a forecast of the probable consequences of each alternative, and then making the choice (**9n**). Here are some personal examples:

Henry was an important head of a major international development cooperation project. He had been traveling on home leave, and then to international headquarters, through several changes in climate. By the time he reached his work station, he seemed to be suffering from a severe cold. After several days of combined rest and work, however, his health worsened instead of improving. He ran a high temperature, and couldn't sleep. As he lived alone, his local counterpart tried to convince Henry to see a doctor, but he refused. The counterpart convinced his housekeeper to stay in the house overnight, and was telephoned at midnight because Henry seemed to be having convulsions.

When the counterpart took a look at Henry, who was by then unable to carry on a meaningful conversation, he got back in his car, drove to the home of an excellent local physician (at around 2 a.m.) and drove the doctor back to Henry's home. The doctor urged that an ambulance be called to take Henry to the city's main hospital. But Henry, who could only exchange a few words with them, insisted on staying home. What to do?

At this point (about 3 a.m.) the counterpart decided to telephone the administrator accountable for all projects of Henry's organization in the country. That administrator, in turn, got a vehicle and rushed to Henry's home. The doctor and the counterpart explained the situation, and urged that since Henry had no family in the country, and that since he had refused to go to the hospital, it was up to the administrator to decide what to do! The physician pointed out that Henry was in very serious condition, and that only in the intensive care unit of the hospital was there equipment with which a diagnosis could be made.

The administrator leaned down over Henry's head, and whispered in his ear, "Henry, everyone thinks you should be moved to the hospital. Don't you agree?"

Henry grunted, and the administrator declared to the others. "Henry has agreed to go. Call the ambulance immediately."

The decision had been made, but that isn't the end of the story. Omitting details, in the diagnosis process, the physicians and laboratory technicians discovered what no one else in the country, or in Henry's organization knew: Henry had diabetes, had had it for many years, but failed to mention it at the usual physical exams. His blood sugar levels were higher than the physician had ever encountered, and a series of emergency steps were taken, which resulted in his recovery.

There is risk, of course, in all decisions. But managing risk and uncertainty are normal tasks for administrators of international development activities. And while mutually consultative decisions are recommended throughout this book, along with a collaborative style of leadership with full participation of all those concerned, there are times when the accountable administrator must make very difficult decisions. In the normal course of events, administrators have the alternative of delaying a decision. But the delay itself is a decision. These come along when there is an emergency, such as a medical emergency, when the individuals involved do not agree with each other, and when administrators are not able to achieve consensus. Then what?

A rather large group of international staff of one development project, representing many different countries, were all located in a very remote village in an African country. On a warm Sunday afternoon, the local staff and their international counterparts were enjoying outdoor sports for recreation when one of the international staff, called Charlie, collapsed. The local physician suspected a heart attack, but had no instruments to verify that. The project manager made arrangements for a vehicle to race to the nearest city and borrow a portable electro-cardiograph machine.

Charlie had been carried home, where his family and the local nurse kept him lying flat, and made him as comfortable as they could.

The EKG equipment arrived, but it required electric power, and more special arrangements were made. The generator was noisy, but the physician tried to make an electro-cardiogram. In the meanwhile, a cylinder of oxygen was found by some local engineers, and a makeshift arrangement was made so that oxygen could be given to Charlie to ease his breathing.

The physician sought out the Project Manager to inform him that he was unable to confirm the heart attack with the EKG machine, since the electric power was so variable that voltage fluctuations destroyed the credibility. But he recommended that the safest thing was to keep Charlie as quiet and comfortable as possible, and let his body recover.

Soon after the physician left the Project Manager's home, three members of the international team, who happened to be veterinarians, arrived with a suggestion. They said they had a drug which they used on farm animals, and said it would strengthen Charlie's heart. The Project Manager urged them to make this known to the physician. But the group said they already had informed the medical doctor, but that the physician said he lacked the proper equipment to monitor Charlie's vital functions, and the drug was unsafe without that.

A visit to Charlie's home brought bad news to the Project Manager. He was informed that Charlie's heartbeat, which had been irregular, was slowing down gradually. A consultation with the physician let the Project Manager know that Charlie was weakening. But the professional opinion was that the safest thing to do was not to administer the drug, but merely wait, and hope that Charlie's body would regain its strength.

The Project Manager went home to wait it out (by now late in the evening). But soon a group at his door insisted on a meeting. They were wives of other international team members who claimed that Charlie's heart rate was continuing to slow down, and that the international veterinarians had the only hope for Charlie with their drug. When the Project Manager reminded them that the medical doctor had good reasons not to use the drug, the group became angry. "Charlie is going to die", they said, pointing fingers at the Project Manager, "and it will be your fault!"

After this group left, the international Project Manager went to see his counterpart, the local chief executive. The Project Manager asked his advice, both as an old friend and as co-leader of the project. But the local colleague merely said, "You are the Project Manager. Officially you are the administrative head of the international group here, and you must make the decision. I cannot even give you my opinion, as that would be inappropriate."

During that night, delegations of colleagues on both sides of this issue came to the Project Manager's home to plead their case. Reports from Charlie's house were of gradual decreases in his heart rate. It was still slowly, slowly, going down. Occasional conferences with the physician, who stayed with the case all night, all indicated his clear preference not to administer the drugs.

Administration is often a lonely task, particularly for individuals at the top of any organization. And, as some have suggested, decision-making is relatively easy when there are clear alternatives and there is good evidence by means of which to predict the consequences of the decision. But there is a tendency that the more important the decision, the less valid evidence there is by means of which to predict the outcome of any particular choice. Thus, the tougher the decision, the less likely that the results will be predictable in advance. (In everyone's life there are such important decisions, like whom to marry.) For administrators, the more critical the decision, the more lonely the administrator is likely to be. And when the consequences of the decision may be a matter of life or death, it can be very lonely.

Towards morning, with Charlie's pulse rate still going down, the Project Manager made tentative arrangements for some space in a refrigerated cold room to be cleaned and reserved. This was preparation for the unlikely event that Charlie might die, as there were no embalming facilities available, and the family would want the body preserved and sent to his home country for burial.

Fortunately, these arrangements were not needed. Soon after dawn, a runner came to the Project Manager's home to inform him that Charlie's pulse rate was beginning to rise again. Rushing to the home, the Project Manager found the doctor, who confirmed that pulse rate was continuing to rise, and he happily announced that Charlie had survived the crisis, and was beginning to recover. As the weeks went by, Charlie recovered sufficient health to be medically evacuated to his home country. There he regained full health, and was able to work successfully for many more years before retirement.

Thus, the administrative task of decision-making has its risks and uncertainties. Most decisions are not as challenging as Charlie's case. But all mistakes have a price, and the successful administrator makes more good decisions than bad ones. However, it is not the proportion of good decisions which is the measure of successful administration; it is the importance of the decisions. Thus, one bad decision in a life-threatening, or an organizational survival-threatening situation, may bring about the dismissal or resignation of an administrator.

On the positive side, an important successful decision can result in promotions in salary and responsibility level for the administrator. More important, good decisions can result in successful achievement of project and program goals!

Administrative decisions always relate to both ends and means (**9o**). Here are some suggestions from experienced administrators:

1. *Make decisions about what to do and how to do it at all levels.*
2. *Emphasize* how *at working level.*
3. *Emphasize* what *further up, but leave much of* what *to do for all levels.*
4. *Decentralize participation and policy-making as much as possible to all levels where the knowledge is. Then make specific delegations of operating responsibility and authority.*
5. *Never make decisions before you need to make them. If you wait, you may not have to make them.*
6. *If you make decisions and make them fast, you must be right more often.*
7. *If you make decisions slowly, you must be right even more often.*
8. *It is the importance of the decision, not the percentage, that makes success or failure.*
9. *One major wrong decision can be final.*
10. *Decisions which relate to morale of human beings are key decisions.*
11. *If postponed too long, decisions will be made by someone further down the line.*

9.2.3 Resource Management

Resource-management and budget-control decisions are important in any organization. In situations where all members collaborate in such decisions, support to administration is enhanced. But administrators at every level have responsibility for such resources as people, money, equipment, facilities, and supplies. While the duties of accounting for these can be delegated to others, administrators have continuous need to be informed about the status of each resource. And since budget is the main instrument for control in most organizations, participation in the budget-making process is normally one of the leadership tasks. Because of its significance to both leadership and management, we discuss it in some detail.

Like most other types of organized human activity, international development functions by means of the flow of money from unit to unit, and from individual to individual. Money is not the organization's reason for being, but it is a means by which its functions are fueled. It is like the blood which carries oxygen and food throughout the body and without which the body cannot survive. If money is the lifeblood of an organization, then its management is critical. Thus, financial planning of development activities is singled out here for special attention.

There are normal tasks for any organization operating in several different nation states. But if the leadership of an international development organization chooses to work in a *collaborative mode* with partner organizations in other countries, the complexity increases. Several of the challenges in collaboration have been mentioned in earlier chapters. With regard to money, there are special problems. First, in any partnership, if one partner is rich and the other is poor, it will be difficult for the poor partner to feel and act like it is an equal partner. But if a (perceived to be) wealthy NGO, for example, from the USA enters into a collaboration with a (relatively) poor NGO in a "poor" country, how can the two collaborate as partners? Their goal may be to select projects jointly and to implement them only when both partners agree that a particular project is the right thing to do in the right place at the right time. However, there will be a tendency for each to realize its "relative power" in the discussion. It is like a partnership between an elephant and a mouse. Of course they may be the only two animals working together toward a common good. But experience suggests that it is easier for the mouse to listen to the elephant than for the elephant to listen to the mouse.

This situation is not easy to overcome even when both partners realize it exists and jointly agree to try to transcend it. Ignoring the wide financial differences does not work. Accepting the differences, and then making special arrangements to take them into account in financial planning, is better.

In one case, the partners made an agreement that when any new money became available, half would be deposited with the operating unit in each country. Sometimes expenditures overlapped, but at least each controlled equal amounts from each donor at the beginning of each financial year. Others have made more specific small operating agreements. Salaries are a typical point of contention. If each individual assigned to a project expects to be paid at the salary rate of her/his home country, there will be great disparities among team members. On the other hand, paying them both the same salary has problems. Each staff member may have, for example, home mortgages, school fees, and health insurance to pay in her/his home country, in that country's currency. There could be an agreement that while working in the field together, all members of an international team of collaborators will receive the same travel reimbursements. But even that is problematic. One may be able to survive very nicely eating local food in local shops and drinking local water. Another might require bottled (purified) drinking water and meals only at "international standard" restaurants.

These little differences and requirements are real. Our purpose here is not to attempt to list them all and provide recipes for overcoming them. Instead, attention is called to the diversity of financial requirements, and to the need for each group of international collaborators and those who administer their organizations, programs, and finances, to respect the differences. Perhaps then they can manage with sufficient flexibility so that the programmatic collaboration can be genuine.

9.2.3.1 Estimates, Budgets, and Financial Control

One responsibility of top administrators in all but the smallest of organizations is financial control. Political mechanisms in governments, governing bodies of corporations, NGOs, and universities hold leaders accountable for controlling the finances. A major mechanism for controlling money, and keeping track of income allocations and expenditures, is a financial plan. These plans are known as *estimates* or *budgets*. The word *budget* is used here to refer to both.

A budget is a plan expressed in fiscal terms. It is also a report. A budget is the major instrument of control in many organizations (**9p**).

Writing from the perspective of governments, Albert Waterson put it this way:

> Since annual budgets are the principal means by which governments authorize and control most of their expenditures, most outlays provided for in the public sector portion of a development plan must be incorporated into these budgets if the plan is to be carried out. From a practical point of view, therefore, the conversion of a public development plan into a series of annual budgets is likely to be the most important stage in the planning process. It is by examining the link between a plan and a budget that one can tell whether or not a government means to carry out a plan.... A government's budget is therefore a key element in converting a development plan into a program for action (Waterson 1965/1979: 201).

What Waterson has written about governments may also be said about most of the non-government organizations which participate in international development cooperation. These include international development banks, UN specialized agencies, private charitable foundations, educational institutions, cooperatives, and others. By studying the operating budget of an organization, or of one of its projects or programs, one can determine what it actually intends to implement.

The many types of budgets used in international development are illustrated below. One of the most common is known as the "line item budget". Here the major types of expenditures to be made are grouped. *Categories within a budget will tend to facilitate accounting if they are organized for ease of record keeping* (**9q**). Development project budgets will group financial allocations by such categories as salaries, travel, supplies and equipment, and facilities.

The simplest kind of budget, for example, for a watershed management project, might look like the one shown in Table 9.1.

This illustration informs a reader that the total amount of money allocated to this project, for a three-year period, in US currency, is $ 1,015,000. And for the purpose of the financial commitment, as mentioned, it can be a useful document. However, for actual operations, more details would be needed. For example, how is this money

Table 9.1
Simple Line Item Budget
Rollings Hills Watershed Management Project 1997–99

(All figures in US$)

Line Item	Amount
Salaries	600,000
Travel	250,000
Supplies and Equipment	30,000
Facilities (Rental)	45,000
Contingency (Miscellaneous)	90,000
TOTAL	1,015,000

to be spent over the three-year period? Will each year be the same as the other two? Will most money be spent in the first year, and then smaller amounts later? A time-phased annual budget could answer those questions, as shown in Table 9.2.

Table 9.2
Time-phased Annual Budget
Rolling Hills Watershed Management Project 1997–99

(All figures in US$)

Line Item	1997	1998	1999	Total
Salaries	100,000	250,000	250,000	600,000
Travel	90,000	110,000	50,000	250,000
Supplies and Equipment	15,000	10,000	5,000	30,000
Facilities (Rental)	15,000	15,000	15,000	45,000
Contingency	22,000	38,000	30,000	90,000
TOTAL	242,000	423,000	350,000	1,015,000

Much more about the operating plan for the project is revealed in this time-phased budget. One might look at this budget and safely assume that there is, in fact, a time-phased action plan for the project, and this budget reflects it. For example, the project planners probably assume that they would not be able to recruit and assign the entire staff to the project by the first year. They may have allowed some time in the first year for the first few members of the project staff to study the local situation, work with collaborators, and then decide what specific types of individuals would be needed in the next two years.

This budget suggests that travel would also not be spread evenly over the three years. It provides for quite a bit of travel in the first year, probably including more trips by fewer people. Then in the second year, probably because several families might be moved to the project site, there is the largest expenditure for travel. And in the final year, with fewer short planning trips necessary, the travel budget is smallest of the three years.

For this particular project, supplies and equipment are different from travel. First-year expenditures may include purchase of some small equipment for measuring flow and sedimentation in the river, and possibly a computer to process that information, along with other field tools. Thus the largest expenditure is in the first year, with gradually diminishing expenditures for the following years.

Since the project may rent the same facilities for the whole three-year period, the facilities item stays the same for the three years. But the contingency item, set aside for unexpected needs which might arise during operations, seems to vary in a different pattern. Since this item is just under 10 percent of the total budget, it seems that the financial planners have decided (in this case) to maintain it at approximately 10 percent for each of the three years.

Both the illustrations above (Tables 9.1 and 9.2) are over-simplifications. One aspect of the oversimplification is that the line items themselves are large generalizations. For each there can be much greater detail. For example, in the salary item, someone has to estimate what types of people would be needed. How many person-months might be arranged in each year? What would the cost for each position be? In fact, the detail of that item, for the first year alone, might look something like this:

SALARIES
  Professional
      Team Leader   12 person months
      Soil/Water Conservationist   3 person months
      Forester   3 person months
      Livestock Specialist   1 person month
      Rural Sociologist   1 person month

Administrative

Administrative Officer/Accountant   9 person months
Clerk   8 person months

Similarly, the more detailed version of the time-phased line item budget might show as many or more subitems under each main line item. Some budgets attempt to be as precise as possible in the first year, and then less specific in the later years. *In a time-phased budget, the greatest detail is needed for expenditures to be made soon; much less detail is appropriate for time periods much further in the future* (**9r**). Thus, in a ten-year budget, since the future is not predictable, it is safer to be much less specific in the beginning when describing anticipated expenditures in the later years.

Another type of oversimplification in these budget illustrations relates to the source of the funds. At one stage of planning the simple budgets can be useful. But for other purposes, people want to know where the money is coming from. And if there are two or more sources, who is paying for what. The simplest budget showing source of funds might merely report:

International Agency Share   US$ 750,000
Host Country Agency Share[1] US$ 265,000
TOTAL   US$ 1,015,000

A more complete display could break down each line item into its components, and then show which subitems and what proportions come from each source. For the watershed management project, the first-year budget might look something like Table 9.3.

For a project using a collaborative mode, the cost-sharing budget might become even more complex, indicating ways in which two or more partners attempt to share costs and benefits evenly. If an institution in one country were collaborating with an institution in a second country, they might jointly build a budget which shows equivalent contributions of each in terms of such items as time of personnel, use of facilities and equipment, etc. Then there might be one or more income columns for "donor" agencies on the budget sheets. Instead of the simple two column headings in Table 9.3,

[1] In local currency or in kind (in kind referring to contributions of labor, materials, housing, commodities, etc., being the estimated cash value of those).

Table 9.3
First Year Expected Income Budget
Rolling Hills Watershed Management Project, 1997

(All figures in US$ Equivalents)*

Line Item	International Agency	Host Institution	Total
Salaries			100,000
International Staff	80,000	–	
Local Staff	–	20,000	
Travel			90,000
International	75,000	–	
Local	–	15,000	
Supplies and Equipment			15,000
Scientific Instruments	10,000	–	
Notebook Computer	5,000	–	·
Facilities			15,000
Office Rental	–	15,000	
Contingency	11,000	11,000	22,000
TOTAL	181,000	61,000	242,000

* Currency exchange rate on date of this budget was US$ 1.00 = Gs 17.24.
("G" is an invented fictional symbol for the host country currency.)

there might be five or more columns for each year, with headings such as: Collaborating Agency A, Collaborating Agency B, Local Donor C, International Donor D, and Total (Table 9.4).

Operators of international development projects encounter special problems when there is more than one outside agency "helping" the project by providing funds. Each agency may have a different budget year (for example, one may be on the calendar year, while another begins each year on the first day of June), and they might even require a different breakdown in the definitions of line items. (One might combine supplies and equipment; the other might insist on separate lines.) Such projects may refuse to accept additional money from "well-meaning donors" in order to avoid the excessive costs of, for example, employing an additional accountant just to fulfill the requirements of a variety of supporters.

As an example, our field notes show that in 1986, the following international development agencies were all providing financial support or volunteers to the Production Credit for Rural Women program of the Women's Development Section in Nepal:

Table 9.4
Collaborative Mode Budget
Rollings Hills Watershed Management Project, 1997

(All figures in US$ Equivalents)*

Line Item	Agency A	Agency B	Local Donor C	Int. Donor D	Total
Salaries					100,000
International Staff	—	—	20,000	60,000	
Local Staff	10,000	10,000	—	—	
Travel					90,000
International	—	—	10,000	65,000	
Local	—	5,000	10,000	—	
Supplies and Equipment					15,000
Scientific Instruments	—	—	—	10,000	
Notebook Computer	5,000	—	—	—	
Facilities					15,000
Office Rental	7,500	7,500	—	—	
Contingency	3,000	4,000	5,000	10,000	22,000
TOTAL	25,500	26,500	45,000	145,000	242,000

* Currency exchange rate on date of this budget was US$ 1.00 = Gs 17.24. ("G" is an invented fictional symbol for the host country currency.)

UNICEF   Major support, personnel and program
SNV   The Netherlands government through noted funds to UNICEF, volunteers, and direct program funding
USA   Peace Corps Volunteers, USAID support in certain districts
FPIA   Support for family planning in certain districts
GTZ   Support for program in one district and specialized volunteers
ILO   Support for special program for women-headed households in one district
UNDP   Support for Water Decade program in one district
UK   VSO volunteers
WIF   Communication assistance in one district

The complications in planning, management, and reporting in this case were increased because the official calendar in Nepal was different from the Gregorian calendar, which specified 1986 for that year. The local calendar had a different and higher number to specify the year, and its months had different names and began and ended about half way through those of most of the "donors". This resulted in the need for one accounting system based on the local official calendar, and different systems for each of the "donors" listed above based on their calendar and their specified financial reporting year. It also resulted in an increase of the size of the accounting staff as well as the numbers of extra evening hours required of top leadership.

Very small projects may rely heavily on work contributions and local materials supplied by village people. For some international partners, it is useful to convert these into "best estimate" of their cash value. For others, words like "contributed in kind", instead of numbers, are inserted in the budget.

All of the types of budgets illustrated above have featured the *line item*. However, it is also possible to rearrange the same budgets according to the major features of the program. *Categories within a budget will tend to facilitate program implementation if they are organized by program areas* (**9s**). A program budget may be less convenient for financial auditors, but it is highly useful to project implementation staff as they monitor progress on different aspects of their work. It is also valuable when leadership is trying to convince their financial supporters that the project is a good investment. Those who contribute financial support to international development activities, in their own country or abroad, are often more interested in such considerations as how many people will be fed, or how much soil and water will be saved, than in *line items* like *salaries* or how much is spent on *travel*. Thus a simple program budget for the Rolling Hills Watershed Management Project, comparable in simplicity to Table 9.2, is shown in Table 9.5.

Table 9.5
Simple Program Budget
Rolling Hills Watershed Management Program 1997–99

	US$ (or equivalent)
Upstream Soil and Water Loss Measurement	55,000
Check Dams and Other Water and Soil Loss Prevention	380,000
Livestock Development on Hillsides	160,000
Village Drinking Water Supply	315,000
Tree Fruit Development	105,000
TOTAL	1,015,000

A simple program budget can be useful in the planning stages, as different vested interests and professional experts can debate the relative value of the different program components. Certain donors might be found who are interested in soil and water loss prevention and who might be willing to contribute to that program line, while other donors might be interested only in safe drinking water. Also, if potential collaborators are exploring each other's interests, competence, and commitment, a program budget will add realism to their assessments.

Like the other oversimplified budgets (Tables 9.1 and 9.2), Table 9.5 is an oversimplification. Each of the program items could be divided into many operating components: a time-phased version could spread various program lines over the three-year period, or even into twelve-monthly units in the first year, and funds could be disaggregated by source, as was illustrated in the line item budgets.

One value in program budgets is their utility in presenting the amounts of money as *investments* rather than merely as *expenditures*. At local levels, people may be more willing to contribute their time and energy if it is for safe drinking water than if it is to make up 50 percent of a budgeted labor item. Internationally, development agency leadership might be more interested in participating in conserving soil and water than in paying the cost of scientific equipment and computers. Even from the perspective of the enthusiasm and concerns of the personnel of the organizations involved, the leadership may find it more feasible to demonstrate that the program budget lines fit the basic *doctrine* of the organizations involved, than to stimulate interest in administratively routine line items.

As in other aspects of administration, it is not appropriate to choose between *either* line item budgets *or* program budgets. It is usually possible to construct *both* line item budgets *and* program budgets, and good financial management of development activities usually requires both.

9.2.3.2 Indirect Cost Items

Another type of item, found in many international development project budgets, has a name like "indirect costs" or "overhead". This item tends to be included when either the funding agency or an executing agency has contracted with another organization to implement, or execute, part or all of the project. Sometimes, such a contracting organization might even subcontract a portion of the work to a third organization. In such situations, the contract may be for the contractor to perform certain tasks (like build 10 km of road, or train five people to use a certain computer software program) in exchange for which the contractor would receive a certain fixed sum of money. In this situation the overall budget might show that sum of money for the contract. This type of contract is called a "fixed cost" contract.

Often, however, the contract specifies a maximum amount to be paid to the contractor, but only as reimbursement for expenditures the contractor has made on the project. In such situations, the contractor is expected to incur the expenditures in doing the work specified in the contract, and then request reimbursement from the development agency. These are called "cost-reimbursement" contracts. (Sometimes such contracts provide for a cash advance to the contractor, and sometimes for withholding the final reimbursement until the work has been satisfactorily completed.) Planners of such projects attempt to anticipate what actual costs are likely to be, and then specify these in line items on a budget attached to the ontract. However, there are so many different items that planners find it more convenient to list the major items like salaries, travel, equipment, etc.

in the contract; group some smaller ones under a heading like miscellaneous; and then group other costs under an item called "indirect costs". Then the indirect costs can be specified as a proportion of the total, or a percentage.

For example, suppose a university contracts with a development agency to supply five professors, each to work three months on a project. The contract might specify reimbursement to the university of the salaries of the professors, their travel costs, their food and lodging costs, and perhaps a general item for supplies and equipment. But the university has other costs. After all, for each professor, there is probably a department chairperson and a dean with certain administrative responsibilities, the costs of which are not reduced when the professor is away on this assignment. The professor may continue to use the services of his/her university library while on this assignment, as well as the services of a purchasing department and a payroll office. And if annual leave is not included in the contract, for each month the professor is on this assignment, s/he accumulates annual leave which the university must later pay. Because it would be impractical to calculate all of these small items for each individual professor and put them in the contract, they are normally grouped for the entire university as a basis for estimate. Then this becomes the basis for the budget item called "indirect costs" which is part of the contract. Sometimes it is calculated on the basis of a percentage of salaries; at other times it is calculated as a percentage of the total contract cost. If the development organization contracted with a private consulting firm for similar work, that firm might also have an item in its budget for its normal profit. It might be named "profit", or it might be included in the indirect cost calculation and be a part of that percentage. Sometimes that item is called "overhead" and includes all of these normal costs of doing business as support to the major items being provided.

At any rate, items with names like "indirect costs" not included in the budget illustrations in this chapter are normally found in budgets or annual estimates for international development cooperation activities.

9.2.4 Monitoring and Evaluation

Similarly, while monitoring the flow of inputs and outputs for any project may be delegated to others within the organization, administrators need to keep themselves informed on these matters. Parallel to monitoring such flows, there is another function of evaluating the impact of projects, both in terms of their stated goals and objectives, and in terms of consequences of the project for the environment, the community, the economy, the political and diplomatic situations, etc. While monitoring can usually be done within an organization, and communication between monitors and other operating personnel should be continuous, evaluation is another matter. Since members of an organization tend to have a vested interest in its success, separate outside agencies are often contracted to do the evaluation of the project's impacts. Chapter 5 has a more detailed discussion of monitoring and evaluation.

9.2.5 Issues of Seriousness

In international development administration, *seriousness* is a key variable. Too often, persons and agencies involved, BOTH in the host country where activities are being planned and implemented AND in the international organizations involved, may not be *serious*. Of course such persons may be serious about something, but it may not be the particular project to which they are assigned. For international personnel, they may be involved, for example, not because they care about achieving the project's goals, but:

- because they need to be away from their home country, or
- because they cannot find employment in their home country, or
- because they can earn more money by being abroad, or
- because they love the country of assignment and want to see it as tourists, or
- because it will look good on their biodata later on, or
- for any other unrelated reason.

Local personnel, for example, may be involved not because they care about achieving the project's goals, but:

- because their regular organization of appointment would like to be rid of them for a few years, or
- because they can make much more money working on an international project than in their normal work, or

- because it looks like a step toward later employment in an international agency, or
- because they hope for a scholarship for international training, or
- because the international project offers a higher level of such perquisites as housing, healthcare for the family, personal transportation, etc., or
- for any other unrelated reason.

Seriousness is an important consideration in any type of organization. However, the complexities of international development activities make seriousness a special concern in international administration. *The effectiveness of a development program usually varies directly with the extent of discipline and seriousness built into the program* (**9t**).

The examples above focus on personal seriousness. There is also the matter of organizational seriousness. In international development cooperation, seriousness can be broken down into three major categories: (*a*) project seriousness; (*b*) personnel seriousness; and (*c*) international supporting agency seriousness.

On the project seriousness side, there are matters such as:

- Whether or not the head of the implementing unit is highly committed to project goals.
- Whether or not the head of the relevant government ministry (for government projects) is committed to project goals.
- Whether or not the project fits host country plans.
- For government projects, whether or not there is a continuing line item in the government budget after the project terminates.
- Whether staff assigned to the project from the local side are on temporary transfers from their regular assignments, or staff are assigned "permanently" to the project.
- The nature of incentives provided for staff performance on the project.
- The extent to which non-project personnel have been sent on international study or travel with project resources.
- The extent of unnecessary personnel in the budget.
- The extent of inclusion of unnecessary buildings and equipment in the budget.
- The extent to which project vehicles are co-opted for non-project use.

With respect to seriousness on the personnel side, such matters as the following provide an assessment:

- The extent to which an individual is committed to the goals of the project.
- The extent of preparation (training) for project implementation.
- The relevance of individual skill and experience for implementation.
- The extent of personal interest in implementation.
- The extent of individual interest in private short-term (financial) gain.
- The extent of individual interest in private long-term (financial) gain.
- The willingness to invest personal time (beyond usual hours and days) in the project.

These are all delicate matters, and information about them is not normally discussed in public, nor is it put in written form. Thus the task of the administrator in estimating personnel seriousness is always difficult.

Then there is the matter of the seriousness of the international funding and/or implementing agencies, often called "donors". Such matters as the following may be assessed:

- The extent to which the head of the agency is highly committed to project goals.
- The extent to which the head of the implementation team is highly committed to project goals.
- The extent to which the project is responsive to the needs of the host country, rather than only to the needs of the international agency.
- The frequency with which agency supervisory personnel visit the field.
- The extent to which the agency subcontracts for implementation personnel, rather than supply them from its regular staff.
- The extent to which the agency subcontracts for services, rather than provide them with its regular personnel.
- The extent to which available funds far exceed what could be used in implementation.

These criteria are merely suggestive, based on personal experience. In any particular international development project, criteria for assessing seriousness will vary. But *the ease of administration is directly related to the seriousness found in the project, its personnel, and the supporting international agencies* (**9u**).

9.2.6 Public Relations

Finally, since every organization has diffuse linkages to various public elements, every administrator must be concerned with public relations. Some large formal organizations have a separate staff department with a name like public relations, public information, or public education. In small, informal organizations, it is expected that the top administrator will pay attention to the public image of the organization. S/he may be expected to take steps to develop a positive attitude toward the organization with groups in the community who may have no direct program interaction with it.

This leadership task is different from many of the others already mentioned, as it has a less direct relationship with implementation of project activities and achievement of project goals. Nevertheless, since a positive working atmosphere can contribute significantly to organizational achievement, public relations is an inescapable part of administration. Successful administrators usually share public relations responsibilities with all other members of the organization, and attempt to keep the entire staff concerned about the public's views of the organization.

9.3 Implications for Professional Practitioners

All professional personnel in international development have a stake in the *directing* aspect of administration. Leadership styles and the skill of administrators with leadership tasks can have a significant impact on achievement of project and program goals. Practitioners in international development who take a professional approach realize that there are always administrative forces in the directions of both continuity and change. Without bringing along those who direct development agencies, practitioners are likely to encounter unnecessary difficulties. And, since at some time in their careers successful practitioners who stay in the field tend to have management and leadership responsibilities themselves, the abilities and skills of directing an organization are part of professionalism.

In the second half of the 20th century, those concerned with financial management of development activities have usually outnumbered others with specialized skills relating to technical aspects of development. The dominance of economists and accountants was an early strength, and perhaps a later weakness, in the global effort to strengthen weaker countries and human groups within them. If anything, there may have been too much concern with money flows, and not enough concern with changing the human condition.

One reason for that problem, however, was the tendency for practitioners involved with international development cooperation to be too specialized in their perspectives and competence. Each thought his/her own field would make the most difference, and the others were somehow less important. As professionals make the transition to the 21st century, it is becoming more apparent that development itself requires cooperation among the various special fields involved.

Therefore, serious practitioners, whatever their individual fields may be, will increasingly need to understand financial planning and other aspects of management. Budget-making is a necessary component of all international cooperative undertakings, and some grasp of the alternatives is useful to various types of specialists. Without it, development professionals will continue to be outwitted by financial specialists and be blamed for the inadequacies of their financial planning and budgeting. Fortunately, as in other specialized areas like personnel management and communication, there are many books on the subject, and opportunities for special courses if required. Since the specifics of financial management vary from donor to donor, and from recipient to recipient, our purpose here is merely to alert development practitioners to the importance of this dimension of the field, and to reassure them that more information is available. When all practitioners involved have some grasp of budget-making possibilities, the probability of the mutual respect required for genuine collaboration will be greatly enhanced.

With a movement in development work toward more collaborative arrangements, especially between host country organizations and international organizations, the need for understanding, appreciation, and skills of both management and leadership in the early phases of the 21st century is likely to be even greater than it has been in the later years of the 20th century. In collaborative leadership, for example, transcending cultural clashes will provide new opportunities for personal creativity. Thus the professional practitioner of collaborative international development in the future will be both an analyst and a critic of the directing done by others, and, from time to time, hopefully, a demonstrator of excellent performance in directing roles.

PART 4

Epilogue

CHAPTER 10

Changing Approaches for a Changing Globe

New occasions teach new duties,
Time makes ancient good uncouth;
They must upward still and onward,
Who would keep abreast of truth!

James Russell Lowell 1819–91

Toward the close of the 20th century, people who have made a career in international development activities are sometimes asked, "But is development assistance being reduced all over the world? Was it a feature of the post-World War II world? Is it now over?"

To the extent that "it" refers to the 1950s model of "foreign aid"—which in the spirit of global charity featured the wealthy western countries "giving" help to their poor neighbors—then "it" should be over. That view of international development has been obsolete for several decades. While it still persists in the minds of some in both the rich and the poor places, we see it as having been replaced by an acknowledgment of *global interdependence*.

We are all passengers on spaceship Earth. While some may, at the moment, have first class seats, and most are crammed into smaller seats (or have standing room only), we are all breathing the same oxygen and drinking from the same global water supply. Without it, none of us can survive.

Whenever and wherever members of one family are fighting among themselves and mistreating each other, others are at risk as the violence grows. Whenever or wherever one family, one clan, one tribe, one ethnic group, one community, or one nation state suffers a breakdown in society and turns to violence, *we are all at risk*. Wherever civil insurrection breaks out, *we are all at risk.*

Wherever people are hungry and starving, *we are all at risk.* Wherever some people are cruelly exploited by others, *we are all at risk.*

At the end of the 20th century it has become increasingly clear that even with great diversity among the peoples of this Earth, we are all interdependent. In spite of the hopes for a world without wars, the evidence toward the close of the 20th century has been that human greed and fear result in dozens of local conflicts, and they are violent and destructive.

At some future time people may accept the idea of a global governance system, with a global police force designed to protect humanity from its own weaknesses. But in the next half century we may, at least, evolve in the direction of more effective global caring—and more global sharing. We have much to learn from each other, and we all need each other's support. It is this global caring and sharing that earlier chapters of this book have referred to as *international development collaboration.*

In some situations, collaboration in international rural development has already replaced international development assistance. We see that as a positive movement, and have written this book to help move the process along. As stated earlier, collaboration between *insiders* and *outsiders*, and collaboration among professionals with different disciplines, different languages, different cultures, etc. is difficult and time-consuming. But the high transaction costs of such collaboration lead to more successful collaboration, and are necessary. Without such genuine collaboration, the professional practice which is necessary will not be achieved!

There is room for optimism about the future. The transition will not be rapid or easy. Instead, realizing that we do not know the future, we anticipate a turbulent and difficult transition. But our optimism pervades our forecast.

Complexity is not new to this planet. Complex physical, biological and human systems have been evolving for a long time. And individuals have been able to ignore them, to deny them, to acknowledge them, or to try to cope with them. Increasingly, the willingness to accept complexity and the systemic nature of our universe encourages our optimism.

The computer scientist John Henry Holland has commented on the emerging field of complexity.

Many of our most troubling long-range problems—trade balances, sustainability, genetic defects, mental health, computer viruses—center on systems of extraordinary complexity. The systems that host these problems—economies, ecologies, immune systems, embryos, nervous systems, computer networks—appear to be as diverse as the problems. But there may be some hidden order, some fundamental characteristics and common interactions inherent in all these systems (Blakeslee 1995).

As part of the initiative of the International Food Policy Research Institute to look ahead to the first two decades of the 21st century, its director-general, Per Pinstrup-Andersen writes:

Actions that the international community, national governments, and nongovernmental organizations take—or do not take—to address integral challenges of poverty, food insecurity, and degraded environments will influence the well-being of current and future generations. For some, including many of the 1 billion poor people, the consequences of inappropriate action or inaction may be more misery and death. The degree of success of our actions will depend on our understanding not only of the nature and causes of the problems we must solve, but also of the linkages between them. These fundamental problems do not exist in compartments waiting to be solved sequentially. They are linked. Attempting to solve one problem in isolation may be inappropriate (Pinstrup-Andersen and Pandya-Lorch 1994: v).

The discussions of continuity and change, of changing perceptions of development, and of the development cycle in Chapter 2 have taken a systems approach, and the analyses and propositions offered in other chapters maintain that approach. Awareness that everything is related to everything else has not prevented the examination of individual components of larger systems. But it has driven us to urge readers in any particular section to look back at some earlier discussion and ahead for some ideas. The written word has the limitation, like a string of pearls, of being linear—each word is preceded by only one other word and followed by only one other word. Different from an artist who paints murals and can show a viewer the whole picture all at one time; those who attempt to convey ideas through the written word must struggle to transcend this limitation.

Nevertheless, acknowledging the complexity of development as the unfolding of the possible, assuming a continuing struggle between continuity and change, is the essence of the professional practitioner's task in international development. In that spirit, we turn again to the series of issues discussed in Chapter 3 and attempt to cast them in an appropriate perspective of the future.

10.1 The Issues Revisited

Sustainability has been used as an abbreviation of everything related to the environment and the need to protect the ecosystem on this planet for future generations. And sustainability, in that sense, is an issue which is likely to become one of the most important aspects of development policies, strategies, and programs in the future. But a broader view of sustainability has to do with the sustainability of the patterns of human behavior and the assumptions about the development process discussed earlier in this book. In an ever-unfolding world, these too will not last forever. They will change, and they should change.

The need for a new orientation in development policy was addressed in an essay in the foreign assistance periodical published by the German government. Ingomar Hauchler points to the low effectiveness of international economic and development policy, and suggests that it is rooted in two outdated paradigms on which the present world-wide strategy of economic development is based, namely that:

1. The western social and economic model optimizes the activation of productive forces—independent of the development stage of a country or its culture—and therefore is best suited to satisfy basic needs.
2. It is possible to launch the development of a society from outside within a few decades—without regard to its cultural and historical background—through external input of money, goods, technology, expertise, and personnel (Hauchler 1994: 4).

He concludes that these two paradigms

have led international cooperation and development down the wrong path.... In the future, development policy must do all it can to stop the loss of skills and self-reliance, the plunder of natural resources, the erosion of cultural values, the violation of human dignity and human rights. Initiatives must prevail which are orientated on these values, and not just on the gross national product.... There must be an end to the manic fixation of development strategy on external inputs and external markets (Hauchler 1994: 4).

Nancy J. Adler has identified another revealing and useful dimension of the changing scene:

As the complexity, turbulence and rates of change in the economic and political arenas increase, societal observers note that people worldwide appear to be retrenching into more and more narrowly defined cultural identities (Adler 1995: 526).

Proprioception means staying in balance with the outside world by using the strength of your inside world...the ability to respond to the constant complexity, chaos, and turbulence of the outside world by using the strength of our competence, professionalism, and most of all, our personal vision from our inside world (Adler 1995: 534–35).

David Korten pushes the challenge to an economic growth perspective:

We are coming to realize that the extravagant promises of the advocates of the global economy are based on a number of myths that have become so deeply embedded in Western industrial culture that we have grown to accept them without examination.

- The myth that growth in GNP is a valid measure of human well-being and progress.
- The myth that free unregulated markets efficiently allocate a society's resources.
- The myth that growth in trade benefits ordinary people.
- The myth that economic globalization is inevitable.
- The myth that global corporations are benevolent institutions that if freed from governmental interference will provide a clean environment for all and good jobs for the poor.
- The myth that absentee investors create local prosperity (Korten 1996: 4–5).

As explained in the UNDP's *Human Development Report, 1996,*

> Human development is the end—economic growth a means. So, the purpose of growth should be to enrich people's lives. But far too often it does not. The recent decades show all too clearly that there is no automatic link between growth and human development. And even when links are established, they may gradually be eroded—unless regularly fortified by skillful and intelligent policy management (UNDP 1996: 1).

The report goes on to compare countries with each other on the seven criteria which make up the human development index: health, education, income and poverty, women, children, environment, and politics and conflicts.

Participation is another continuing issue which is likely to be manifest in different ways in the years ahead. As suggested in earlier chapters, development is not development if those most affected by it have not participated in its planning and implementation. Writing on the "mislaid mission" of adult education, Paul Miller makes this plea for participation:

> Adult educators as leaders will recognize that the United States and the global system have entered an epochal period of change. Political orientations the world over move toward democratic practice, however many the nuances. The future of democratic civil society depends broadly upon the will, the understanding, and responses of citizens. These citizens must now face the gap between technological and institutional innovation, a crisis in urban governance, high rates of more violent crime, the jeopardy of losing a high proportion of youth as productive citizens, the stubbornness of racial and ethnic polarization, and, as mysterious as it is persistent, the spread of cynicism about public life and its leaders. Something resembling a civic entropy now knocks at the gate.... Thus may adult educators, joined in a collective movement, help recover, design, sustain, and animate civic endeavor (Miller 1995: 51).

A similar, perhaps even more global perspective on participation was expressed by Pope John Paul II in his talk to the United Nations in October 1995. He said:

The international economic scene needs an ethic of solidarity, if participation, economic growth and a just distribution of goods are to characterize the future of humanity. The international co-operation called for by the Charter of the United Nations for "solving international problems of an economic, social, cultural or humanitarian character" cannot be conceived exclusively in terms of help and assistance, or even by considering the eventual returns on the resources provided.

When millions of people are suffering from a poverty which means hunger, malnutrition, sickness, illiteracy and degradation, we must not only remind ourselves that no one has the right to exploit another for his own advantage, but also and above all we must recommit ourselves to that solidarity which enables others to live out, in the actual circumstances of their economic and political lives, the creativity which is a distinguishing mark of the human person and the true source of the wealth of nations in today's world (Pope John Paul II 1995: A16).

The *participation* required for development in the 21st century may be more global than merely local. Ideally, people from different communities, different nations, and other different perspectives will increasingly participate with each other. This may be a characteristic of participation in the next half century. It will fit other aspects of globalization as defined by Paul Robertson: "Globalization as a concept refers both to the compression of the world and the inten-sification of consciousness of the world as a whole" (Robertson 1992: 8).

As discussed in Chapter 3, *participation*, *decentralization*, and *accountability* are intimately related issues. For organizations, de-centralization is a way of encouraging more participation and of encouraging accountability to local people. And accountability to local people is a rationale for having them participate, and for decentralizing. These three issues are not likely to go away in the decades ahead. Ideally, practitioners in international rural develop-ment will increase their appreciation for, and abilities and skills to deal with, these issues. They may even receive more support from those at policy levels for this kind of work than was characteristic of the last half century.

The importance of equity for, and the empowerment of, those who have been most disadvantaged and weak is perhaps the most significant conceptual achievement in the practice of international development in this last decade of the 20th century. The logic was stated by the UNDP this way:

> Such national soul-searching has moved human development concerns to the center of national policy debates in many countries. What is the meaning of growth if it is not translated into the lives of people? In the era of opening markets and globalization of trade, does the comparative advantage of developing countries not rest on an intelligent investment in their people? Can development be sustainable if people do not take part in the processes that influence their lives? Are there not alternatives to conventional wisdom in setting development priorities, managing the process and distributing the outcome? (UNDP 1995: 118).

Much of the strategic thinking and planning in international development of the last five decades has stressed increases in production and productivity. Certainly, in the agricultural side of rural development, it was assumed that if farmers could produce more, their families would also consume more, and they would be better off. But the experience in rural development suggests that such is not always the case. Even increasing the efficiency of production sometimes does not result in a better life for those who are the producers. As discussed in Chapter 1, this is especially valid for those who produce large quantities of crops for commercial export, rather than food for home consumption. Equity is a different matter than either efficiency or productivity. And without equity for those affected, they are not likely to perceive change as development.

From this reasoning flows the issue of *gender*, which dominates the UNDP *Human Development Report, 1995*. The issue also received global attention during the Beijing Global Conference on Women.

> Equality is not a technocratic goal—it is a wholesale political commitment. Achieving it requires a long-term process in which all cultural, social, political and economic norms undergo fundamental change. It also requires an entirely new way of thinking—in which the stereotyping of women and men no longer limits their choices, but gives way to a new philosophy that regards all people as essential agents of change and that views

development as a process of enlarging the choices of both sexes, not just one. Providing equal rights and equal access to resources and opportunities to women and girls—as well as to men and boys—is crucial to the goal of reducing poverty, illiteracy and disease among all people. Gender equality is an essential aspect of human development (UNDP 1995: 99).

Writing about women and water resources, Frances Cleaver and Diane Elson made some suggestions for the future which are applicable to many other types of development efforts. Here are their conclusions:

This paper has discussed in detail the potential threats posed by the new policy climate to women's roles in water resources management and the likely consequences for equity and efficiency. In conclusion, the marginalisation of women can largely be avoided if the following key areas are recognised, understood and taken into account by policy-makers:

- that all data should be disaggregated by gender;
- that markets and meetings structure the system but that the situations of women and men in relation to these differ;
- that matching ability to pay and willingness to pay may require redistribution of income to women;
- that not only water but also women's time is an economic good—and that markets are likely to undervalue women's time;
- that gender-barriers to effective and equitable management of water resources are more likely to be overcome if women are organised into movements for change (Cleaver and Elson 1995: 13).

The Beijing Conference was a significant milestone. Martha Chen comments:

By far the most conspicuous change over the decade (1975–1985) was the phenomenal increase in the number and types of women's NGOs in every country of the world and the complex of alliances, networks, and coalitions set up to unite them. A new breed of NGOs, quite distinct from the established international women's NGOs which had long had consultative status with the UN, brought with them a shift in leadership of the international women's movement...although not entirely...from women in the

North to women in the South…this process mobilized thousands more (women) around the world. Another significant result of the many national and international meetings which were part of the Decade was that women came to know one another better and became more widely listened to. Over the past decade (1985–1995), the international women's movement has been very successful in forging remarkable consensus and coalitions around a variety of issues affecting women (Chen 1995: 6).

Writing about women entrepreneurs in Tanzania, but with much wider relevance, Marja-Liisa Swantz says:

The most profound change in Third World societies in recent decades relates to women. Women have entered into public life of African societies as significant actors, although their major contributions to economy are often not recognized as such. Rather than depicting the women of the developing world as deprived creatures, overworked and lacking basic rights, a picture often painted, we have illustrated women's ways of creatively expand[ing] their productive activities into other economic and social fields. In order to maintain economic viability economics must be reshaped to accommodate sustaining economies which simultaneously allow different modes of livelihood (Swantz 1995: 59).

Devaki Jain summarizes the personal side of development:

Economics is about power. Politics is about the control of that power. Poverty is a political issue and has to be sorted out politically. The poor and the powerless have to be brought into political processes if we expect economics to adjust itself to equity. The "poor" know it. It is the elites that can afford an aseptic view of politics. Such a view of politics has to be abandoned. The accumulation of doubt has to be discarded and a commitment forged to support the groundswell especially as it gets an opportunity to express itself constitutionally. Notions of trust in the capability of social groupings—whether bound by geographical or cultural space, including gender—have to be firmly supported (Jain 1995: 33).

The *collaborative mode* of international development activity, as we have been advocating throughout this book, can address the complexity of global needs and the systemic requirements. While far short of a majority, a few of the organizations involved in international development have attempted collaboration as a central strategy. And among these, we see significant achievement.

Within the UN system of specialized agencies, several are involved in collaborative activities including both NGOs and bilateral government development agencies, as well as local governments. FAO, for example, supports many country programs where several local institutions are in collaborative partnerships with similar institutions in other countries, and both national bilateral assistance agencies and international development banks are providing financial support.

From the USA, the Agency for International Development has more than a decade of experience of support for Collaborative Research Support Programs (CRSPs) in which several US universities enter into collaborative relationships with each other and with several overseas partners in other countries. Together they focus on research problem areas, such as production and use of beans and cowpeas, small ruminants, or grain sorghums. The CRSPs have established enduring scientific linkages among scholars and practitioners on a global basis, and promise to contribute long after the agencies which created them have ceased to operate.

In the UK, the Overseas Development Institute (ODI) has sponsored several studies which have focused on collaboration between government development organizations and NGOs (see Arnaiz 1995 and Farrington et al. 1993). A growing consensus seems to indicate that collaboration is an appropriate and necessary aspect of international development activity. The issue now is how to implement more of it.

After an intensive review of one university's attempt to involve itself in collaborative relationships in international rural development, we have suggested that collaborative relationships appear to develop more easily when the faculty members have at least some of these characteristics:

- focus on a problem which is important to the host country collaborator;
- work at maintaining communication channels;
- observe the social norms or protocol of the collaborating institutions;

- share authorship; and
- respect the scientists with whom they are working.

In that particular study, these characteristics were found more often among young and among female faculty members (Axinn and Axinn 1994).

Collaboration in international development in the future is likely to involve new kinds of arrangements in which local people participate in deciding who their outside collaborators may be. Those outsiders may include persons from a variety of different specializations from a combination of NGOs, government units, universities or other educational institutions, banks and private commercial firms, and perhaps people from international agencies. And the local participants will help decide what is to be done, how it is to be done, where and when it is to be done, and by whom. Such decision-making, in a collaborative mode, will not be a one-time affair. It is likely to be a continuous series of iterations before, during, and after the development project.

Practitioners in international development, along with professionals in social and biological sciences, may increasingly take the lead in developing appropriate programs in their own countries. What are the implications of that for international practitioners and scholars? The collaborative mode may become the primary entry point.

The issue of *human greed and corruption*, mentioned in Chapter 3, is not likely to fade away in the next several decades. It is a serious matter and an area of opportunity for creative professional practice. Whether corruption is less in a centralized system or a decentralized system is yet to be demonstrated. While there is hope that accountability to local people is likely to reduce this problem and not increase it, the case for that has not been proven. It remains a challenge to professional practitioners, as well as to administrative leaders and the power centers of each society.

10.2 The Professional Practitioner in Collaborative International Rural Development

A vigorous, dynamic, creative, and insightful response to the issues of international rural development in the 21st century will certainly

demand collaboration, and will require active long-term involvement of professional practitioners and scholars. There are plenty of challenges which promise to be demanding, exciting, and rewarding.
The UNDP summary says:

History is likely to judge the progress in the 21st century by one major yardstick: is there a growing equality of opportunity between people and among nations? This is the issue that has begun to dominate the development debate in the final decade of the 20th century. That is entirely appropriate, since the pace of development—robust as it was in the past five decades—has been accompanied by rising disparities *within* nations and *between* nations.

The most persistent of these has been gender disparity, despite a relentless struggle to equalize opportunities between women and men. The unfinished agenda for change is still considerable. Women still constitute 70% of the world's poor and two-thirds of the world's illiterates. They occupy only 14% of managerial and administrative jobs, 10% of parliamentary seats and 6% of cabinet positions. In many legal systems, they are still unequal. They often work longer hours than men, but much of their work remains unvalued, unrecognized and unappreciated. And the threat of violence stalks their lives from cradle to grave (UNDP 1995: iii).

While this challenge is apparently recognized in an increasing number of agencies and organizations, there are other serious challenges about which the same organizations may be less aware. One of these is the overwhelming dominance of traditional economic thinking among development professionals. The UNDP report also points out:

- Economic growth is necessary but not sufficient for human development. The right kind of economic environment and policies are required to translate the benefits of growth into the lives of people.
- Commitment and political will, not always resources, are often the main constraints to taking care of economic growth and human development simultaneously (UNDP, 1995: 124).

The myth that economic growth is basic to development still pervades the field. Our concept of a development cycle challenges this, as does the deepening concern for the limited ecosystem of space-ship Earth. But the simple idea of economic growth continues to be more powerful than the concerns for equity or sustainability. Practitioners in the 21st century are likely to wrestle with the issue of the conflict between economic growth and empowerment of the poor. Perhaps new paradigms will arise which offer more manageable paths to equity?

Hazel Henderson suggests this approach for the future:

If we are to redirect our paths to people-centered development and a newly defined global security, we must create a climate that fosters human creativity and social innovation. This, in turn, means the fostering of global civil society and strengthening the connecting peoples' organizations globally. We are talking nothing less than reinventing ourselves, re-framing our perceptions, reshaping our beliefs and behaviour, composting our knowledge, restructuring our institutions and recycling our societies. This is not an impossibly tall order. Rather, it is routine in the repertoire of human behaviour. Indeed, such systemic social change is the stuff of all human society (Henderson 1994: 27).

Ever since the industrial revolution began some three hundred years ago, its goal has been to produce more goods with fewer people—and this goal is being achieved today on a world scale. Few now pay attention to the debates of the 1960s about how the fruits of all this productive technological virtuosity could be purchased by unemployed people (Henderson 1994: 29).

In a plea for broad transformation, Klaus M. Leisinger writes:

Because hunger and undernourishment are first and foremost a consequence of flawed or inadequate social and economic development, they will require broad social and political transformation to overcome them lastingly. To this end, people must first be mobilized to amend static traditional modes of thinking and behaving; adoption of economic and technical innovations must follow (Leisinger 1995: 3).

The second half of the 20th century can be characterized as the era when amateurs in international development agencies outnumbered professionals. The next half century may be a period of transition, with professionals outnumbering amateurs. Their careers are likely to be more creative and constructive, and less prescriptive than their predecessors. Young practitioners will be encouraged to be more imaginative, rather than particularistic, in their approach to development. The winds of change in this direction include:

- Growing literature and formal training and actual experience opportunities which can produce professional practitioners.
- Increasing emphasis on strategies and programs based more on human resources than on money.
- An ambivalence which combines both pessimistic and optimistic perspectives.
- The diminishing acceptance of those who pretend to know the future.
- Opening up of science to go beyond the reductionist to the holistic and systemic ways of thinking and understanding.
- Increasing interest in collaboration, including interdisciplinary collaboration.
- More awareness of the complexities of development.
- Recognition that development of an improved situation typically requires subversion (if not destruction) of the old situation.
- Increasing need to recognize the diversity of physical and biological resources, and human groups.
- The concept of a *rural renaissance*, which might overtake the notion of *rural development*.
- Increasing opportunities for and demand for professional practitioners.

Human greed and corruption will not go away, but perhaps more accountability at all levels to those who live and work at the grassroots will reduce their incidence. Optimistically, out of the destruction of those portions of a development cycle in which each generation converts more and more of the energy available to them, will come a creative new development, as a human group moves down the other side of the cycle. This fits the view of development as not a one-dimensional process, which moves only to grow bigger and bigger in every respect, but rather a zigzag process which goes back and forth over time. The history of human settlements is testimony to this. And just as human societies become more developed or less developed over time, so do the agencies and organizations which work in the field. They keep changing and embrace new paradigms in a gradual institutionalization process in which some replace others as time goes by.

Like other writers, we acknowledge that we do not know the future and that our knowledge of the past and the present is quite limited. We also realize that *we live in the world, but we do not control it*. But we are well aware of the conditions of hunger and poverty which characterize the weaker majority of humanity, and we are committed to change toward more equity in the global human condition. Strategies discussed in earlier chapters have a bias toward stimulation of the *empowerment* of the weak, particularly those who till the soil and tend the livestock on the small mixed-farming systems of this globe, and especially women and their families.

One of the global changes which contributes to our optimism is the expanding use of electronic communication systems, such as the internet. The exchange of information and knowledge among agricultural scientists has grown exponentially in the last decade of the 20th century. Development professionals are increasingly able to access the global experience through a growing number of networks such as the world wide web. And professionals within individual international development organizations are able to keep each other informed on an instantaneous international basis.

The potential for exciting changes is evident as people of the world community transition into the 21st century. After a half century of global power polarization and neglect of the weak, the old ways of thinking are changing. Old social, political, and economic structures are fragmenting. Those who reflect on the conceptualizations and the practices in rural development, in international development, and particularly in international development collaboration, may see a dramatic evolution of challenging and positive possibilities which are the focus of this book. The authors' goal was to enhance the reader's understanding of these critical phenomena and empower that reader to contribute significantly in the 21st century. Serious professional practitioners should be able to find useful ideas in the references cited.

Continuing in our optimism, as the pendulum of development moves back and forth, perhaps from underdevelopment to overdevelopment to underdevelopment in various places on planet Earth, opportunities for the practitioner of international development in the future are bright.

We have learned from some of the Buddhists of the high Himalayas that there is a perfect city, a *Shambhala*, or a Shangri-la (as westerners call it), but it is found deep within one's self, not in a hidden valley. The thought was expressed much better by the winner of the Nobel Prize for Literature in 1913, Rabindranath Tagore (1965: 27) in these words:

Where the mind is without fear and the head is held high;
Where knowledge is free;
Where the world has not been broken up into fragments by narrow
    domestic walls;
Where words come out from the depth of truth;
Where tireless striving stretches its arms toward perfection;
Where the clear stream of reason has not lost its way into the dreary
    desert sand of dead habit;
Where the mind is led forward by thee into ever-widening thought
    and action—
Into that heaven of freedom, let my country awake.

References and Select Bibliography

Abel, Martin E., 1975, 'Irrigation Systems in Taiwan: Management of a Decentralized Public Enterprise', Minneapolis, Department of Agricultural and Applied Economics, University of Minnesota, Staff Paper.

Acharya, Meena and **Lynn Bennett**, 1981, *The Rural Women of Nepal: An Aggregate Analysis and Summary of Eight Village Studies. The Status of Women in Nepal*, vol. 2, Field Studies, Part 9, Kathmandu, Centre for Economic Development and Administration, Tribhuvan University.

Adams, William M., 1990, *Green Development—Environment and Sustainability in the Third World*, London and New York, Routledge.

Adler, Nancy J., 1995, 'Competitive Frontiers: Cross-cultural Management and the 21st Century', in *International Journal of Intercultural Relations*, vol. 19, no. 4, Fall: 523–37.

Altieri, Miguel, 1995, 'Escaping the Treadmill—Agro-ecology Puts Synergy to Work to Create Self-sustaining "Agro-ecosystems"', in *Ceres, The FAO Review*, no. 154 (vol. 27, no. 4): 15–23.

Antholt, Charles H., 1991, 'Agricultural Extension in the 21st Century: Lessons from South Asia', in Rivera, W. and Dan Gustafsen (eds), *Agricultural Extension: Worldwide Institutional Evolution and Forces for Change*, New York, Elsevier: 203–18.

Arnaiz, Maria E. O., 1995, *Farmers' Organizations in the Technology Change Process—An Annotated Bibliography*, Network Paper 53, London, Agricultural Administration Research and Extension Network, Overseas Development Institute.

Axinn, George H., 1991a, 'Sustainable Development Reconsidered', in *Development, Journal of the Society for International Development*, vol. 1: 120–23.

——————, 1991b, 'Potential Contribution of FSRE to Institution Development', in *Journal of the Asian Farming Systems Association*, vol. 1, no. 1: 69–78.

——————, 1988a, *Guide on Alternative Extension Approaches*, Rome, Food and Agriculture Organization of the United Nations.

——————, 1988b, 'International Technical Interventions in Agriculture and Rural Development: Some Basic Trends, Issues, and Questions', in *Agriculture and Human Values*, Winter–Spring: 6–15.

——————, 1978, *New Strategies for Rural Development*, Kathmandu and East Lansing, Rural Life Associates.

——————, 1977a, 'The Development Cycle: New Strategies from an Ancient Concept', in *International Development Review*, no. 4: 9–15.

——————, 1977b, 'Tagore for Today', in *International Development Review*, no. 4: 28–29.

Axinn, George H., 1975, 'Rural Renaissance—A Perspective and a Process', Paper Presented at the Third International Conference of the East–West Communication Institute on Integrated Communication for Rural Development. (Conference Proceedings, *Integrated Communication—Bringing People and Rural Development Together*, Honolulu, East–West Center.)

——————, 1969, 'A Strategy of Communication in the Development Process', Paper Presented at the Eleventh World Conference of the Society for International Development, New Delhi, India. (Published in the Proceedings, *International Development*, Washington, DC, 1970.)

——————, 1957, 'The Milieu Theory of Control', *Public Administration Review*, vol. XVII, no. 2: 97–105.

Axinn, George H. and **Nancy W. Axinn**, 1969, 'An African Village in Transition: Research into Behavior Patterns', in *Journal of Modern African Studies*, vol. 7, no. 3: 527–34.

Axinn, Nancy W., 1990a, 'Involving Women Farmers in FSR/E—Separate Projects vs Integrating Gender: The South Asian Experience', Paper Presented at the Tenth Annual Symposium, Association for Farming Systems Research/Extension, Michigan State University.

——————, 1990b, 'Agricultural Extension for Women Farmers in South Asia', Special Report to The World Bank, Washington, DC.

Axinn, Nancy W. and **George H. Axinn**, 1994, *External Review Report*, Cornell International Institute for Food, Agriculture, and Development (CIIFAD), Ithaca, NY.

——————, 1987, 'The Recycling Ratio: A Useful Tool in Farming Systems Analysis', in *How Systems Work, Proceedings of the Farming Systems Research Symposium*, Fayetteville, University of Arkansas.

——————, 1984a, 'Energy and Food Relationships in Developing Countries: A Perspective from the Social Sciences', in Pimental, D. and C.W. Hall (eds), *Food and Energy Relationships*, Orlando, Academic Press: 121–46.

——————, 1984b, 'Social Impact, Economic Change, Development and Energy—With Some Illustrations from Nepal', in Derman, W. and S. Whiteford (eds), *Social Impact Analysis and Development Planning in the Third World*, Boulder, Westview Press: 97–118.

Axinn, William G., 1992, 'Rural Income-generating Programs and Fertility Limitation: Evidence from a Microdemographic Study in Nepal', in *Rural Sociology*, vol. 57, no. 3: 396–413.

Ball, J.B., S. Braatz and **C. Chandrasekharan**, 1995, 'It Starts with "F", and that Stands For Food!', in *Ceres, The FAO Review*, no. 154 (vol. 27, no. 4): 39–44.

Bawden, Richard J., 1991, 'Systems Thinking and Practice in Agriculture', in *Journal of Dairy Science*, vol. 74: 2362–373.

——————, 1990, 'Of Agricultural Systems and Systems Agriculture: Systems Methodologies in Agricultural Education', in Jones, J.G.W. and P.R. Street (eds), *Systems Theory Applied to Agriculture and the Food Chain*, London and New York, Elsevier.

Baylor, Byrd, 1972, *Yes is Better Than No*, Tucson, Treasure Chest Publications.

Bista, Dor Bahadur, 1991, *Fatalism and Development: Nepal's Struggle for Modernization*, Calcutta, Orient Longman Ltd.

Black, Jan Knippers, 1991, *Development in Theory & Practice—Bridging the Gap*, Boulder, Westview Press.

Blakeslee, Sandra, 1995, 'Searching for Simple Rules of Complexity', in *New York Times*, December 26: B5&B9.

Borton, Raymond E. (ed.), 1966, *Selected Readings to Accompany Getting Agriculture Moving*, New York, The Agricultural Development Council.

Boulding, Elise, 1977, *Women in the Twentieth Century World*, New York, John Wiley & Sons.

Brokensha, D.W. and **P.D. Little** (eds), 1988, *Anthropology of Development and Change in East Africa*, Boulder, Westview Press.

Brokensha, D.W., D.M. Warren and **Oswald Werner**, 1980, *Indigenous Knowledge Systems and Development*, Lanham, MD, University Press of America.

Bruntland, Gro Harlem, 1989, 'Sustainable Development: An Overview', in *Development, Journal of the Society of International Development*, nos 2 and 3: 13–14.

Bryant, Coralie and **Louise G. White**, 1984, *Managing Rural Development with Small Farmer Participation*, West Hartford, Kumarian Press.

Cano, Jairo, 1981, 'Formation of Human Resources for Agricultural Research in Latin America, and Participation in Research Networks: Training Researchers at CIAT', Ph.D. Dissertation, East Lansing, Michigan State University.

Carley, Michael and **Ian Christie**, 1992, *Managing Sustainable Development*, London, Earthscan Publications, Ltd.

Carney, Diana, 1995, 'Management and Supply in Agriculture and Natural Resources: Is Decentralisation the Answer?', in *ODI Natural Resource Perspectives*, no. 4: 1–4.

Ceres, 1995, 'A First: NGOs Advise FAO on Forestry', in *Ceres, The FAO Review*, vol. 27, no. 4: 14.

Cernea, Michael M., 1995, 'Malinowski Award Lecture—Social Organization and Development Anthropology', in *Human Organization*, vol. 54, no. 3: 340–52.

Chambers, Robert, 1995, 'The Professionals and the Powerless: Whose Reality Counts?', in *CHOICES—The Human Development Magazine*, vol. 4, no. 1: 14–15.

————————, 1994, 'All Power Deceives', in *Ids bulletin*, vol. 25, no. 2: 14–26.

————————, 1993, *Challenging the Professions—Frontiers for Rural Development*, London, Intermediate Technology Publications.

————————, 1983, *Rural Development—Putting the Last First*, London, Longman.

Chen, Martha, 1995, 'Beijing!', in *AWID, The Newsletter of the Association for Women in Development*, vol. 9, no. 4, August: 1 and 6.

Chhetri, Ram B., 1995, 'Rotating Credit Associations in Nepal: Dhikuri as Capital, Credit, Saving, and Investment', in *Human Organization*, vol. 54, no. 4: 449–54.

Clark, Cameron, 1975, *Integrated Approach to Agricultural and Rural Development: Asia and the Far East*, Rome, Food and Agriculture Organization of the United Nations.

Clark, John, 1991, *Democratizing Development—The Role of Voluntary Organizations*, West Hartford, Kumarian Press.

Cleaver, Frances and **Diane Elson**, 1995, *Women and Water Resources: Continued Marginalisation and New Policies*, Gatekeeper Series no. 49, London, International Institute for Environment and Development.

Cloud, Kathleen, 1989, 'Women, Development, Equity, and Efficiency: In Pursuit of Constrained Bliss', in Clubb, Deborah and Polly C. Lignon (eds), *Food, Hunger, and Agricultural Issues*, Morrilton, AR, Winrock International Institute for Agricultural Development.

Collins, Jane L., 1991, 'Women and the Environment: Social Reproduction and Sustainable Development', in Gallin, Rita and Anne Ferguson (eds), *The Women and International Development Annual*, vol. 2, Boulder, Westview Press.

Conway, Gordon R., 1990, 'Agroecosystems', in Jones, J.G.W. and P.R. Street (eds), *Systems Theory Applied to Agriculture and the Food Chain*, New York, Elsevier: 205–33.

Cottrell, Fred, 1955, *Energy and Society—The Relation Between Energy, Social Change, and Economic Development*, New York, McGraw-Hill Book Co.

Coward, E. Walter, Jr. (ed.), 1980, *Irrigation and Agricultural Development in Asia: Perspectives from the Social Sciences*, Ithaca, NY, Cornell University Press.

Crossette, Barbara, 1995, 'New Watchdog Group Ranks Nations in "Corruption Index"', in *New York Times*, August 13: 8.

Crowley, David and **David Mitchell** (eds), 1994, *Communication Theory Today*, Stanford, Stanford University Press.

Daily, Gretchen C., H. Anne and **Paul E. Ehrlich**, 1995, 'Socioeconomic Equity: A Critical Element in Sustainability', in *AMBIO*, vol. 24, no. 1, February: 59.

Daly, Herman, 1995, 'An Open Letter: Advice for a Would-be Reformer', in *Ceres, The FAO Review*, vol. 27, no. 6: 10–12.

Danforth, Nick, 1995, 'Let's Not Forget About the Men', in *Choices*, vol. 2, no. 2, August: 33–34.

De Janvry, Alain, 1981, *The Agrarian Question and Reformism in Latin America*, Baltimore, The Johns Hopkins University Press.

De Soto, Hernando, 1989, *The Other Path—The Invisible Revolution in the Third World*, New York, Harper & Row.

Dewey, Kathryn G., 1985, 'Nutrition, Social Impact, and Development: A Mexican Case', in Derman, William and Scott Whiteford (eds), *Social Impact Analysis and Development Planning in the Third World*, Boulder, Westview Press: 160–77.

Dias, Clarence J., 1995, 'The UN and Development—Business as Usual', in *D + C, Development and Cooperation*, no. 3: 15–16.

Edens, Tom, Cynthia Fridgen and **S. Battenfield**, 1985, *Sustainable Agriculture and Integrated Farming Systems*, East Lansing, Michigan State University Press.

Eicher, Carl K. and **John M. Staatz**, 1984, *Agricultural Development in the Third World*, Baltimore, The Johns Hopkins University Press.

Escobar, Arturo, 1995, *Encountering Development—The Making and Unmaking of the Third World*, Princeton, Princeton University Press.

Esman, Milton J., 1991, *Management Dimensions of Development: Perspectives and Strategies*, West Hartford, Kumarian Press.

Esman, Milton J. and **Norman Uphoff**, 1984, *Local Organizations: Intermediaries in Rural Development*, Ithaça, Cornell University Press.

Esman, Milton J. and **William J. Siffin**, 1975, 'Major Properties and Purposes of the IB Perspective', in Mann, Amy G. (ed.), *Institution Building: A Reader*, Bloomington, Indiana, PASITAM: 17–27.

Farrington, J., A. Bebbington, K. Wellard and **D. Lewis**, 1993, *Reluctant Partners? NGOs and the State in Sustainable Agricultural Development*, London, Routledge.

Farrington, John and **A. Martin**, 1987, 'Farmer Participatory Research: A Review of Concepts and Practices', in *Agricultural Research and Extension*, Discussion Paper no. 19, London, Overseas Development Institute.

Flora, Cornelia Butler, 1992, 'Evaluation and Impact of the Global Synthesis and Networking', Paper Presented at the Twelfth Annual Farming Systems Symposium, East Lansing, Michigan State University.

Freire, Paulo, 1970, *Pedagogy of the Oppressed*, New York, The Seabury Press.

Gamser, Mathew S., Helen Appleton and **Nicola Carter** (eds), 1990, *Tinker, Tiller, Technical Change*, London, Intermediate Technology Publications.

George, Susan, 1992, *The Debt Boomerang*, Boulder, Westview Press.

————, 1988, *A Fate Worse than Debt*, London, Penguin Books.

————, 1984, *Ill Fares the Land: Essays on Food, Hunger, and Power*, Washington, DC, Institute of Policy Studies.

George, Susan and **Fabrizio Sabelli**, 1994, *Faith and Credit: The World Bank's Secular Empire*, Boulder & San Francisco, Westview Press.

Hancock, Graham, 1989, *Lords of Poverty—The Power, Prestige, and Corruption on the International Aid Business*, New York, The Atlantic Monthly Press.

Harris, Marvin, 1977, *Cannibals and Kings—The Origins of Cultures*, New York, Random House.

Hauchler, Ingomar, 1994, 'Crisis and New Orientation of Development Policy', in *D + C, Development and Cooperation*, nos 5 and 6: 4–5.

Heady, Ferrel, 1966, *Public Administration: A Comparative Perspective*, Englewood Cliffs, Prentice-Hall.

Henderson, Hazel, 1994, 'Development Imperatives for the Future', in *Development*, no. 4: 27–32.

Hildebrand, Peter, 1986, *Perspectives on Farming Systems Research and Extension*, Boulder, Lynn Rienner Publishers.

India Today (periodical), April 30, 1993, New Delhi, India.

Ingham, Barbara, 1993, 'The Meaning of Development: Interactions Between "New" and "Old" Ideas', in *World Development* (Pergamon Press), vol. 21, no. 11: 1803–821.

Islam, Nural (ed.), 1974, *Agricultural Policy in Developing Countries*, New York, John Wiley & Sons.

Jacobson, Jodi L., 1992, *Gender Bias: Roadblock to Sustainable Development*, Worldwatch Paper 110, Washington, DC, Worldwatch Institute.

Jain, Devaki, 1995, 'Gripping Development', in *Development*, no. 1: 30–33.

Jiggins, Janice, 1994, *Changing the Boundaries—Women-centered Perspectives on Population and the Environment*, Washington, DC and Covelo, California, Island Press.

Kaimowitz, David, 1991, 'The Evolution of Links Between Extension and Research in Developing Countries', in Rivera, William M. and Daniel J. Gustafson (eds), *Agricultural Extension: Worldwide Institutional Evolution and Forces for Change*, Amsterdam, Elsevier: 101–12.

Kardam, Nuket, 1991, *Bringing Women In: Women's Issues in International Development Programs*, Boulder, Lynne Rienner Publishers.

Khan, Akhtar Hameed, 1996, *Orangi Pilot Project—Reminiscences and Reflections*, Karachi, Oxford University Press.

Korten, David, 1996, 'The Truth about Global Competition—The Economic Myths behind Globalization', in *D + C, Development and Cooperation*, no. 3, March: 4, 5 and 23.

——————, 1986, *Community Management—Asian Experience and Perspectives*, West Hartford, Kumarian Press.

Korten, David C. and **George Carner**, 1984, 'Planning Frameworks for People-centered Development', in Korten, David C. and Rudi Klauss (eds), *People-centered Development*, West Hartford, Kumarian Press: 201–9.

Korten, D.C. and **R. Klauss** (eds), 1984, *People-centered Development*, West Hartford, Kumarian Press.

Kothari, Rajni, 1988, *Rethinking Development—In Search of Humane Alternatives*, New Delhi, Ajanta Publications.

Leisinger, Klaus M., 1995, *Sociopolitical Effects of New Biotechnologies in Developing Countries*, Food, Agriculture, and the Environment Discussion Paper no. 2, Washington, DC, International Food Policy Research Institute.

Lerner, David and **Wilbur Schramm**, 1967, *Communication and Change in the Developing Countries*, Honolulu, East–West Center Press.

Lewin, Kurt, 1951, *Field Theory in Social Science: Selected Theoretical Papers*, New York, Harper.

Lightfoot, Clive, Shelley Feldman and **M. Zainul Abedin**, 1991, *Households, Agroecosystems and Rural Resources Management—A Guidebook for Broadening the Concepts of Gender and Farming Systems*, Manila, International Center for Living Aquatic Resources Management (ICLARM) and Bangladesh Agricultural Research Institute (BARI).

Lull, James, 1995, *Media, Communication, Culture: A Global Approach*, New York, Columbia University Press.

Lynam, John K., 1992, 'Sustainability: The Challenges for International Agricultural Research', in *Proceedings of the Workshop on Social Science Research and the CRSPs*, June 9–11, Lexington, University of Kentucky: 119–39.

Lynam, John K. and **Robert W. Herdt**, 1992, 'Sense and Sustainability: Sustainability as an Objective in International Agricultural Research', in Moock, Joyce Lewinger and Robert E. Rhodes (eds), *Diversity, Farmer Knowledge and Sustainability*, Ithaca, Cornell University Press.

Martin, Edward D., 1986, 'Resource Mobilization, Water Allocation, and Farmer Organization in Hill Irrigation Systems in Nepal', Ph.D. Dissertation, Ithaca, NY, Cornell University.

Martin, Edward D. and **Robert Yoder**, 1987, *Institutions for Irrigation Management in Farmer Managed Systems: Examples from the Hills of Nepal*, Kathmandu, International Irrigation Management Institute.

Mattelart, Armand, 1994, *Mapping World Communication: War, Progress, Culture*, Minneapolis, University of Minnesota Press.

Meadows, Donella H., Dennis L. Meadows, Jorgen Randers and **William W. Behrens III**, 1972, *The Limits to Growth—A Report for the Club of Rome's Project on the Predicament of Mankind*, New York, Universe Books.

Merrill-Sands, D., P. Ewell, S. Biggs and **J. McAllister**, 1989, *Issues in Institutionalizing On-farm Client-oriented Research: A Review of Experiences from Nine National Agricultural Research Systems*, Staff Notes: 57–89, The Hague, ISNAR.

Miller, Paul A., 1995, 'Adult Education's Mislaid Mission', in *Adult Education Quarterly*, vol. 46, no. 1, Fall: 43–52.

Mosher, Arthur T., 1969, *Creating a Progressive Rural Structure—To Serve Modern Agriculture*, New York, Agricultural Development Council.

NASULGC, 1969, *International Development Assistance*, a statement by the TASK FORCE on International Development Assistance and International Education, Washington, DC, National Association of State Universities and Land Grant Colleges.

New Internationalist, 1995, 'African Village— Lending a Hand', no. 268, June: 30.

New York Times (newspaper), 1995a, Section 3: 1, April 2.

―――――――, 1995b, Section A: 5, March 13.

Newby, Howard, 1978, *International Perspectives in Rural Sociology*, Chichester, John Wiley & Sons.

Newman, William H., 1951, *Administrative Action—The Techniques of Organization and Management*, New York, Prentice-Hall.

Niehoff, Arthur H. (ed.), 1966, *A Casebook of Social Change*, Chicago, Aldine Publishing Company.

Obasanjo, General, 1995, Interview in *2020 Views*, February, Washington, DC, International Food Policy Research Institute.

Ostrom, Elinor, 1992, *Crafting Institutions for Self-governing Irrigation Systems*, San Francisco, Institute for Contemporary Studies Press.

O'Sullivan, Tim, John Hartley, Danny Saunders, Martin Montgomery and **John Fiske**, 1994, *Key Concepts in Communication and Cultural Studies*, London and New York, Routledge.

Oxford Paperback Dictionary, 1983, Oxford, Oxford University Press.

Pinstrup-Andersen, Per and **Rajul Pandya-Lorch**, 1994, *Alleviating Poverty, Intensifying Agriculture, and Effectively Managing Natural Resources*, Food, Agriculture, and the Environment Discussion Paper 1, Washington, International Food Policy Research Institute.

Pope John Paul II, 1995, 'The Pope Speaks at UN: Human Rights and "the Risk of Freedom"', *New York Times*, October 6: A16.

Pretty, Jules N. and **Robert Chambers**, 1993, *Towards a Learning Paradigm: New Professionalism and Institutions for Agriculture*, Sussex, Institute of Development Studies.

Rao, Y.V. Lakshmana, 1966, *Communication and Development: A Study of Two Indian Villages*, Minneapolis, University of Minnesota Press.

Reeves, Floyd, 1956, Class Lectures at Michigan State University.

Robertson, Roland, 1992, *Globalization—Social Theory and Global Culture*, London, Sage Publications.

Rogers, E.M. and **Lynne Svenning**, 1968, *Modernization Among Peasants: The Impact of Communication*, New York, Holt, Rinehart and Winston.

Röling, Niels, 1994, 'Communication Support for Sustainable Natural Resource Management', in *Ids bulletin*, vol. 25, no. 2: 125–33.

Ropetto, Robert, 1985, *The Global Possible*, Washington, World Resources Institute.

Ruddle, Kenneth and **Dennis A. Rondinelli**, 1983, *Transforming Natural Resources for Human Development: A Resource Systems Framework for Development*

Policy, Resource Systems Theory and Methodology Series no. 1, Tokyo, The United Nations University.

Schensul, Jean J., 1995, 'SIAA President's Letter', in *Society of Applied Anthropology Newsletter*, vol. 6, no. 2: 1–3.

Schuler, Randall S., 1986, *Effective Personnel Management*, St Paul, West Publishing Co.

Sen, Amartya Kumar, 1981, *Poverty and Famines: An Essay on Entitlement and Deprivation*, Oxford, Clarendon Press; New York, Oxford University Press.

Sen, Gita, 1995a, 'Alternative Economics from a Gender Perspective', in *Development*, no. 1: 10–13.

—————————, 1995b, 'Creating Common Ground Between Environmentalists and Women: Thinking Locally, Acting Globally?', in *AMBIO*, vol. 24, no. 1: 65.

Sen, Gita and **Caren Grown**, 1987, *Development, Crises, and Alternative Visions: Third World Women's Perspectives*, New York, Monthly Review Press.

Shaner, W.W., P.F. Philipp and **W.R. Schmehl**, 1982, *Farming Systems Research and Development—Guidelines for Developing Countries*, Boulder, Westview Press.

Shiva, Vandana, 1991, *Most Farmers in India are Women*, New Delhi, FAO.

—————————, 1989, *Staying Alive—Women, Ecology, and Survival in India*, New Delhi, Kali for Women; London, Zed Books Ltd.

Shivakoti, Ganesh Prasad, 1991, 'Organizational Effectiveness of User and Non-user Controlled Irrigation Systems in Nepal', Ph.D. Dissertation, East Lansing, Michigan State University.

Shrestha, Bihari K., 1983, 'Technical Assistance and the Growth of Administrative Capability in Nepal', in Panday, Devendra Raj, *Foreign Aid and Development in Nepal*, Kathmandu, Integrated Development Systems: 219–49.

Smith-Sreen, Poonam, 1995, *Accountability in Development Organizations—Experiences of Women's Organizations in India*, New Delhi, Sage Publicatons.

—————————, 1992, 'The Relationship of Member-accountability in Organizations with the Economic and Social Benefits Accrued by Members—A Comparative Study of Four Women's Development Organizations in India', vols I and II, Ph.D. Dissertation, East Lansing, Michigan State University.

Stiller, Ludwig F. and **Ram Prakash Yadav**, 1979, *Planning for People: A Study of Nepal's Planning Experience*, Kathmandu, Tribhuvan University.

Swaminathan, M.S., 1994, Spoken at the International Conference on Population and Development in Cairo in 1994, and quoted in *Ceres, The FAO Review*, no. 151 (vol. 27, no. 1): 11.

Swantz, Marja-Liisa, 1995, 'Women Entrepreneurs in Tanzania: A Path to Sustainable Livelihoods', in *Development*, no. 1: 55–60.

Tagore, Rabindranath, 1965, *Gitanjali* ('Song Offerings'), New York, St Martin's Press.

—————————, 1941, *Rabindranath Tagore on Rural Reconstruction*, New Delhi, Government of India.

The Independent (newspaper), August 28, 1993, Kathmandu, Nepal.

Thiel, Reinhold E., 1994, 'NGOs: Better than the State?', in *D + C, Development and Cooperation*, no. 1: 3.

Thoreau, Henry David, 1958, *Walden*, New York, Harper & Row.

Thrupp, Lori Ann, 1993, 'Political Ecology of Sustainable Rural Development: Dynamics of Social and Natural Resource Degradation', in Allen, Patricia (ed.), *Food for the Future: Conditions and Contradictions of Sustainability*, New York, John Wiley & Sons.

Thrupp, Lori Ann, Bruce Cabarle and **Aaron Zazueta**, 1994, 'Participatory Methods in Planning and Political Process: Linking the Grassroots and Policies for Sustainable Development', in *Agriculture and Human Values*, vol. 11, nos 2 and 3, Spring–Summer: 77–84.

Thrupp, Lori Ann and **Richard Haynes**, 1994, 'From the Editors—Participation and Empowerment in Sustainable Rural Development', in *Agriculture and Human Values*, vol. 11, nos 2 and 3, Spring–Summer: 1–3.

Tyler, Ralph W., 1950, *Basic Principles of Curriculum and Instruction*, Syllabus for Education 305, Chicago, University of Chicago Press.

UN (United Nations), 1995, *Beijing Declaration and Platform for Action, Fourth World Conference on Women, Beijing*, New York, United Nations.

UNA–USA, 1995, *The United Nations at a Glance*, New York, United Nations Association of the United States of America.

UNDP, 1996, *Human Development Report*, New York, Oxford University Press.

——————, 1995, *Human Development Report*, New York, Oxford University Press.

——————, 1993, *Human Development Report*, New York, Oxford University Press.

Uphoff, Norman T., 1992, *Learning from Gal Oya—Possibilities for Participatory Development and Post-Newtonian Social Science*, Ithaca and London, Cornell University Press.

——————, 1986, *Local Institutional Development: An Analytic Sourcebook with Cases*, West Hartford, Kumarian Press.

Useem, John and **Ruth Useem**, 1955, *The Western-educated Man in India*, New York, The Dryden Press.

Useem, John, Ruth Useem and **John Donahue**, 1963, 'Men in the Middle of the Third Culture: Roles of American and Non-Western People in Cross-cultural Administration', in *Human Organization*, vol. 22, Fall: 169–80.

Vahlhans, Martina, 1994, 'The New Popularity of NGOs—Will the Enthusiasm Last?', in *D + C, Development and Cooperation*, no. 3, May–June: 20–22.

Waterson, Albert, 1965/1979, *Development Planning—Lessons of Experience*, Baltimore, The Johns Hopkins University Press.

Whyte, William Foote, 1991, *Social Theory for Action—How Individuals and Organizations Learn to Change*, Thousand Oaks, CA, Sage Publications.

Wignaraja, Ponna, 1990, *Women, Poverty, and Resources*, New Delhi, Sage Publications.

Wimberley, Ronald C., 1993, 'Policy Perspectives on Social, Agricultural, and Rural Sustainability', in *Rural Sociology*, vol. 58, no. 1: 1–29. (Presidential Address to the 55th Annual Meeting of the Rural Sociological Society, August 16.)

Women's Watch, 1996, 'The Next Phase', in *The Women's Watch*, vol. 9, no. 3, January: 1–8, Minneapolis, International Women's Rights Action Watch, Humphrey Institute of Public Affairs.

Yoder, R.W., 1986, 'The Performance of Farmer-managed Irrigation Systems in the Hills of Nepal', Ph.D. Dissertation, Ithaca, NY, Cornell University.

Index